THE BEVERAGE SERVICE WORLD

Wallace Rande Ed.D., C.H.E
*School of Hotel and
Restaurant Management
Northern Arizona University*

Luciani Valentino, C.H.E
*William F. Harrah College
of Hotel Administration
University of Nevada, Las Vegas*

Prentice Hall

Upper Saddle River, New Jersey 07458

Library of Congress Cataloging-in-Publication Data

Rande, Wallace L.
  The beverage service world / Wallace Rande, Valentino Luciani.
    p. cm.
  Includes index.
  ISBN 0-13-375924-5
    1. Bars (Drinking establishments)—Management.   2. Alcoholic beverages.   I. Luciani,
  Valentino.   II. Title.
  TX950.7 .R36 2001
  647.95'068—dc21

                                                                00-032405

Publisher: Dava Garza
Production Editor: Patty Donovan, Pine Tree Composition
Production Liaison: Barbara Marttine Cappuccio
Director of Manufacturing
  and Production: Bruce Johnson
Managing Editor: Mary Carnis
Manufacturing Manager: Ed O'Dougherty
Art Director: Marianne Frasco
Cover Design Coordinator: Miguel Ortiz
Cover Designer: Joe Sengotta
Cover illustration: Andrew Bylo / SIS / Image.com
Marketing Manager: Ryan DeGrote
Editorial Assistant: Susan Kegler
Interior Design, art production
  and page layout: Pine Tree Composition
Printing and Binding: R. R. Donnely & Sons

I would like to thank my family, Holly, Sarah, and Jason for their patience and support through the production of this book.
                            Wallace Rande

I would like to thank my family, Mary Helen, Jino, and Rigel, for all their love and support.
                            Luciani Valentino

Prentice-Hall International (UK) Limited, *London*
Prentice-Hall of Australia Pty. Limited, *Sydney*
Prentice-Hall Canada Inc., *Toronto*
Prentice-Hall Hispanoamericana, S.A., *Mexico*
Prentice-Hall of India Private Limited, *New Delhi*
Prentice-Hall of Japan, Inc., *Tokyo*
Prentice-Hall Singapore Pte. Ltd
Editora Prentice-Hall do Brasil, Ltda., *Rio de Janeiro*

Prentice Hall

10   9   8   7   6   5   4   3   2   1
ISBN 0-13-375924-5

CONTENTS

Chapter 2
The Role of the Customer in a Food-Service Operation

20

Chapter 3
The Planning Stage

32

Chapter 4
Bar and Beverage Equipment

44

Chapter 11
Promoting Responsible Drinking and Alcohol Awareness   188

Chapter 12
Legal Factors in Beverage Service   203

Chapter 13
Costing, Pricing, and Control   217

Chapter 14
Purchasing, Receiving, Storing, and Issuing   235

Chapter 15
Controlling Internal Theft   248

Chapter 16
A Look at Tomorrow's Beverage World

Appendix 1
Glossary

Appendix 2
Practical and Useful Forms and Plans

Appendix 3
Useful Websites by Chapter

Index

FOREWORD

The beverage sector is one of the more exciting areas in the hospitality business today. In the past, except for specialized sectors of the business, beverage management was not necessarily considered a separate are; it was normally combined with food—as in food and beverage management. Now one can increasingly speak of beverage management as a specialized are of hospitality administration.

Several factors are contributing to this.

- The increased interest in wine professionals exhibited by the dramatic growth in the number of individuals who have attained the coveted designation of *Master Sommelier.*
- Increasing importance being placed on wine programs in the high end of the dining spectrum.
- Distilled spirits have become skewed to the super-premium end of the quality spectrum. The introductions of more and more "high end" products have come at a dizzying rapid pace over recent years and shows no signs of slowing. Traditional levels of product knowledge are no longer adequate.
- More and more hospitality organizations are separating food and beverage, with specialists in charge of each.

There is ample evidence of professionalism in the food end of the business. There have been culinary certification programs available world-wide for many years, and hospitality educational institutions have historically emphasized food service management (although they often call themselves *Hotel and Restaurant Management* programs, most have leaned more towards the Restaurant part of the industry). Beverage study was limited to an occasional wine course and a limited role in food and beverage cost control courses. This is changing however. Research Conducted at UNLV indicates that the industry perceives a need for beverage professionals, and the Harrah Hotel College is about to offer a major in Beverage Management.

The Beverage Service World is therefore especially welcome at this time. It provides an excellent overview of the various elements making up a beverage program. These would include: planning and organizing beverage operations, equipment, basic knowledge of the various types of alcoholic beverages, how they are made and what their characteristics are, mixology, and the important management concerns of staffing, purchasing, receiving, storing and issuing of alcoholic beverages, and beverage costing, pricing and theft control. An important element of the beverage business today is the legal environment and the necessity of responsible beverage business. A glossary is provided along with several examples of forms and bar operating procedures. Students and practitioners alike will find this book both useful and interesting.

Donald Bell Ph.D.

PREFACE

This book is intended as a text for college level courses in bar and beverage operations management. Its chapters provide, first, a brief history and an overview of the beverage industry. They then cover the fundamental areas of beverage operations—the planning of the bar, staffing the bar, legal factors, drink costing, purchasing, receiving and storage, beverage production methods, as well as mixology.

The book also contains several chapters not normally covered in beverage operation management texts: the role of the customer in the success of the business, controlling internal theft, and the promotion of responsible drinking. An extensive glossary is included to assist students in the class as well as managers in the field. Management forms were added to assist students in the understanding of the material, as well as to assist them in setting up and operating a beverage operation. The bar and beverage operation business is very dynamic and always changing. These chapters were included to reflect trends that, we believe, will be crucial to the industry.

To be successful in the ever increasingly competitive arena, beverage operations need to be customer-driven. The text stresses the importance of the customer to the success of an operation. Chapter Two is dedicated specifically to the role of customer. The importance of the customer and the role of customer service is surprisingly left out of most beverage operation texts, but future managers (and those currently working in the industry) must respond to their customers in all aspects of the running of the business.

The text is broken up in four segments:

1. Introduction to the Beverage Industry and the Role of the Customer,
2. The Running of the Bar,

3. Beverage Product Knowledge and Mixology,
4. Management of the Bar Operations

The material on the planning of a bar covers the different types of bars and the determining of target markets and market segments. Market and feasibility studies are included. The importance of a clear-cut concept as well as the setting of atmosphere, décor and layout is emphasized. The equipment chapter explains and displays the major pieces of both large and small equipment crucial to the operation of a bar.

Bar managers need to be knowledgeable about the products they serve in their operations. The product knowledge segment of the text covers the mechanics of both fermentation and distillation as well as the key factors that affect quality. There are chapters for the major beverage the classifications: spirits/cordials, wines, and beer. Each chapter includes materials on how the products are made and what distinguishes them from other beverages in their classifications. The basics of mixology is covered so students understand the key drink classifications, behind the bar procedures, garnishing, etc.

There are both similarities and differences between the running of a beverage operation and the running of a food service operation. The last segment of the text covers materials managers and future managers must know to successfully run an operation selling alcoholic beverages. Key topics such as staffing, legal factors, drink costing and pricing, and purchasing / storage all require special attention and are covered it individual chapters.

Promoting the responsible consumption of alcohol is a major concern to operations serving alcohol in a time where people are so quick to look to the courts. Managers must understand the importance of controlling the consumption of alcohol to their guests, and how to promote non-alcoholic beverages in their operations.

Another major concern to bar operators is theft by employees. Bartenders and servers have the opportunity to steal both cash and inventory from their employers as well as their guests. Studies show most of the theft from an operation is from employees not from outsiders. The chapter on internal theft helps the student and future manager to determine why employees steal, how they steal, and how to develop policies and procedures to control the theft.

The text is organized in a manner that facilitates both teaching and learning. Each segment provides the student with the key material they need in the crucial areas. The chapters begin with objectives and outlines to prepare the reader for what follows and to help identify the key concepts. Each chapter has questions to help the student better grasp the material. The chapters include pictures and diagrams to better illustrate the key points of the text. Key terms are highlighted in the text and included in a comprehensive glossary at the end of the book.

The idea for the book came from many years of combined working experience coupled with many years of teaching beverage operation management class. The book was written with both the future and present manager in mind. The material presented is timely and presented in a way that is easy to understand. The test bank and overhead masters provided in the instructor's manual will be a great benefit to those teaching the course.

We are grateful to the educators who reviewed the manuscript, and our friends and colleagues who shared materials with us. The editorial staff of Prentice Hall needs to be commended for their patience through the long and arduous task of writing and re-writing the manuscript. A special thanks goes to all of the companies that assisted us by sharing the pictures and diagrams used throughout the text. We both would like to thank our students for allowing us to share our experiences and knowledge with them and for sharing their knowledge and experiences with us.

Most of all we would both like to thank our families for their assistance in this project. Without their patience and support this project would not have been completed.

chapter one

THE HISTORY
OF THE BEVERAGE INDUSTRY

chapter outline

chapter objectives

Upon completion of this chapter you will be able to:

- Describe the high regard that alcohol has been held in throughout history.

- State the approximate dates of the first records of distillation and fermentation.

- Explain why problems with alcohol consumption did not begin until distilled spirits became more available.

- Elaborate on the effect of absinthe on the culture of drinking in the world.

- Assess the evolution of drinking from the infancy of the United States.

- Describe the role of the tavern in early America and its relevance to the culture of drinking.

- Explain how the westward movement of Americans affected drinking preferences.

- Identify the origin of the name for the whisky called bourbon.

- Explain the importance of the Volstead Act (Prohibition) on the beverage industry.

- Analyze why Prohibition was considered a failure.

- Describe the ways in which alcohol is an integral part of our society.

- State the approximate percent of the retail cost of alcohol that goes to taxes.

- Differentiate the contradictory views governments have toward the consumption of alcoholic beverages.

- Explain the importance of the service of alcoholic beverages to the success of food and beverage operations.

- Describe the consumption patterns of Americans and how they can benefit the proprietor of a bar or restaurant.

- State the effect of ethanol on the human body.

- Relate how the consumption of alcohol influences the level of intoxication.

- Describe how it is possible for a person to drink alcohol without getting intoxicated.

- Sketch how alcohol travels around the human body.

- Identify how alcohol is removed from the body.

- Explain why drinking coffee, taking a shower, and so on, will not help sober a person.

- State what unit is used as the legal measure of alcohol.

- List the legal BAC level indicating intoxication in most states.

- Describe the effect of alcohol on human physiology.

- State the amount of alcohol in common types and sizes of drinks.

- List the seven factors affecting the absorption of alcohol into the body.

- Explain the effect of third-party liability and dramshop laws on the beverage industry.

- Analyze the reasons behind the growth of neo-Prohibitionist movements in the U.S.

- List several of the responses of the beverage industry toward increased legal regulations of their business.

The production and consumption of alcohol goes back almost as far as the earliest recorded history. It has been written that a brewer was held in higher esteem than a baker in early Egyptian villages. Unfortunately, the history and background of alcohol is not without its negative side, and over-consumption continues to cause problems worldwide. There is a certain portion of the human population that cannot control its intake of alcohol; this behavior casts a shadow on an industry and a group of products that employ many people, provide tax dollars, and bring pleasure to most of the rest of the population.

Although alcohol has its dark side, it is a common and, even in some instances, a traditional part of many celebrations and rituals. For example, champagne plays an important role at New Year's Eve celebrations and weddings and wine is found on the dinner table in many cultures, as well as being a part of the Christian Mass. Alcoholic beverages are part of many of the joyous times in cultures worldwide.

Throughout history in most of the world alcohol has been held in high regard. The word vodka in the Russian language, as well as the word whisky in the Scottish Gaelic language, literally translates into "water of life." Moderate consumption of alcohol has rarely been challenged or chastised in the majority of countries and cultures worldwide.

There are several reasons why alcohol has historically been held in such high esteem. The quality of water throughout the world was often questionable, and liquid beverage alternatives to beer and wine did not appear until the mid-seventeenth century. Beer and wine provided necessary nutrients to the diet. Alcohol was first valued for its perceived medicinal characteristics. People were rewarded for their hard work with a drink; it apparently helped them relax after a hard day's work and brought relief to the drudgery of their everyday lives. Drinking and socializing were often two of the few forms of entertainment.

Alcohol has a dramatic effect on human physiology. It first acts like a stimulant, then as a depressant. There are many misconceptions about the effect of alcohol on people. People who work in bars and beverage operations should know how alcohol affects their clients so that they can control over-consumption.

Many governments are conflicted about alcohol. On one hand they benefit from the taxes that the production and sale of alcoholic beverages provide to both state and federal governments. Beverage alcohol is one of the most heavily taxed commodities in our country. The only other items taxed at a similar rate are cigarettes. Politicians often look to the taxes on alcohol when they want more revenue, because they realize that there is often little resistance to such a raise. On the other hand they are faced with the costs to society from the consumption of beverage alcohol: broken families, lost work time, alcohol–related traffic deaths, and so on.

Future managers and workers in the beverage industry should be aware of the checkered history of alcohol so that they can better adapt to the environment in which they will be involved. The saying, "It is always good to know where you have been before you look to see where you are going" is appropriate.

THE CULTURAL HISTORY OF DRINKING

The history of alcohol is almost as old as the history of mankind. The production of alcoholic beverages pretty much followed the spread of Christianity throughout the world. The invention of alcoholic beverages made from fermented grain is generally attributed to the Egyptians more than 5,000 years ago. For thousands of years alcohol has been used as both a healing medicine and an agent to help kill pain. Beer was known to many early civilizations, particularly those in climates that could not produce grapes. Beer has been a popular beverage partly because it does not deteriorate during long periods of storage and is adaptable to most climates. A law in Babylon, in about 1770 BC, imposed the penalty of death on those who watered down the beer they sold. Brewing was mostly done in the home and in monasteries prior to becoming a commercial product in the Middle Ages in Europe. Vineyards were known as early as 4000–6000 BC. Wine supplanted beer as the favorite alcoholic beverage of Mesopotamia as early as 3000 BC. Alcohol was considered a gift of the gods and a sign of wisdom.

For most of history the type of alcohol consumed was some form of beer or wine produced by simple fermentation. Distillation, a much more complicated process of separating the alcohol from the liquid, did not occur until 3000–4000 years later. General drinking "for fun," or recreational drinking, did not start until the sixteenth century and did not become a significant activity in most countries of the world until the eighteenth century. For most of history recreational drinking was limited to the ruling classes, an upper crust of society who had plenty of time on their hands, although condemnation of the evils of drinking dates almost as far back as the history of drinking itself.

References to the consumption of alcohol appear throughout history. The Greco-Romans sang praise to the glories of wine but worked to encourage moderation. Over–consumption of alcohol was also a problem in Athens during the fifth century BC. Excessive drinking was considered on a par with overeating, greed and love of luxury during that period. However, concerns about overdrinking were generally overshadowed by the appreciation of wine's value to life.

Early Christians considered wine to be inherently good because it was one of God's creations. They felt that the problem was not with the beverage but with the people who consumed too much. Christians held that drunkenness was a sin that endangered one's soul and hampered one's chance for everlasting life. Drunkenness was also condemned in the Old Testament.

The drinking of wine and beer was commonplace in the Middle Ages. Alcohol was commonly provided at public feasts and banquets. Villagers considered festive drinking to be part of their community's self-consciousness. There

The drinking of wine and beer was commonplace in the Middle Ages.

are several references and complaints about drunkenness in medieval literature. Although the Church officially condemned drunkenness, many people
would host dinner parties where beer or wine was served to raise money for the
Church. However, most of the laws of the time pertaining to alcohol were di-
rected at protecting drinkers from unsavory sales practices and producers
rather than controlling or limiting consumption. The level of drinking rose during the late Middle Ages as living standards increased after the Plague. The citizens of Western Europe reportedly drank much more than they do now.

The first distilled spirits were expensive and were reserved for the ruling classes. The problems with alcohol consumption did not become widespread until distilled spirits became lower in price and therefore more
available to the masses. The higher alcohol content of spirits made people intoxicated faster. The lower alcohol content of beer and wine was not a problem for most people and did not contribute to widespread alcoholism.

During the 1700s alcohol began to cause problems worldwide.

The monks can be given credit for most of the improvements to the production and quality of both wine and spirits. For example, the name given to a popular quality champagne, Dom Perignon, was that of a monk who is credited with inventing both champagne and the wire cage that goes over the cork to keep it in the bottle, and which is still in use today. The Christian Brothers, an order of monks in California, is credited with helping foster the wine industry in that state and as the maker of the most popular American brandy.

During the 1700s alcohol began to cause problems worldwide. The popular French drink absinthe was only allowed to be served watered down because of the increasing number of cases of blindness and death it caused, particularly in the poorer classes. The early gin mills of England, who advertised their product with the slogan, "Drunk for a penny, dead drunk for tuppence," contributed to public drunkenness, and opposition grew. Many countries passed laws to curb the consumption of alcohol; several nations started with full prohibition, or the outlawing of all alcohol, and then later reconsidered and eased the laws.

THE HISTORY OF DRINKING IN AMERICA

Our forefathers landed on the shores of North America with both a desire for freedom and a thirst for alcoholic beverages. Native Americans were reportedly brewing beer in America before the arrival of Columbus. Upon leaving their homes for the colonies, the passengers as well as the ship's captain brought a supply of beer for the journey. Colonists were by no means teetotalers (people who do not drink beverage alcohol). There had been growing panic on Columbus's ship as they approached land because the supply of beverages was declining to what they considered to be alarmingly low levels. Later arrivals to the colonies were eager to produce their own alcoholic drinks.

Because the harsh climate of New England made the growing of European grapes impossible and the soil would not support the growing of grains, most of the supplies needed to make beer and wine had to be imported. This increased the cost, as well as furthering the colonists' dependence on the very lands that they had fled from. Also, accustomed as they were to unhealthy, densely developed areas in Europe, colonists doubted the quality of the water they found in the New World. Water was considered to be a carrier of disease and only to be drunk as a last resort.

Madeira, a wine that was fortified with the addition of a distilled spirit, was the favorite drink of the early American colonists. The addition of alcohol to the wine helped it withstand the transatlantic journey. In addition, Madeira was a product of what was considered part of Africa at the time, and so did not have to be shipped on European vessels, as was the law for European-produced goods, which helped keep the price more affordable.

As the population of the colonies grew it was harder and harder to import enough beer and wine to satisfy the thirst of the growing nation. Early colonists were encouraged to brew beer as an alternative to the consumption of spirits. They tried to reproduce the beverages they were accustomed to from Europe. The lack of available ingredients caused them to improvise with the products they found in their new home. One example of their creativity was the fermenting and distilling of cider from the abundant apples found growing in New England.

Columbus brought sugarcane cuttings on one of his journeys from the Old World. The sugarcanes grew well in the West Indies and trade in sugar products began to develop between the colonies of the Americas. People began to prefer rum over Madeira. This ushered in one of the darker periods of the history of beverage alcohol in North America, the slave triangle. Some recent research, however, seems to contradict earlier accounts of the significance of the slave triangle, arguing that the colonists in the Americas had little need for slaves during that period.

The slave triangle worked as a three-way exchange of goods and people. People from Africa were taken from their native lands and exchanged as slaves in the West Indies for molasses, a product made by processing and boiling sugar cane. The molasses was shipped to New England to make rum, which in turn was shipped back to Africa and traded for slaves, therefore completing the triangle. By 1763, there were reportedly 176 rum distilleries in New England.

Taverns

The early taverns of the colonies were about a day's ride apart, and they served travellers on the original network of roads. Taverns also served as community meeting places and the general focal point of many towns. Planning for the American Revolution probably took place in the taverns of the colonies.

These taverns served multiple purposes. They were often used as courthouses before towns could afford their own. Besides being the places where most of the drinking took place in colonial times, they served as lodging places, municipal buildings and places where mail was distributed. They were a place where travelers could get "room and board," the latter being a board set up with dinner for the guests. The term "cold shoulder" originated in taverns—it applied to a guest who showed up late, after the meal was put away, who would get only a cold shoulder of meat instead of the more complete meals that other guests were offered.

The liquid refreshments served at taverns were basic. This was before ice was available. Thirsty locals and guests had the choice of Madeira, American-made beers, rum either straight or mixed, imported gin, brandy, and cider.

Americans Move West

As the population continued to grow, Americans began to move west from where they originally settled by the coast. With the expansion to the "new territories," rum was left behind and work was done to perfect the making of whisky. Irish and Scottish immigrants to the area lent expertise brought from their native lands. The soil to the west of the early colonies proved better suited to the growing of grains, the essential ingredient for making whisky.

Producers found that it was more efficient to transport the grain in the form of whisky from these western regions to the eastern colonies.

Both George Washington and Thomas Jefferson operated distilleries on their estates. The increased interest and production in whisky was aided by several factors:

- There was an increase in the number of Irish and Scottish immigrants who brought knowledge of whisky making with them,
- British blockades of the shipping lanes during the Revolutionary War cut off the supply of molasses,
- Demand for spirits rose as a growing number of men enlisted in the army to fight in the Revolutionary War.

So much grain was being used to make spirits that the supply of flour for bread was threatened. One of the first tests of the federal power of the new republic came in 1794, when a new government in need of funds after the Revolution decided to place a tax on distilled spirits. Farmers in Pennsylvania protested the new tax on the whisky they made and refused to pay it. Protest turned into rebellion, the Whisky Rebellion, as local groups drove the tax collectors out of the area. President Washington sent in troops to quell the disturbance and the protesters disbanded quickly at the sight of federal troops. The collection of taxes and the involvement by the federal government sent the distillers into the hills to distill their spirits illegally to avoid paying taxes, thereby fostering one of the longest running illegal industries in the United States—moonshining.

The Whisky Rebellion arose from a disagreement over the collection of taxes, unlike the temperance movement, which aimed to limit the production and consumption of alcohol. Alcohol consumption was higher after the Revolutionary War than it was in colonial times. Drinking generally was not looked down upon, although public drunkenness was considered unsavory, as it had been throughout history. Proud after its triumph in the Revolution, the new republic viewed the drinking of American-produced liquor as a matter of pride. It was considered both patriotic and loyal to drink American-produced corn whisky rather than imported brandy.

AMERICA'S CONTRIBUTION TO THE SPIRIT INDUSTRY

The first American whisky was made from rye, a common grain of the area. The exact origin of rye whisky, as well as who is credited with first making it, is unknown. Today rye whisky is made from a combination of grains, rye, corn, and barley malt, which improve and moderate the flavor.

The abundance of corn grown in America provided the innovative distillers of the time with the idea to use it to make corn whisky, the predecessor to bourbon. The person responsible for first making bourbon is not known for sure, but it is generally credited to Reverend Elijah Craig. In those times the name of the whisky was generally credited to the county in which it was made. The public took such a liking to the whisky made in Bourbon County, Kentucky, that the name stood for all whiskies made in a similar manner from a combination of corn and grains.

Bourbon, by law, must be made from 51–74 per cent corn. The remainder is a combination of barley malt, rye, and wheat. The product gets its dark color and some of its distinctive flavor from aging in charred oak barrels. By the early nineteenth century, bourbon was a strong regional industry and was considered the national drink of the era.

The golden age of American bars and the beverage industry began in the late 1800s and lasted until the early 1900s, coming to an abrupt end with Prohibition in 1920. There was an evolution from the tavern of the colonial era, to the western saloon, to the bar, as Americans became more sophisticated. Bars were popping up in both hotels and restaurants across the nation. The most elegant bars were found in the luxury hotels. Contributing to this golden age was availability of ice, which was stored in insulated areas to maintain a supply throughout the year. With ice came the cocktail, or mixed drink. Creative bartenders would make fancy concoctions to attract customers to their bars. The roots of the original martini, Manhattan, and Bronx cocktail can be traced to this era.

The anti-alcohol forces in the U.S. Congress finally got their way in 1920 when they passed the Eighteenth Amendment to the Constitution, the Volstead Act, which outlawed the production and consumption of alcohol. This act was passed despite the lack of success of similar laws attempting to outlaw alcohol in other nations of the world. The Volstead Act achieved the opposite effect to that intended, fueling both the growth of, and desire for, alcoholic beverages. Prohibition also made many people wealthy, those who produced and sold illegal alcohol, and gave a healthy boost to organized crime in our nation.

The resounding failure of Prohibition in the United States demonstrates that alcohol is a part of our culture. The prohibition legislation was considered a failure by all the parties involved, and the Twenty-first Amendment repealed it. Although outright banning of the sale and consumption of alcohol did not work, people still think that government should have a role in controlling the use of alcohol and the problems it causes.

THE ROLE OF ALCOHOL IN OUR SOCIETY

The consumption of alcohol in many instances is an integral part of our social life. The amount of alcohol one can consume is considered a measure of maturity by a certain segment of our population. Consumption of certain brands of alcohol is a status symbol to some groups. Beverage companies often try to advertise their product to portray a certain image. Beer companies use advertisements that portray people having fun as a way of implying that alcohol is an important component of having a good time.

Alcohol plays a role in many of the celebrations of our culture. New Year's Eve, weddings, and other times of celebration would almost be considered incomplete without the customary champagne toast. Wine and food are a natural combination in many homes and restaurants. Beer is a customary accompaniment to pizza and with hot dogs at sporting events. Alcohol is the most easily available legal drug in our society.

The distinction between social and religious uses of alcohol has always been unclear. Despite the close ties with religious services, most church leaders have seen drinking liquor as evil. In Islam the consumption of alcohol is forbidden. As the strength of the church has diminished throughout history, the consumption of alcohol has tended to increase accordingly.

The sale, production, distribution, and consumption of alcohol provides a huge revenue for the government. One study found that approximately 65 per cent of the retail cost of distilled spirits goes to pay the local, state, and federal taxes. The beverage industry employs many people who work and pay taxes in a variety of jobs. The alcoholic beverage industry is a major source of both revenue and jobs for our country. According to an estimate by the Distilled Spirits Council of the United States, federal, state and local governments collect more than 6.5 billion dollars a year in taxes from the production, distribution, and sale of alcohol.

Governments generally have contradictory views toward alcoholic beverages and their consumption. On the one hand they believe that alcoholic beverage production should be encouraged because it generates a large amount of tax revenue. On the other side all levels of government are faced with the problems that alcohol causes. Alcohol addiction is a serious problem that plagues all levels of society. Drunk drivers and drunken behavior cost many innocent lives, billions of dollars in damage, broken relationships, and dysfunctional families. There are an estimated 97,000 deaths per year attributed to excessive drinking, and the estimated economic impact approaches 100 billion dollars.

Many food-service operations could not stay open without the profits generated by the sale of alcohol. The general profit mark-up on alcohol is almost twice that on food items that are sold in food service establishments. Together with the fact that people like to drink alcoholic beverages while dining and during entertainment, the sale of alcohol constitutes an integral part of the hospitality industry. Many companies have had to rethink their business plan to compensate for the reduction in alcoholic beverage consumption that has occurred in the last 20 years as Americans have become more aware of the health concerns associated with liquor and the increased legal problems of driving while intoxicated.

Problems Faced by Governments: How to Balance

$Tax revenues generated by alcohol	$Cost of the problems of alcohol

Table 1–1 Popular Sources of Alcohol in the World

1. Beer
2. Wine
3. Spirits

Source: Brewer's Association of Canada, 1996.

SOME FACTS ABOUT ALCOHOL CONSUMPTION

The consumption of alcohol has generally increased with the level of affluence in the Western world. The Western influence on Asia has opened up its market to Western spirits. However, alcohol sales peaked worldwide in the 1980s. There has since been a decline in consumption of all alcoholic beverages except sparkling wines. This reduction in worldwide consumption can be partly attributed to economic recession and to the increased concern for healthy living. Once considered off limits for those with health problems, alcohol may be gaining in popularity again due to the possible benefits attributed to consumption of red wine in reducing cholesterol buildup in the arteries.

Americans generally do not have the daily tradition of drinking with meals that is found in many other cultures. In many European cultures it is customary to consume wine as a part of the meal. There has been a shift in consumption patterns in the U.S. from bars to the home. In most of the country there is a stigma attached to those who admit that they drink too much or drink at home alone.

While some people seek entertainment while they drink they generally go to a bar. They generally prefer the social nature of a bar or lounge. Bars have changed and adapted to make the surroundings more accessible to people who enjoy going out for a drink. The invention of the sports bar has made for an easy transition from watching sports at home to watching sports at the bar.

There are no reliable figures on the worldwide production and consumption of alcohol. A study by the Brewer's Association of Canada found that only about one fourth of the alcohol consumed in the world is in the form of liquor or distilled spirits. Beer and wine rank first and second as the most popular sources of alcohol in the world.

The top five nations in the developed (or 'Western') world for per capita (per person) total consumption of alcohol are Luxembourg, France, Portugal, Hungary, and Spain. The lowest five are Malaysia, Tunisia, Algeria, Morocco, and Vietnam. The United States ranks 24th in total alcohol consumption at 6.8 gallons per person per year, slightly below the 32-nation average. This is up 0.1 gallons from 1993–1995 consumption levels.

THE AMOUNT OF ALCOHOL IN VARIOUS BEVERAGES

Servers and managers of locations that sell alcoholic beverages need to understand the alcohol equivalencies of the various alcoholic drinks to better assist them in the control of intoxication of the patrons they serve. The

Table 1–2 Total Alcohol Consumption by World Region (1990–1995)

Region	Number of Countries Included	Total Alcohol Consumption per Capita 1990 (LPA)	Total Alcohol Consumption per Capita 1995 (LPA)	Percentage Change 1990–95
Western Europe	19	8.56	8.12	−5.2
European Union	16	9.76	9.29	−4.9
Eastern Europe	8	5.92	5.79	−2.1
Latin America	10	3.95	3.95	2.7
North America	2	7.35	6.74	−8.4
Australasia	2	7.98	7.50	−6.1
Rest of World[1]	12	2.45	4.02	64.4
World Total	53	4.39	5.07	15.5

Source: World Drink Trends, 1996 Edition.
[1]Includes Algeria, China, Iceland, India, Israel, Japan, Malaysia, Morocco, Singapore, South Africa, Taiwan, Thailand, Tunisia and Vietnam.

equivalencies of alcoholic beverages are frequently misunderstood by both bar employees and drinkers.

> *There is approximately a half an ounce of pure alcohol in each of the following drinks:*
>
> 12 oz beer = 4 oz wine = 1.25 oz. 80–proof liquor = 1.0 oz 100–proof liquor

THE EFFECT OF ALCOHOL ON THE HUMAN BODY

The alcohol found in alcoholic beverages is actually ethanol, or ethyl alcohol. Ethanol has a sedative effect on the body. In small doses, the human body is able to handle the alcohol. In large doses, alcohol can be deadly. People become intoxicated when they consume more alcohol than their body can metabolize or break down. If a person consumes less than the amount that the body can metabolize, they will not become intoxicated. When a person consumes more alcohol than their body can metabolize, the alcohol remains in their system, causing the person to become intoxicated until the body can break down the alcohol.

The ethanol consumed as part of a drink gets absorbed into the bloodstream in several places as it travels through the body. A small portion of the alcohol is absorbed directly into the bloodstream through the mouth. Twenty percent of the alcohol is absorbed in the stomach, and the remaining 80 percent is absorbed in the intestines. When the alcohol is absorbed into the bloodstream it moves quickly throughout the body.

Although some alcohol passes into the urine without being absorbed, the only way for the majority of alcohol to leave the body is through the body's metabolic process. Most of the alcohol is metabolized in the liver at a constant rate of about one drink an hour. When a person has consumed more alcohol than the body can metabolize, the alcohol circulates in the bloodstream until the liver can process it. Nothing will speed up the rate of metabolism in the liver, or the rate at which a person sobers up. Showers, drinking coffee, exercise, or dancing are common misconceptions that some people have for ways to sober up, but actually they do not affect the rate at which the liver removes the alcohol from the human system.

 Drinking coffee, exercise, showers, or dancing does *not* speed up the rate at which the body sobers up.

The human body is sensitive to alcohol. The legal measurement for intoxication and the amount of alcohol in the body is called Blood Alcohol Concentration (BAC), which is calculated as the percentage of alcohol in the blood. Most states consider a BAC of 0.10 percent or higher as legally intoxicated, while some states have set the limit of 0.08. A BAC of 0.10 percent represents a ratio of alcohol in the body of a thousand to one. A BAC of 0.30 percent can cause a person to fall into a coma, while a BAC of 0.40 percent could cause death.

The ways that alcohol affects the human body include the following:

- Alcohol depresses the central nervous system. The first part of the brain to be affected is the area that controls inhibitions. Then as consumption continues and more alcohol is absorbed, other parts of the brain are affected, such as those that control memory, coordination, sensory perceptions, and motor skills.
- Alcohol causes the person to become thirsty and want to drink more. Its chemical properties help to deplete the body of its fluids. Serving water with a drink helps dilute the amount of alcohol in the blood and partially satisfies the body's craving for liquids.
- Alcohol causes the body to feel warm as the small blood vessels on the surface of the skin dilate. Actually, however, the process cools the body down.

Table 1–3 The Significance of Various Blood Alcohol Concentrations (BACs)

BAC	Legal Definition/Effect on the Human Body
0.08%	Legal level for intoxication in some states
0.10%	Legal level for intoxication in some states
0.30%	Could cause coma
0.40%	Could cause death

THE FACTORS AFFECTING THE ABSORPTION
OF ALCOHOL IN THE BODY

The speed at which alcohol is absorbed into the system and begins to cause the symptoms of intoxication is influenced by several factors. The greater the amount of alcohol in the human system, the faster it will be absorbed. Remember that the alcohol in excess of what the liver can metabolize remains circulating in the body. The rate of consumption and the amount of alcohol consumed go hand in hand to affect absorption and intoxication. There will be a vastly different level of intoxication if a person consumes four glasses of beer in one hour compared to the same person consuming four glasses of beer over a span of four or more hours.

The advice "never drink on an empty stomach" is very wise. The amount and type of food in one's stomach has a direct effect on how quickly one will begin to feel the effects of the alcohol. The presence of food in the system coupled with the time spent actually eating the food slows down the rate at which people drink. The amount and type of food are two important factors affecting the rate of absorption. Food in the stomach helps absorb the alcohol and slows its rate of absorption into the system. Food also helps to protect the stomach from the possible irritating effect of the alcohol.

The type of food also has an effect on the rate of absorption. Fatty foods, such as items that are deep-fried or most cheeses, help to coat the stomach and slow down absorption. Foods that are high in protein are not digested quickly, which also slows down the absorption of alcohol.

The type and composition of the drink can also have an effect on the rate of absorption. Obviously, the more diluted the drink the more slowly the alcohol is absorbed. Although there is the same amount of alcohol in a shot of whisky and a whisky and water, the alcohol in the shot of whisky will be absorbed quicker because it is not diluted as much.

A drink made with a carbonated mixer will be absorbed more quickly than one without. Drinks made with mixers, such as tonic water or carbonated soft drinks like Coke and 7-Up, will pass through the system and into the blood faster than the same amount of alcohol prepared with a non-carbonated mixer, such as juice or water.

The larger the person, the more blood in the system; the smaller the person, the less blood in the system. Since BAC is a measure of the percentage of alcohol in the blood, a bigger person can consume more alcohol than a smaller person can to produce a similar BAC. Women are generally smaller than men are, and coupled with the fact that women's bodies do not metabolize alcohol as efficiently as men's do, women generally become intoxicated faster.

A drinker who is depressed, under stress, or fatigued will react differently to alcohol than someone who is not. The mental state of the person can have a profound effect on their physiology, causing the alcohol to also have a greater effect. A person who is depressed or under more stress than normal may tend to drink more, which further complicates the problem. Fatigue can also produce the effect of the alcohol entering the person's system faster, causing quicker intoxication.

Drugs and medications can have a major effect when mixed with the drinking of alcohol. Some medications intensify the action of the alcohol on the body, while other combinations of drugs and alcohol can be deadly. Some customers may not be aware of the effects on them of combinations of medication and alcohol.

The human body and brain can build up a tolerance to the effects of alcohol over a period of time. The "experienced" or long-term drinker can learn to hide the effects of alcohol and thereby delay the detection of intoxication by the server. Since intoxication is measured legally by the percentage of alcohol in the blood, the experienced drinker can thus have a BAC in the legally intoxicated category and not display the normal signs of intoxication.

DRAMSHOP AND THIRD–PARTY LIABILITY AND THEIR EFFECT ON THE BEVERAGE INDUSTRY

One of the biggest problems facing the beverage service industry is the increase in third-party liability and dramshop-related lawsuits. Although the consumption of alcohol has been reduced in bars, the number of lawsuits filed by people, or the families of people, who are injured by drunk drivers has increased.

It is against the law in all states to serve an intoxicated person. Many states have dramshop laws that hold the business that serves alcoholic beverages liable for the damages caused by an intoxicated guest. In states that do not have dramshop laws, people can sue the business that served the guests until they became intoxicated for damages under the common law of negligence.

Third-party liability transfers the responsibility for the damages and injury caused by a drunk driver to the server, manager, and owner of the operation that served the guest. Lawyers for the injured party will first go after the intoxicated person to cover the expense of the damages. If they find that the guest does not have the large sum of money needed to cover the expenses, they may go after the third party, the seller of the alcohol. Going after the bar, or the bar's insurance policy, is called the deep-pocket theory; one sues the party that has the deepest pocket, or the most money, when trying to get a settlement for damages. Third-party liability and dramshop law issues will be covered in more detail in Chapter 12.

INCREASED PUBLIC AWARENESS AGAINST THE ALCOHOL INDUSTRY

Since before Prohibition there have been groups in the country who have actively campaigned against alcoholic beverages. The miserable failure of Prohibition proved that alcohol is ingrained in our culture. Even so, there are groups today that are calling for a return to Prohibition. They cite the many problems that alcohol causes in our society and to our nation. Although it is a pretty commonly held view that alcohol will never be totally banned here, the neo-Prohibitionists have caught the attention of some lawmakers. The result is stiffer laws and enforcement concerning alcohol.

One group that has had a dramatic effect on the laws pertaining to alcohol is MADD, or Mothers Against Drunk Driving. MADD was founded by a mother whose young daughter was killed by a drunk driver who had been arrested on several prior occasions for drunk driving. MADD has mobilized into a nationwide group that has raised the public awareness of the problems with alcohol. Their actions have brought about stiffer laws and penalties for those convicted of drunk driving, resulting in a reduced number of repeat offenders on the road. Their current project is working with states to lower the legal BAC of intoxication from 0.10 percent to 0.08 percent.

Beverage Industry Responses to the Increased Number of Lawsuits and Public Awareness

The increase in alcohol-related lawsuits coupled with heightened public awareness of the problems that alcohol causes has resulted in major changes by both beverage suppliers and servers. The beverage industry is producing advertisements advising people to drink more responsibly, fearing government intervention. Beer companies, for example, are producing advertisements encouraging people to consume their products in a responsible fashion, with phrases such as "Know when to say when."

Beverage service operations are adapting with their own procedures and policies to help control the abuse of alcohol. An overview of these programs to promote responsible drinking is presented in a later chapter.

The Problems of Alcoholism

Alcoholism is a chronic and generally progressive disease involving the excessive consumption of ethanol. It is characterized by both an emotional and physical dependency on alcohol and often leads to brain damage and early death. The cause is traced to psychological, social, and genetic factors. Approximately ten percent of drinkers in the United States are considered to be alcoholics or to have what is considered a drinking problem. This problem plagues males more than females and is spreading at an alarming rate among teenagers.

Alcoholism generally develops over a prolonged period. The problem is more than excessive or irresponsible drinking—it is a complex disease with many factors. Although the causes of alcoholism are not completely known, it is believed to be partially hereditary.

SUMMARY

Making and consuming alcoholic beverages has gone on for all of recorded history. Equally enduring has been the certain portion of the population that feels alcohol should be banned or severely limited to control the problems it causes for society. The facts that Egyptians accorded the village brewer higher esteem than the baker, and that several religious groups include alcohol as part of their rituals while condemning over-consumption, illustrate the high esteem that alcohol has enjoyed. The historical perspective of this chapter gives the future manager a basic understanding of the historical role of alcohol in our culture.

Alcohol has a dramatic effect on the human body. Those employed in the beverage industry need to be aware of how alcohol flows through the body and the factors that affect absorption, so they can better protect their guests and reduce the potential for lawsuits. The perils of alcoholism are often not included in beverage management texts; future managers need to be informed about some of the resistance they may face and some of the opposition to drinking in general.

KEY TERMS

Dom Perignon	Whisky Rebellion	Eighteenth
Bourbon	Ethyl Alcohol	Amendment
BAC	Tavern	Third-Party Liability
Absinthe	Volstead Act	Rye
Reverend Elijah Craig	MADD	Ethanol
Tolerance	Corn Whisky	Teetotaler
Distillery	Metabolize	Prohibition
Twenty-first Amendment	Madeira	Dramshop Laws
Alcoholism		

CHAPTER QUESTIONS

1. Explain what is meant by the phrase, "alcohol has a mixed history."
2. Why is it fairly accurate to say that the government will not ban alcohol again?
3. How does alcohol affect human physiology?
4. Explain government's contradictory view of alcohol.
5. Why did Prohibition fail in the United States?
6. What has caused the increase of alcohol consumption in the Western world until recently?

7. Where is alcohol absorbed into your bloodstream and where is the majority metabolized?
8. What speeds up the metabolizing of alcohol in the human system?
9. What is the legal BAC of intoxication?
10. What is the equivalent measure of the following drinks: beer, 80–proof alcohol, 100–proof alcohol?
11. Explain why one should not drink alcohol on an empty stomach.
12. Explain two of the factors that affect the absorption of alcohol into the body.
13. What is causing the neo-Prohibitionist movement?
14. What effect is MADD having on the beverage industry?
15. How is the beverage industry reacting to the neo-Prohibitionist movement?
16. Explain the problems with alcoholism.

SUGGESTED READINGS

1. Austin, G. *Alcohol in Western Society from Antiquity to 1800, A Chronological History.* Santa Barbara, CA: ABC–Clio Information Services, 1985.
2. Lender, M. and J. Kirby. *Drinking in America.* New York, NY: The Free Press, 1987.

chapter two

THE ROLE OF THE CUSTOMER
IN A FOOD-SERVICE OPERATION

chapter objectives

This chapter should help you:

- Describe the importance and implications of service in the food and beverage industry.

- Discuss the importance of the customer in a beverage operation.

- State the problems with customers not voicing their dissatisfaction when at a beverage establishment.

- Understand the importance of making an operation customer-driven.

- State the four reasons for making an operation customer-driven.

- Distinguish between the characteristics of goods and services.

- Recognize the various components of the customer-service transaction.

- Improve customer service by understanding the importance of the customer's anticipation of the meal, the actual experience, and the residual feelings and thoughts they have when they leave the establishment.

INTRODUCTION

The economic base of the United States has shifted from industry and manufacturing to service-oriented business in the last few decades. This has changed the emphasis from how well we, as a nation, produce things to how well we perform things. This rather abrupt switch in the business world has caused many problems, and some think it may be partially to blame for the reduction in the competitiveness of American companies in world markets.

The poor state of "service" in America is the brunt of jokes and the subject of many editorials and magazine articles. This may partly be because service positions are often at the lowest rung of the salary scale and are most likely plagued with poorly motivated employees. For service to improve, service employees need to be made aware of the great importance of customers to their business and therefore their jobs.

The purpose of this chapter is to provide future beverage-service managers with information to better understand their customers. A satisfied customer is more likely to return. The majority of the training that managers receive covers the procedural points of running the business rather than the personal aspects of the business. Managers and owners often lose track of the ultimate objective of service operations: *satisfying the customer*.

THE IMPLICATIONS OF SERVICE
FOR THE HOSPITALITY INDUSTRY

Service plays an important role in the hospitality industry. People go out for an evening of entertainment and service. They could just as easily stay home and enjoy a few cocktails with friends, but instead they choose to go out to a club or bar for the surroundings and the service. All those involved in the hospitality industry, whether it be food, beverage, or lodging, must realize that service is the foundation of the hospitality industry. Customers seek service when they go out for a drink or when they order a drink with their meal. If customers desired a drink without service, they could simply buy their favorite beverage at the grocery or liquor store. Customers are willing to pay a premium for the service that is provided along with the cost of their cocktail or drink.

"Service" is the buzzword of the decade. When economic times are tight, customers become more conservative about their spending. Most customers view an evening out as a luxury, rather than a necessity. So in tight times most people demand more value, or try to make their dollar stretch further. To please the increasing number of value-conscious customers, businesses must meet or exceed their customers' service expectations.

A 1996 study by the U.S. Office of Consumer Affairs found that 39 to 46 percent of all service customers were dissatisfied but did NOT complain, and of those, 30 percent do not return to patronize that business. Customers who do not voice their complaints, thereby allowing management to remedy the problem, are unfair to the beverage-service operation. They make the job of ensuring customer satisfaction more difficult because they condemn the operation without allowing it the opportunity to acknowledge and correct the problem. The management and service staff are therefore forced to become more observant with regard to customers' non-verbal actions so problems can be detected and corrected.

The beverage-service industry employs many people in a variety of positions; most are in parts of the operation that customers see and interact with, and a few are in the back parts of the operation that customers do not generally see. One problem is that most of the employees do not view their job or their role as a "customer pleaser." Instead many people in customer-service positions view customers as pests, or "not my job," rather than as the providers of the capital that keeps their place of work in business and that guarantees their paychecks. An example of this is the general reaction by the staff at a bar when a customer arrives ten minutes before closing. The customer gets rushed service from both servers and bartenders, who would rather be cleaning up so they can go home, and mediocre drinks below the quality that the operation generally serves. The result is a dissatisfied customers who will probably never return to that beverage operation and who will probably be more than glad to pass the news of the poor experience on to their friends.

THE IMPORTANCE OF THE CUSTOMER, AND THE CUSTOMER-DRIVEN OPERATION

The definition of a customer, according to Webster's New Collegiate Dictionary, is "one that is a patron (as of a restaurant) or that uses the services (as of a store)." In other words, a patron or customer is someone that exchanges their money for goods and services. The customers' patronage of the food-service operation provides the money which is the lifeblood of the business. They provide the money that pays the bills, the payroll, and generally keeps the doors open for business.

This definition of a customer does not adequately stress the importance of customers to a beverage-service operation. To attract and then retain customers, they must be treated as the most important component of the business. The whole operation must be designed around the customers and their needs. It must, in fact, be *customer-driven.*

Why Make an Operation Customer-Driven?

Beverage-service operations cannot afford NOT to make their operations customer-driven for the following reasons:

- *To distinguish the operation from its competitors.* Customers remember good attentive service. In similar types of beverage-service operation there is not usually much difference in price (for example, between TGI Friday's and Houlihan's), and not much difference in the choice or quality of the products offered. Generally, with all other items being relatively equal, the main reason people choose one place over another is because one does a better job of meeting their needs, whether it be through the speed or effectiveness of the server, the friendliness of the bartender, or the efficient way their occasional complaint gets handled. When they leave the location, it is the level of service received that they will remember the longest.
- *To build "market share,"* the percentage of the market that a particular operation has in the locality. Market share is first gained by offering a product that is different from that offered by a competitor. Most new bars are busy when they first open—they are offering something different that customers seek. Once the competition catches up, and matches the attractions of the new place, the differences between the operations are minimized. Excellent service, and the striving to maintain loyal customers, will allow the customer-driven operation to increase its share of the market even in the face of attractive competition.
- *To build customer loyalty.* Customer loyalty and profitability go hand in hand. Repeat guests are the best advertisement—they bring in new customers through positive "word of mouth," whereas negative word of mouth has a detrimental effect. Prospective customers are more likely to believe what their friends say about the place than what they read in an advertisement. Repeat customers know the operation's menu and services, and are therefore generally easier to serve.
- *To help find mistakes before they happen.* This will help serve the customer better and save time and money for the business. All employees should become "quality inspectors," and the little extra time spent checking will be well worth the effort.

How to Make an Operation Customer-Driven

Where does an operation begin the customer-driven service process? The aligning of an entire organization toward taking care of its customers is more than just the declaration of a new strategy or policy. It requires a focusing of all of the company's resources and personnel. It involves evaluating such things as company priorities, management and staff attitudes, behaviors, and policies.

Improving and maintaining high service standards should not be viewed just as a goal to meet, but rather as an ongoing and unending process. The ultimate measure of an operation's success in satisfying their guests is also the most effective form of advertising for a beverage-service operation— word-of mouth-recommendation. The guests or customers will judge whether the program is successful, as they are the people who must ultimately be satisfied.

Customer service must be made a commitment. Quality service has to be viewed as more than just a passing fad, and in fact as a matter of survival, in an ever-more-competitive business environment. All employees of the operation from the top management to the hourly staff must be aware of the new focus of the company. Commitment must start at the top and filter down. The whole process will collapse if top management only feebly supports the program rather than getting totally involved with it.

Many managers have the misconception that quality and efficient service are too costly to implement; therefore, they do not attempt to set it in motion. This notion could not be further from the truth: *quality service does not cost, it pays.* Benefits are gained both in tangible ways with the improvement of sales and profit, and in intangible ways through boosted customer goodwill and the increased morale of the staff.

Listen and pay attention to the customers. A recent Massachusetts Institute of Technology (MIT) study found that 80 percent of technological innovations came from customer suggestions. Managers and operators need to ask the customer, whose satisfaction is the goal, what they can do to provide better service. Rather than guessing what the customers want, it is best to go right to the source.

Since customers generally do not voice their satisfaction or dissatisfaction, employees need to be aware of actions that may indicate customers' feelings. For example, food that was not eaten or barely touched, or a drink that may have only been sipped a small amount, could signal a problem and warrant a question from the server. Why was the food item not eaten? Was something wrong with the drink? Bartenders and servers, who spend more time with the operation's customers than managers do, can be an excellent source of information concerning customer opinions.

Any information obtained from the customer, through direct observation or conversation, must be communicated to management and the other levels of staff. Information must flow freely along a clear path between all of the people involved, including management, preparation staff (bartenders), service staff (servers, bus people, host or hostess), and customers. For example, numerous customer complaints on a certain evening shift that the Bloody Mary mix is too spicy should be relayed to the bartenders and management so that the problem can be resolved. If the server does not pass on the information, the problem will not be taken care of and other customers who order a Bloody Mary that evening may be dissatisfied. Gathering information from all staff members is crucial to the detection and correction of problems so that customers receive the highest possible level of service.

Recognizing and rewarding good service. In order to keep employees committed to providing good service, they must be given recognition and rewarded. Customer service should be included in the evaluation criteria for all staff. Customer comments and direct observations provide valuable information to judge the quality of customer service that employees are providing. Major ceremonies are not required for the recognition to be successful. Employees just like to be acknowledged among their fellow workers with a certificate or gift, such as a free meal or drink. Some bars and restaurants trade dining certificates so that they can offer employees dinners at other dining places at minimal costs.

MARQUARDT'S LOUNGE

EMPLOYEE EVALUATION - BAR DEPT.

NAME: _____

POSITION: _____

	Score
Promptness	
Appearance & Hygiene	
Customer Service Attitude	
Towards Co-Workers	
Towards Guests	
Initiative	
Teamwork	
Organization	
Work Quality	
Communication	
Sanitation	
Following Supervisors' Instructions	
Computer & Cash Handling	
Total	

Additional Comments:

_____

_____

_____

_____

Customer service should be included in the evaluation of items for all staff.

CHARACTERISTICS OF GOODS AND SERVICES

There are *two* things bundled together in the menu item that customers order: goods *and* services. To understand better the concept and importance of making an operation customer-driven, and how the operation can better serve its guests, we must thoroughly examine these two aspects.

Goods (the actual food or drink) and service (the preparation and delivery of the product) are generally inseparable. Most customers are willing to pay at least four to five times the actual cost of the beverage because of the service provided with it. While the quality of the goods is important, the service is usually what leaves a more lasting impression with the customer and can make or break the visit to the location.

Service differs from goods—service is intangible, something that cannot be physically touched or grasped. In contrast, goods are things that can be handled or consumed. To illustrate the difference, consider a hamburger dinner: the *goods* are the alcoholic beverage, the mixer, garnish, the burger, and all of the things that the customer actually consumes. The *service* is the preparation of the drink and food, placement of the garnish, and the delivery to the guest.

Services

In a food-service operation, both service and goods are required to make the transaction complete. Beverage servers cannot perform their jobs without food or drink to serve to their guests. What distinguishes one operation from the rest is how the goods and services are provided together.

Service is also important because of its crucial role in determining the customer's perception of the value of the beverages. The higher the level of service provided with the drink, the more the customer is generally willing to pay. The significant price difference between a drink from a neighborhood bar and a four-star table-service restaurant illustrates this point.

Goods

The goods include food and beverages—the things that customers eat and drink. The quality of the food served is important to customers. Beverage-service operations have options on the quality of the items they serve—either name-brand items that have customer recognition, such as Absolut vodka and Pepsi-Cola, or items with brand names that customers do not recognize.

While the quality of the beverages served is important, the level and quality of the service provided will have a more lasting effect on most customers. All other factors being similar, a mediocre drink that is served with superbly attentive service will result in a satisfied guest. In contrast, an excellently prepared drink made of high-quality ingredients that is served poorly will generally result in a dissatisfied guest.

COMPONENTS OF THE CUSTOMER-SERVICE TRANSACTION

To be successful in satisfying guests, managers must focus on all segments of the interactions and exchanges between their guests and the various components of their business. Once the managers understand the aspects of each step in the transaction, they can better serve their guests. The exchange that occurs between a guest, or customer, and the service operation comprises three steps:

1. Anticipation, or the expectation prior to visiting the location.
2. The Actual Experience, or what happens during the evening.
3. Residue, or what impression, positive or negative, the customer leaves with.

Anticipation

Before actually visiting the bar, many customers will have formed expectations about the drinks and experience they are about to purchase. Those expectations will then be compared with the actual service provided. For the customer to be satisfied the service they receive must meet or exceed their expectations. The problem is that sometimes customers have unrealistic expectations about the location, based on advertisements or from what they have heard from other people, making them very hard to satisfy.

Customers anticipate the value they will receive for the money they spend; people are generally concerned with what they get for their money, or the price/value relationship. The higher the price paid, the more value is expected. This is of particular concern in difficult economic times when customers are trying to make their money stretch as far as possible.

If the customer is visiting a location for the first time they may view the upcoming experience with some anxiety. This feeling is amplified if the customer is entertaining friends or business acquaintances and where the success of the function (meeting, convention, or wedding) is partly dependent on the quality of drinks and service provided.

The Actual Experience

When the customers have arrived, the "actual experience" segment of the transaction begins. This comprises both tangible things, such as the quality of the food, and intangible things, such as the atmosphere of the establishment. The customer's experience is influenced by more than just the drink.

As the customer approaches the location, they first perceive the condition and upkeep of the outside of the building. A sign with burned out lights or flaking paint, or a run-down building, may cause the customer to think less of the operation, already prejudicing their experience.

Once the customer has entered the building, the atmosphere of the operation is evaluated. The background music, the level of lighting, the type and

The initial contact with the personnel of the beverage operation makes a lasting impression on most guests.

condition of interior furnishings are all judged and compared to their expectations. The service provided by the host/hostess also influences the customer. Customers expect to be greeted promptly, or at least acknowledged, upon arriving. The initial contact with the personnel of the beverage operation makes a lasting impression on most guests.

Customers use all five senses to survey and evaluate the beverage-service operation. Sight provides the most information and things for customers to survey. People might make inferences from what the operation allows them to see and what the operation does not allow them to see.

The temperature of the lounge or bar also affects the customer's enjoyment. A room that is either too cold or too warm will cause the customer discomfort and will detract from the other components of the operation. Sounds can either complement the experience or detract from it. Background music must be chosen carefully. Different people have different tastes in music and one must be careful not to offend one group while trying to satisfy another. The volume of the music is also important and must be carefully considered. The noise of an ice machine, a dish machine, or the group in the next booth may disappoint guests looking for a quiet evening out.

Once the guests are seated at the table, they begin to evaluate the actual delivery of the service. The server is the most important component of this part of the experience. Customers expect prompt and courteous service. The server must be knowledgeable about the menu offerings and be able to make suggestions if requested. To maintain and improve the level of service, cus-

A bar theme can be plain or lavish, conservative or flashy.

tomers appreciate a return visit by the server to the table shortly after the drinks are delivered to remedy any problems and to allow them to make corrections quickly.

Residue

The customer's feelings and impressions upon leaving the location will have a lasting effect. A "please come back" sign on the door is not enough to bring back a customer who was not treated the way they thought they should have been treated. Decisions to revisit the operation, or to recommend the place to friends or family, are determined once the customer evaluates all aspects of the dining experience. Most customers will compare their expectations with what they actually experienced. The management and staff of the operation must work hard to make sure that the customer's problems, if any, are resolved and that the customer leaves satisfied. A satisfied customer will probably be back.

Summary of the Customer-Service Transaction

Most managers concentrate on the "actual experience" segment of the service transaction. While this is important, the other two segments have a critical impact on the customer's satisfaction. Care must be taken that advertising portrays the operation in accurate terms so the customer does not have artificially high expectations or anticipations that are impossible to fulfill. Both management and service staff must be well-versed in non-verbal cues to recognize guest dissatisfaction and remedy it, so the guest leaves with a good impression.

SUMMARY

The customer must be viewed as the most important component of the business. The customer provides the capital and funds for the business to operate. Customers can detect when a trader is not concerned with them or keeping their business, and they will take their business elsewhere. Managers need to understand the implications of good or bad service to the hospitality industry, the importance of making an operation customer-driven, the characteristics of goods and services, and the components of the customer-service transaction.

By understanding these concepts and understanding better the reasons customers have for dining out, managers can operate more efficiently and set appropriate priorities and goals.

Improving service does not mean changing recipes or ingredients, although both are important if your customers are dissatisfied with them. Improving service is accomplished by realigning the goals and objectives of the operation toward meeting and exceeding the guests' expectations. All areas and personnel of the operation, from the executives and top managers to the staff and support personnel, must be dedicated to the cause. Training and recognition must be geared toward achieving and maintaining a high level of customer service.

KEY TERMS

Service	Goods	Perception of Value
Customer	Services	Anticipation
Customer-Driven	Tangible	Actual Experience
Market Share	Intangible	Residue

CHAPTER QUESTIONS

1. Why is it important that all employees of a beverage-service operation view one of their roles as customer pleasers? What is the potential problem if they do not?

2. Why is Webster's definition of the word "customer" inadequate for a beverage-service operation? What is the meaning of customer in food-service terms?

3. You are assigned the role of training the new staff in a beverage-service operation. How would you explain to the new staff members the four reasons

for making the operation customer-driven? Include an example of each reason.

4. The owner of the place where you work does not understand why success depends on all levels of staff being committed to making the location customer-driven. How would you explain this key point to him/her?

5. Explain the relationships between goods and services in a beverage-service operation, and the concepts of tangibility and intangibility.

6. Explain the three components of the customer-service transaction. Explain which parts of the transaction the manager has control over and which parts he does not. What potential problems can occur with elements of the transaction that management cannot control?

7. Explain why a PLEASE COME BACK sign on the door is not sufficient to bring customers back.

chapter three

THE PLANNING STAGE

chapter outline

chapter objectives

Reading this chapter will enable you to:

- Discuss the fundamentals of planning a bar and beverage operation.
- Define the American Bar Concept.
- Become familiar with the various types of bars.
- Define feasibility study.

- Establish a marketing strategy.

- Discuss the fundamentals of interior design and practical layouts.

- Discuss project planning before architectural/engineering plans are drawn up.

- Offer an inviting atmosphere by creating an attractive décor.

- Plan a safe, entertaining, and functional environment for bar patrons.

- Define marketing research.

PLANNING THE BAR AND BEVERAGE OPERATION

As in most businesses, a bar and beverage operation requires careful consideration and intelligent planning to achieve success. The wise entrepreneur should consider, above all, the human factor. The deciding issues in the planning turn upon answering questions such as: "What type of person is going to patronize the establishment? What is the nature of the potential patrons? What are their preferences and their social habits? In which income bracket are they? What is the potential-patron percentage for each of the income levels? What are their educational levels, average age, ethnic background and type of residence? What price structure should the establishment adopt? Is there competition in the area? What are the competitor's main features? Is the location urban or rural? Is there adequate accessibility and visibility?" A satisfactory answer to each of the above questions will greatly facilitate the planning task. Only then will the project acquire a distinct shape. Specific and precise project descriptions will simplify the architectural/engineering task, and general contractors will not have to guess and approximate when executing the physical aspect of the plans. The sum total of all this preparation effort is commonly called **Market Research.** Competently conducted market research will leave little doubt as to physical appearance of the building, the landscaping, the interior design and décor, the selection of furnishings, and the overall appointment of the facility. Market research will also reveal the most effective marketing strategy to be adopted, and determine the type of service that will be featured. It will also simplify the staffing task and facilitate the operator's decisions concerning the selection of beverage products to be offered to potential patrons.

Taking over an existing operation is not nearly as demanding as building a new one, (with the possible exception of marketing and/or managing-competence issues if the existing operation has not proven consistently successful). Modifying, improving and upgrading an existing facility certainly requires time and know how. However, more creativity, expertise and greater overall effort is to be expected when building a new enterprise. A new building and an untapped market with an unknown potential clientele carries no history of past performance. The "unexpected" should always be considered, but it is encouraging to note that, traditionally, beverage operations show a very low rate of failure and are generally not considered high-risk investments. Banking executives report that family-owned bar and beverage operations rank low in the bankruptcy charts and that they seldom experience financial problems. In a typical medium to large size hotel where food, taken by itself, usually generates 15–18 percent profit or turnover, the beverage department may well generate a profit of 50–55 percent of sales.

In the process of planning the building logistics and the overall physical execution of the project, federal, state, and local laws must not be ignored. In general, city and county ordinances are subject to change more frequently than federal ones. Liquor laws are known to be strictly enforced. Failure to comply with regulations, such as submitting proper applications for permits and licenses within a certain period of time, may prove costly for the investor.

It is recommended that the first-time-operator study time-proven planning procedures and obtain the necessary background information from experienced operators. This is particularly valuable when considering the best possible use of the space available. Technical factors, such as the placement of equipment in relation to design and layout constraints, require special attention. People that have planned, owned and/or managed consistently successful beverage operations are obviously the most qualified to advise on these matters.

TYPES OF BARS

Following the completion of the market research as outlined previously, and before hiring an architectural/engineering firm, the operator should become familiar with the different types and concepts of bar and beverage operations. An airport bar is designed to attract a distinct clientele, the traveler. In contrast, a bar designed in the same manner and located in a leisure hotel, may appear lacking and may not offer the characteristics, products and service that patrons expect from a leisure hotel.

Types and styles of beverage operations are classified according to a specific marketing technique called **Beverage Market Segmentation.** In this process each operation is classified according to the type of clientele it wishes to attract. Currently four major segments are recognized: Business, Travel, Recreation, and Luxury.

A "bar" is defined as the counter between the person that is serving and the customer. In the U.S. the concept of the bar as we know it today originated from the English Pub. "Pub" is an abbreviation of "Public House" (a public drinking place). A century ago bars in the U.S. were called "Taverns." During the gold fever times of the Far West, a bar was commonly referred to as a "Saloon." A few decades ago, the bar was a place where people went primarily to drink alcoholic beverages. Today there are other reasons for visiting bars. Recent surveys report that a great number of patrons believe that the actual drinking should be considered secondary. Their main purposes in visiting bars are socializing, meeting old friends, and making new ones. The social gathering and interaction with others are what makes the bar so popular. For some, entering a bar means escaping a temporary refuge that takes them away from the daily grind and the stress brought about by our faster-paced, vibrant society.

Beverage Market Segmentation categorizes the major types of bars. However to accurately classify bar concepts can be a difficult task, considering that they vary so greatly. There are **piano bars, airport bars, sports bars, discotheque bars, small and medium size neighborhood bars,** and **large operations with spacious lounges that feature a variety of entertainments.** There are bars that offer simple snacks and appetizers, while others feature more elaborate full-length menus. Billiards, pinball machines, and computer games are commonly provided. Some even offer the most up-to-date arcade-type entertainment. Temporary bars may be set up for special functions, such as a sporting event in a stadium. There are also operations that focus on trendy, specialty food and/or beverage items, and are named as such. Thus one can find Quiche bars, Wine bars, Crepe bars or Microbrewery bars. In the last two decades, the "Karaoke" bar has become popular particularly in neighborhood locations.

THE AMERICAN BAR CONCEPT

There are countless physical configurations and designs of bars. They range from straight counter bars to serpentine, rotating horseshoe, L,S,U-shaped, or circular bars. Some have rectangular or oblong configurations. With few exceptions, they all have a common denominator, they derive their basic design from the **"American Bar Concept."** The American bar prototype was developed around the turn of the last century and refined in the post-WWII period. Its typical features are tall bar stools, a wide selection of alcoholic beverages on display, a vast array of types and sizes of glassware, draft beer spigots, and a number of television sets. They can feature an aggressive or a more soothing atmosphere. In most cases, they suggest a distinct theme or motif. In comparison, the typical European bar (often called "cafe") does not include bar stools. Generally, patrons place their orders while standing up. The selection of alcoholic beverages is limited and ice is seldom offered (or a very small amount) in the service of sodas and in the mixing of drinks. The inventory of glassware, equipment, tools, and utensils is generally small. European bar owners/operators do not place emphasis on atmosphere and ambiance in the same way as in U.S. bars. European bars also feature items not common in U.S. bars such as ice creams (gelatos), sweets and chocolates, pastries, aperitifs (beverages consumed before a meal), bitters, digestifs (consumed after a meal to help digestion), and occasionally medicinals (beverages that help balance gastric juices). Espresso-type coffees, cafe au lait, and cappuccinos are popular items. The food offerings often consist of cold sandwiches and various sliced meats made into a sandwich with toasted, sliced white bread.

Today not only in Europe but in Asia, particularly Japan, Taiwan, Korea, and in South America, the American bar concept is expanding to small towns and along the highways. A typical American bar would include in its inventory all of the six principal spirits (vodka, whisky, gin, rum, brandy, and tequila) and from 25 to over one hundred types of cordials and liqueurs (Kahlua, Drambuie, Benedectine, Amaretto, Anisette, Frangelico, Tia Maria, Grand Marnier, Bailey's, etc.). Beers are served in a bottle, can, or on draft. To be noted is the growth of microbrewed products during the past two decades. In the U.S. beer accounts for 52% of total beverage sales. An average bar may offer a long list of brands for each of the spirits discussed in Chapter 6. It is not uncommon to find eight or ten types of vodka and five or six types of gin, rum, tequila, and brandy. On whiskeys alone, a bar may offer several types of Scotch, Bourbon, Canadian, and Irish. This extensive selection of products is one of the most distinctive characteristics of the American Bar Concept. Like their Asian, South American, and African counterparts, European bars offer a limited selection of cocktails. A typical cocktail guide may contain up to fifty mixtures. In comparison, U.S. bartender's guides may, and often do, list over a thousand cocktails. Wines are also abundant in the American bar. Large volume operations often include a "bag in the box" type of wine dispensing and may also feature a well stocked wine cellar. The "Cruvinet" type of wine dispenser, which allows the bartender to serve wine by the glass, from an individual bottle, is becoming increasingly popular, particularly in upper class bars.

The American bar often includes specialty drinks and beverages that may vary according to geographical location and climate. Thus, one may find a bar in Alaska featuring a hot steamed punch with a choice of various liqueurs, while a bar in the southwest desert might offer cool, refreshing drinks such as frozen daiquiris and wine cooler mixes.

Soft drinks are in most cases American-made (Coca Cola was the first carbonated soft drink); thereby a steady selection of soft drinks is always assured. Sodas can be served in cans, bottles or through the gun system. Another unique feature is the around-clock availability of freshly brewed American coffee and decaffeinated coffee.

In larger hotel and restaurant operations, three bar classifications are usually found: the front bar, the service bar, and the portable bar.

THE FRONT BAR

In a front bar beverages are served directly to the patron seated on the barstool, or they are prepared by the bartender and served by a cocktail server to the patron seated at a table. Usually bartenders wear standard uniforms. The bar is managed here more formally than in a service bar, due to the fact that all activities are under the direct scrutiny of the patron. The most visible aspect of the front bar is the liquor display area. The displays can vary dramatically, from a basic one, featuring only standard products, to the more furbished type that can offer well over one hundred brands of spirits and cordials. In many cases, mirror glass and well designed glass shelves are found. The liquor display is the centerpiece. A bar without product display certainly lacks character. Wise bar operators long ago realized that customers prefer to see the unique bottle packaging and often check the label. An attractive display can represent a significant marketing and merchandising tool. The liquor storage area, the dry goods and supplies store rooms, are usually located behind the front bar, away from the patron's view.

The underbar is the area underneath the view of the patron. It serves as a working station where the bar staff keeps the various pieces of equipment and all that is needed for the customer's needs. A well stocked and organized underbar provides the means to the bartender to maintain a steady flow of service. The underbar includes seven main compartments that are individually discussed in the following chapter: The glassrail, the speedrack, the well or jockey boxes, the ice bins, the gun system, the glass washing compartment, and the refrigeration.

THE SERVICE BAR

The majority of service bars are not in the direct view of the patron and are not designed to be accessed by customers. Although the basic equipment set up is the same as in the front bar, they occupy less space and their physical appearance is often informal. Service bars serve a specific purpose: To expedite service and provide beverage needs for banquets, dining rooms, room service outlets, showrooms, and generally, functions that require a "behind the scene" section. Bartenders who operate service bars may or may not be in uniform. They do not have to perform certain tasks that may be necessary when the patron is present. In catering operations and the like, they seldom handle cash. The beverage orders are given to the service bartender directly, either verbally, by ticket or as in locations equipped with the latest technology, via the terminals of computer systems. Service bar types and sizes vary. There may be a semi-permanent banquet table/bar set up to provide beverages in a small restaurant, or a long counter bar staffed with four or five bartenders and set up to handle a large beverage volume.

Free-pouring is adopted mostly in small operations, while larger volume operations require automatic dispensing systems. Large operations may adopt free-pouring when serving premium brands.

THE PORTABLE BAR

The portable or mobile bar is not a new concept but thanks to modern technology it has been developed and made highly functional for today's needs. Portable bars are particularly useful in on- and off-premise catering functions as well as in various kinds of public places such as stadiums and theaters. If properly set up, a typical portable unit is sufficient to service hundreds of guests. A portable bar unit, although in smaller dimensions, includes some of the same equipment found in a stationary bar such as a speedrack, a gun system, an ice bin etc. A large banquet area might feature a multiple-portable bar unit. Because of their versatility and practicality, today, all major hotels carry various types of mobile and transportable bar units.

ESTABLISHING MARKETING TARGETS

In establishing effective marketing parameters, competent operators resort to the market research reports discussed earlier in this chapter; at the same time they should consider customer preferences and expectations. The bar and beverage business is in constant evolution, so it is necessary to continually analyze trends and answer questions about the decor, the physical layout, the selection of bar products, and types of entertainment; for example, "What do people who patronize bars and lounges, enjoy the most today?" These concerns are simpler to address when planning a distinct type of operation such as a bar in an airport, or a piano bar. There are certain paradigms that have long been established and proven to be valid. The wise operator will conduct his/her marketing strategy within such parameters.

Feasibility Studies

A **Feasibility Study** is an invaluable tool for the entrepreneur. Its main purpose is to forecast what type of operation will have the best chance of success, and to find the best possible means of attracting the desired clientele. The study analyzes items that will be vital for the future business, such as location, traffic patterns, geographical considerations, the evaluation of zoning restrictions, signage, accessibility from main roads and highways and parking availability. To an extent, a feasibility study is an itemized expansion of the market research discussed earlier in this chapter. Whereas market research is intended to study and analyze overall demographic data, such as up-to-date information on the potential patrons' occupations, incomes, social habits, ethnic mix, religious affiliations, personal lifestyles and so forth, a feasibility study is more concerned with geographical and physical characteristics that may affect guest patterns. These studies also review the type of community and the local environment, but not extensively as in a wide-open market research study. Put simply, a feasibility study will conclude whether it is *feasible*, convenient, and advantageous to place a type of business in a certain area, keeping in mind that such an area may include physical environments not typical of other areas.

Feasibility studies have always played an important role in the planning stages of businesses. A good example is provided by the fast food industry, which has experienced astonishing growth in the last three decades. This growth, the "Fast Food Phenomenon," came about as a consequence of distinct social changes, and has been nurtured by companies who are known to invest a great deal of time, effort, and capital to ensure that each outlet is strategically placed in the best possible location in regard to accessibility and visibility.

When the planning reaches the advanced phase, the competent operator prepares for **Positioning.** Positioning includes planning to offer potential patrons a particular bar menu. This is an area where an operation can be made to be attractive and unique. A specialty product (frozen drinks, or creative cocktails for example) might give the patron something to remember, particularly when selecting a bar to go to for an evening.

If, for whatever reason, a new bar is to be placed in a location where there are other bars, it is recommended not to rush but to take time to consider a competitor's **Comparison Analysis.** As this name suggests, all those involved in the planning should learn as much as possible about the competitor's operation and people's perception of it. Although operators often react negatively to a competitor (someone who steals part of your business), a competitor can also be viewed as someone who works with other competitors in promoting and ensuring more business in total. A competitor in most cases is not a rival. It is known that competition can be beneficial to a business, instead of detrimental. If a competitor temporarily capitalizes on someone's errors and/or weakness, that person has the opportunity to correct those errors and overcome the weakness. In the process the trader is given an incentive to strive to become more competitive, by offering improved service and better value for money in an attempt to re-gain lost clientele.

INTERIOR DESIGN AND LAYOUT

Design-Establishing a Theme

Following the market research, feasibility study and the execution of preliminary architectural/engineering drawings, the wise operator begins to be envision the interior design and layout logistics. A bar and lounge may feature a standard appearance, typical of many. There are countless operations that are well appointed, clean, spacious, and attractive but do not offer a specific theme or motif. If a distinct theme is to be established, it must be consistent with certain traits and characteristics revealed by the market research and the feasibility study. A bar theme can be plain or lavish, conservative or flashy. Its furnishings can be moderately priced or quite costly. If an interior decorator is consulted, a bar professional with experience in the business, should be consulted at the same time. The purpose of this is both practical and functional. Too often, investors have been subjected to the unpleasant experience of wasting large sums of money in subsequent construction modifications. Rectifications and physical modifications of original plans can be very costly. It is recommended that original plans be reviewed several times. Occasionally, consulting a seasoned bar professional and hiring the temporary services of specialized firms with an established reputation in the field, can be beneficial and cost saving.

A bar theme can be plain or lavish, conservative or flashy.

Theme bar designs are endlessly varied. Motifs of American nostalgia, country and western, nautical, sports heroes, movie stars, entertainment celebrities, cars-of-the-past, and references to personal hobbies and/or collectibles are among the most popular. Some operations go further: they capitalize on the geography of the region and *its climate*. One can find an exotic tropical theme bar in a northern section of Canada, and perhaps another theme built around a cooling, refreshing mountain stream in a bar located in the southwest desert areas.

Layout

The bar layout must take account of important aspects such as efficiency and practicality. It concentrates on physical considerations such as floor space, storage areas, plumbing, electrical, and ventilation systems. A properly planned layout allows for a smooth traffic flow for both staff and customers while assuring that all furnishings and equipment are placed correctly and conveniently throughout the site. Planning a smart layout also means using the space that is available in the best possible manner.

Space is definitely a concern. It is generally accepted that a customer should be entitled to a minimum of 12 square feet of space; in a lounge each person should be allocated a minimum of 18 square feet. On the counter, the patron should be entitled to a minimum of 20 linear inches of space. During peak times, bars are often overcrowded to the delight of the bar operator. However, state and local fire departments will have established a maximum capacity based on the square footage. This means that at any given time the total number of patrons present in the establishment should not exceed the legal maximum imposed by the fire authorities. When taking over an existing operation that has been demonstrated to include a layout that was not functional, the manager can face a challenging task. Among the many inconveniences, a poor layout could also result in a higher payroll cost. For example, if a refrigeration unit, or a larger piece of equipment cannot be easily moved, or reached, that will result in considerable time wasted. "Time and motion studies" clearly show that due to poor layout, a higher number of employees is often necessary to perform the same duties that a smaller number could, had the layout be more functional and more carefully planned.

Generally in smaller operations, the owner/operator plans the layout and participates in the execution of the project. In larger outlets, an architectural firm is customarily hired. The architect will follow up with a general contractor in completing specific physical areas such as plumbing, flooring, and electrical wiring.

Atmosphere and Decor

It is often said that the determining factors that bring a patron back to an establishment are price/value, cleanliness, quality of service, and quality of the product served. Often times the "atmosphere" and ambiance are overlooked. They should be considered equally important factors. Patrons in general share a more personal relationship with a bar or lounge atmosphere than any other public place. Trendy, more flamboyant establishments will attract more of an "upbeat" clientele, while wood-paneled, dimly lit and more conservative outlets will feel more inviting to a sedate clientele. There are patrons who feel that a bar without loud music or lively entertainment lacks "mood" and atmosphere; while there are others who prefer a quiet conversation with friends in more relaxed surroundings.

What sets the atmosphere? We identify two principle factors, the abstract feeling and the physical appearance, which are mainly set by the decor, the colors, and the sound. Obviously, there are instances where, if the establishment is empty it will not be attractive to anyone, no matter what type of atmosphere is offered. As the old adage says: "People go where people are."

Before entering the establishment, patrons must feel that the parking area, surrounding grounds, and the overall outside appearance is clean and well maintained. The feeling of safety is also important. Upscale beverage establishments and hotel operations handle this matter correctly by offering valet parking and uniformed security guards. The competent bar operator knows how crucial first impressions can be. The signs should be well posted, and easy to read. Upon entering, the patron should feel comfortable.

If the furnishings suggest a particular theme, they should blend harmoniously throughout the locale. Good sanitary conditions are an important part of the operation. Today people are more concerned with cleanliness than ever before. There is nothing more unappealing than rest rooms that are poorly maintained, soiled carpets, and bar glassware that is not thoroughly washed and sanitized. Ladies rooms, apart from displaying the highest sanitary standards, should also offer lighter colors, large mirrors, flowers if possible, and in general, amenities that appeal to the female clientele. Wise beverage operators know that the female patron is the deciding factor in selecting one establishment over another. In a lounge, table and chairs should be arranged in an orderly manner and all appointments properly placed and neatly cared for. Environmental control factors such as heating and ventilation should always be in proper functioning condition. Fireproof material and safety devices are usually specified by the local fire code. It is imperative for the establishment to be ready at all times for unannounced visits by the local fire and health inspector. The responsible bar and beverage manager regularly consults a daily opening and closing checklist. The checklist will allow the manager to avoid neglecting items that could later on result in a guest complaint.

Today more than ever, women patronize bar and beverage establishments. Traditionally, bars were designed with the male customer in mind. As pointed out previously the wise operator, when choosing furnishings and appointments for a particular theme, makes certain not to neglect features that are pleasing to the female patron. Flattering lighting, lighter and more subtle colors, wider isles between tables, easy to read bar menu, flowering plants, and art work are attractive to the female clientele. They will in turn attract male clientele resulting in increased sales.

In today's food and beverage industry, the quality of service is an essential part of an operation's success. Service has become the backbone of the hospitality industry. Many patrons believe that the atmosphere of a bar or restaurant is greatly enhanced by the friendly and positive attitude of its staff. A cold, detached bartender or a lounge cocktail server who does not possess the necessary inter-personal skills will not make the patron feel welcome and appreciated.

KEY TERMS

Public Place	Sequencing	Market Research
Saloon	Aperitif	Demographics
Quiche Bar	Concoction	Feasibility Study
Island Bar	Service Bar	Positioning
American Bar Concept	Backbar	Competition
Underbar	Layout	Analysis
Glassrail	Time & Motion Studies	Bag in the Box
Speedrack	Mobile Bar	

CHAPTER QUESTIONS

1. Is it simpler to build a brand new beverage operation or to upgrade an existing one?
2. What is the number one priority for an individual who is planning to invest in a new bar and beverage operation?
3. What is the derivation of the word "Pub"?
4. What are the most common types of bar?
5. Name the three bar categories typical of a large hotel operation.
6. What is the question most often asked, when determining a marketing target?
7. What is a feasibility study?
8. What should be taken into consideration when planning a bar design and layout?
9. Atmosphere is created by two main elements. What are they?
10. For what reasons should a bar operator develop an attractive decor for female patrons?

SUGGESTED READINGS

1. Coltman, M. *Beverage Management.* New York: Van Nostrand, 1989.
2. Kotschevar, L. *Managing Bar and Beverage Operations.* East Lansing, MI: Educational Inst. American Hotel & Motel Association (AHMA), 1991.

chapter four

BAR AND BEVERAGE EQUIPMENT

chapter outline

chapter objectives

Upon completion of this chapter you will be able to:

- Understand why the proper equipment is necessary for a successful operation

- Become familiar with typical bar equipment

- Identify the various units of underbar equipment

- Identify the most common bar tools and utensils

- Identify the various units of backbar equipment

- Understand the importance of equipment upkeep and maintenance

PROPER EQUIPMENT FOR A SUCCESSFUL OPERATION

As discussed in the previous chapter, an attractive decor, a practical layout and a comfortable atmosphere are essential for the success of the operation. However, ensuring that the proper equipment is utilized, can be just as crucial. The basic equipment, such as refrigeration units, ice machines, and cocktail mixing devices, has for the most part, remained unchanged in the last fifty years and is practically the same in most bars. There are, however, many variables according to the type of operation. For example, some bars still use the basic cash register that was prominent in the not-too-distant past, while others adopt more sophisticated computerized equipment. If one were to analyze the evolution and modification of basic bar equipment over the last two decades, the thing that has improved the bar and beverage industry more than any other is, without a doubt, the computerized system using liquor-dispensing units and touch-screen technology. The efficient volume-service beverage operations we see today would have been impossible to realize without these technological marvels. Bar and beverage operators can now obtain quick and accurate financial reports and sales breakdowns at any given time thanks to computer technology. In a thousand-patron showroom setting, operators can now satisfy everyone's beverage needs in a timely manner, by serving portion-controlled drinks using an improved liquor dispensing system.

As a result of the expansion of restaurant and bar supplies centers, which are now fairly well distributed throughout the U.S., bar operators today have a larger selection of equipment and working tools to choose from. Buying quality equipment seems to be the common goal of today's bar owners and managers. Quality equipment often means durability. Refrigeration equipment of inferior quality can represent a serious headache for the bar operator and the staff. In busy bars, items such as blenders and mixers, are subject to continuous use. Anything less than the very best quality will result in breakage and loss of revenue. Equipment that shows the utmost simplicity in design is often strongly built and durable. Knives, that are used to cut and slice fruit for garnishes, should be of high grade steel, serrated and always razor sharp. A condiment tray that has compartments that are easy to pull out and wash, is a more practical item to work with. A speedrack should easily detach from the main unit and be easy to clean, sanitize and put back in place. A metal shaker must be of quality gauge metal and of the correct size.

UNDERBAR EQUIPMENT

Most of the equipment needed by bartenders to service customers is located in the **underbar.** The underbar is located inside the bar counter. Some of the larger equipment such ice machines, walk-in refrigerators and automatic dispensing systems are located in the **back bar.** A typical underbar includes the following compartments:

The **glassrail** is a narrow extension of the counter, usually one inch lower than the regular counter surface. In this area drinks are prepared before service. The glassrail is often seen covered by a plastic or rubber mat for the purpose of containing spillage and maintaining a sanitary appearance.

The **speedrack** is located below the ice bin at waist level. Like most of the working areas in the underbar, the speedrack is made of stainless steel and serves the purpose of holding the bar products most commonly requested by the customer. A good practice for the bar manager and bar staff is to maintain a steady order of *sequencing* so that the bottles of each particular spirit are always in the same spot. The experienced bartender never needs to look at the product label when picking up a bottle out of the speedrack. Although each operation establishes its own working standards, a typical sequence is set up in the following order: 1. vodka 2. bourbon 3. scotch 4. gin 5. rum 6. brandy 7. tequila. One traditional sequencing method listed bourbon first, followed by scotch and gin. Some operations prefer the sequence that does not allow the clear spirits (vodka, gin, rum) to be placed next to each other.

The **wells** or **jockey boxes** are located on both sides of the ice bin and serve the purpose of keeping all supplementary items needed for proper service. The temperature that surrounds the ice bin helps keep these items cold. Unlike the speedrack, in which only liquor is placed, the wells hold items such as grenadine, lime juice, the most common fruit juices (orange, tomato, grapefruit, cranberry, and pineapple), various mixes, sweet and dry vermouth, milk, whipping cream, and so forth.

The **ice bins** located underneath the bar provide the ice needed for the drinks. As the ice melts, the perforated bottom of the bin will drain the

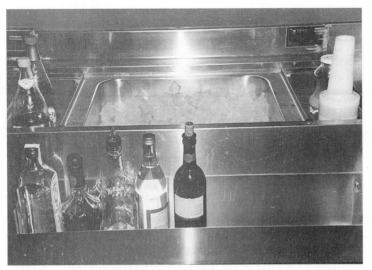

Speedrack (front) and well or jockey boxes (to each side of the ice).

overflow water. Inexperienced or careless bartenders often develop the erroneous habit of placing on the ice items such as fruit juice containers, bottles of wine, can of whipping cream etc. With the exception of the ice scoop, nothing should be placed in the bin. A good sanitation principle is that ice is a food product and should not be contaminated.

The **front gun system** (see liquor dispensing systems later in the chapter)

The **glass washing compartment** can include manual glasswashing, which is done by using three different sinks (a. washing b. rinsing c. sanitizing), and an automatic glasswashing machine. The washing sink may have an electric or a manual glass scrubber. Some operators feel that a fourth sink (the dump sink) allows the bartender to recycle the glassware faster. The dump sink, in which all used garnishes and leftover ice is dumped, is located to the left of the three sinks mentioned above.

Reach-in refrigeration, such as reach-in boxes, beer coolers, and sometimes small freezers are located in the underbar area, conveniently positioned so that the bartender can reach for the item needed in the shortest possible time.

The typical smaller equipment, working tools, and utensils found in the underbar are:

Shakers. For mixing and/or chilling the liquids used to make a cocktail (by shaking the ice and the liquids together.) The shaker can be of the traditional type, which includes a metal and a glass part; or the continental type, which is a single unit entirely made of metal, that can be separated in various pieces.

Jiggers. Devices used to assure the correct measure when pouring. The standard jigger, also called "shot glass," is made of thick glass and will

Two-headed jiggers or measuring cups offer a multitude of measures.

measure up to three ounces. There are also two-headed jiggers or measuring cups that offer a multitude of measures. They are usually made of metal with small imprints on one side indicating the corresponding measures. Experienced bartenders claim to have developed over the years certain techniques, by which they can pour the exact amount of liquor without the need of a jigger or shot glass. One of these techniques involves a systematic counting system when pouring. An example is: counting 1001, 1002, 1003 and 1004 and stopping immediately; this (it is said) will result in pouring exactly one ounce (for each count 0.25 of an ounce is released.) This practice is called **Free Pouring.** It is recommended that management discourage this practice particularly with novice employees. An inexperienced bartender can easily pour a **double shot** without realizing it.

Measured pourers. Colorful pre-measured devices that release the correct amount of liquid when turned upside down. These are not recommended when pouring cordials, liqueurs, or syrupy beverages as they can be easily clogged and become "sticky" by the action of the sugar content in the beverage. Once the pouring spout becomes clogged the measured portion will no longer be accurate. The three most common measures are: **short pour, medium pour** and **long pour.** Generally the short pour consists of a portion from ½ oz. to ¾ oz; the medium pour from ⅞ oz. to 1¼ oz.; the long pour from 1¼ to 2 oz.

Strainers. Metal tools with a round coiled wire. For straining and preventing the ice from being poured from the shaker, or shaker-type container into the customer's glass.

Zesters. Also called strippers, are small tools used to cut small pieces of citrus skin.

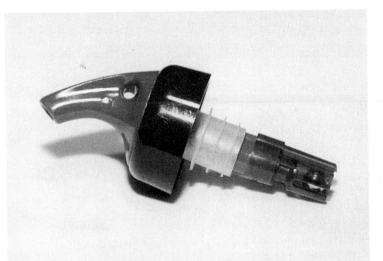

Pre-measured devices release the correct amount of liquid when turned upside down.

Condiment Trays. For keeping fruit and other garnishes necessary to dress cocktails. Usually made of plastic, they can have from five to ten compartments. The most common garnishes are: olives, lemon peels (for "twist"), lemon wedges, maraschino cherries, orange slices, lime wedges, bar onions, pineapple slices, and celery stalks.

Bar Spoons. Small spoons with long, twisted handles, they are used to chill liquids, such as those used in the preparation of a martini or a Manhattan up. They can also be used to layer drinks by using a "floating" technique over the back side of the spoon.

Cutting boards and knives. For slicing and cutting fruit garnishes. The cutting board surface should be of non-pourous material for health reasons. Serrated knives are preferred.

Rimmers. Used to uniformly coat the rim of a glass with salt or sugar, as when making a Margarita cocktail. The coupette type of glass, with its rim wet, is placed upside down on the rimmer for couple of seconds so that the glass rim will evenly salted.

Muddlers. For crushing fruit, such as an orange slice or a cherry, used in the preparation of an "Old Fashioned" cocktail. This tool is usually made of light wood.

Blenders. For crushing the ice while mixing the liquids, as in the preparation of frozen cocktails such as Margaritas and Daiquiris.

Mixers. Used in most modern bars to replace the shaker. Unlike the blender, which breaks and crushes the ice, the mixer kicks the ice around the metal container, allowing the mixing and foaming of liquids, such as those used in the preparation of Collins, Sours, and Fizzes.

A rimmer is used to coat the rim of the glass with salt, as with a Margarita cocktail.

The muddler is used to cruch fruit, such as an orange or cherry, in preparation of an "Old Fashioned" cocktail.

Coffee Makers. Indispensable items in most bars. Coffee makers vary in types and sizes. Operators often obtain coffee makers at no charge, from the company that supplies them with coffee.

Slush Machines. Used to dispense premixed and pre-portioned ingredients particularly for "tropical" cocktails such as Pina Colada.

A mixer and a blender.

Draft Beer Spigots. From the traditional two or three spigots of the past, modern bars may feature up to twenty colorful units offering different kinds of domestic and imported beers, including **ales, stouts,** and **microbrews.**

Wine Dispensers. Wine can be dispensed using the gun system, in the same manner as liquor and juices. In this case it becomes necessary to use a large container, commonly known as "bag in the box," which can hold several gallons. Some beverage operators, aware that wine of superior quality is rarely stored in this type of container, feature the **cuvinet** dispenser in which individual standard-size wine bottles are placed for quality wine dispensing, by the glass.

Juice Containers. For holding juices needed in working areas. The plastic types are preferred for sanitary reasons. The most common type of juice container is not totally transparent; for this reason bar equipment vendors offer color-coded bases or spouts to better identify the type of juice. Tomato juice is easy to identify, but grapefruit and pineapple juices can be easily mistaken if the color-coding is not applied.

Other smaller equipment and working utensils include: **customized pour spouts, stirrers or stir sticks, straws, swords, parasols, ice scoops, salt/sugar/nutmeg/celery salt shakers, margarita salt trays (see rimmers), can openers, bottle openers, small rubber mats, garnish picks, ashtrays, ice scoops.** Among the most frequently used supply items are: **bar menus and/or price lists, wine lists, bartenders guides, bar towels, matches, coasters, cocktail napkins.** On the floor it is typical to find drain covers, and bar mats. Bar mats provide the bartender with a more comfortable cushioning and a non slip surface. In order to comply with sanitary requirements, bar mats have to be cleaned and sanitized frequently.

BACK BAR EQUIPMENT

The **ice making machine** is one of the most vital pieces of equipment of the bar operation. It is usually located in a convenient area away from the patron's view. In some bars a smaller type of ice machine is made to fit underneath the counter, making it more accessible for the bartender or the bartender's helper. Ice machines vary in type and size. The ice produced also varies in size and shape. The most common ice types/shapes are: tube, cube, pillow, crushed, flake, and lens. The competent bar operator knows that the shape of the ice affects how rapidly it will melt, and which shape of ice is more suitable for the type of operation. For example, "flake shaped" ice melts quickly and might dilute the drink too rapidly for some customers drinking habits. "Lens shaped" ice, being a slow melting type, is perferred by many.

According to the health code, ice is a food product and should not be contaminated. In handling it, the only utensil that should be allowed to come in contact with the ice, is the scoop.

The Supplies Store Area contains paper, linen, cleaning supplies, and other working materials and is usually away from the patron's view. Bar managers often delegate to bartenders and cocktail servers the responsibility of seeing that this area is well stocked, and that the par stock of items used everyday, such as bar towels, stirrers, straws, coasters, pretzel/peanuts baskets, paper napkins, and the like, is correctly maintained. Most bars offer freshly brewed coffee; all items needed to make and serve coffee, such as coffee filters, sugar, and sugar containers, are stored here. The same is true of the essential materials to make tea, iced tea, and other common beverages.

Glassware, perhaps more than any other piece of working equipment, makes a direct statement about the type of operation. People often wonder why bars feature such a vast array of glassware. Some operations offer, as part of their service, more than fifty types of glasses all shaped differently. This is one of the aspects that makes the bar business unique. There is a sherry glass, a brandy snifter, a pony, a coupette, a shot, a martini, a high ball, a tall high ball, an old fashioned, a tulip, a flute, and so on. Serving beer alone can require five different types of glasses. The service of wine and champagne may require up to ten types of glassware. Imagine how awkward it would feel if your bartender was to pour wine in a brandy snifter or a shot of tequila in a beer glass or serve a scotch on the rocks in a champagne glass.

Glassware can be an effective means of merchandising bar products and the type of equipment used can directly convey a perception of value to the patron.

Walk-in Refrigeration Units are essential in volume beverage operations to store cold beverage products that cannot be stored in a smaller refrigerator located in the underbar. Beer kegs, individual bottled or canned brews, white, blush, and rose wines, sodas, juices, and bar fruit and dairy products are some of the most common items found in the walk-in units. Walk-in refrigeration temperatures may vary although most display a temperature in the 40–50 degrees range.

Glassware makes a direct statement about the type of operation.

A well stocked glassware case.

Liquor Dispensing Systems. The 1950's saw a major change in the portion control and the service delivery methods of spirits, cordials and soft drinks. The first workable automatic dispensing system was introduced by a manufacturer of soft drinks during the birth of what was later to become the Fast Food Phenomenon. The system was later modified by the liquor industry with the primary purpose of serving portion-controlled drinks. The National Cash Register Corporation improved the system further in the seventies, introducing "Electra Bar" electronic pouring which gave the operator the opportunity to accurately monitor and record sales by the means of a "Meter System." Today's A.L.D.S. (automatic liquor dispensing system) has been made into state-of-the art equipment and it has become essential for many beverage operations, particularly large volume ones.

The A.L.D.S. central system will be found in a room separate from the front bar in an area sometimes referred to as the "pump room." Bottles are inverted in their own reservoir, from which a line of plastic tubing will allow proper measure to be poured into the customer's glass by means of the electronic gun located in the underbar. The bartender, by pressing the key of a specific brand of liquor, will cause a pre-established portion of that liquid to travel through the plastic tubing and arrive at the gun unit in less than a second. The guest charges are automatically registered in the computer system and recorded for inventory and auditing purposes.

Today this system is used not only for liquor, but for fruit juices and soft drinks as well. Although everyone agrees that there is no better system available to expedite service and provide sound bar control, some operators do not favor A.L.D.S. for a variety of reasons. One is that the gun system denies the patron the opportunity to see the label of the product he/she is being served. Other reasons include the exorbitant cost of the more advanced A.L.D.S. systems, the cost of maintenance, and the fact that free pouring is still needed in order to make certain specialty cocktails. The more severe critics of A.L.D.S. claim that many of the spirits and cordials are affected by the plastic tubing. For example, that Beefeater gin loses many of its unique sensory characteristics once poured from a gun and that Chivas Regal scotch whisky doesn't taste any different than a common well brand once it is made to travel through a hundred feet of plastic tubing. The adverse critics also add that all fruit juices served from the gun are of inferior quality and have a synthetic taste. Large volume beverage operators consider these issues small losses compared to the significant gains provided by the A.L.D.S. These include the elimination of illegal practices by dishonest bartenders, more accurate sales, less waste and spillage, reduced bar staff labor cost, and better overall control.

UPKEEP AND MAINTENANCE

The equipment of a bar and beverage operation can be made to last for years if properly maintained and cared for. A responsible preventive maintenance program will not only make the equipment look better and last longer but it will allow the beverage operator to maintain stringent sanitary standards, and at the same time comply with local, state, and federal requirements set by the health and fire authorities. A situation may arise when the conscientious bar and beverage manager has to perform the duties of an engineer. Although in major breakdowns the knowledge of a qualified technical person is required, small repairs and routine inspections can be handled by non-experts. As the old adage goes: "one ounce of prevention is worth a pound of cure," so the manager can save a considerable amount of money in unnecessary repairs later on by maintaining a weekly and/or monthly preventive maintenance checklist.

Vital engineering concerns, such as the proper functioning of plumbing, refrigeration, air conditioning/heating, and electrical systems, if not properly and frequently inspected, can adversely affect individual equipment units. The preventative maintenance checklist becomes easier to manage when combined with the manager's everyday routine opening and closing checklist.

Here is an example of a combination working/preventative maintenance checklist:

1. Bar stools, lounge table, and chairs clean, properly arranged and in good repair?

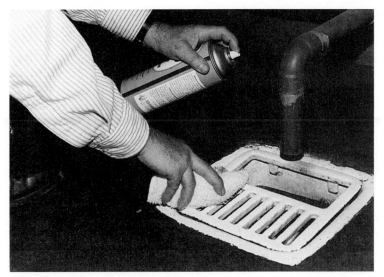

Checking and cleaning bar drains is often overlooked.

2. Bar counter and back bar surfaces wiped down? Glassrail firmly attached to the main counter?
3. Reach-in and walk-in refrigerator temperatures in normal range?
4. Bar stations set up, cleaned, and sanitized properly?
5. Condiments trays clean? Need to be replaced?
6. Daily working equipment and bar utensils in good condition, clean and sanitized?
7. Cash drawer, main register unit, and touch screen terminals properly set up and functioning correctly?
8. Speedrack attached properly? Liquors placed according to proper sequencing order?
9. Lounge carpet clean? In need of repair or replacement?
10. Backbar floor swept and mopped? Trash containers lined?
11. Liquor room temperature correct? Doors locked?
12. Blenders, mixers, set up? Blades cleaned? Slush machine set in proper working order?
13. Bar guns cleaned, keys sticky?
14. Pour spouts soaked and rinsed?
15. Bar sinks draining properly?
16. Glass scrubbers need replacement?
17. All stainless steel surfaces wiped down? Metal working tools clean? Ice machine clean, ice reaching roof? Scoop buried in ice?
18. All deliveries properly stored and par stock checked?
19. All paper and cleaning supplies stored adequately and inventoried?

20. Soda tanks and CO_2 checked?

21. Liquor and beer dispensing systems checked? Stock up to par?

KEY TERMS

Underbar
Back Bar
Glassrail
Wells or Jockey Boxes
Muddler
Bar Mixer
A.L.D.S.
   (Automatic
   Liquor Dispensing
   System)

Footed Pilsner
Tulip Glass
Electra Bar
Bar Towel
Pousse Café
Pre-measure
Free Pouring
Parasols
Bar Nate
Slush Machine

Strainer
Pony Glass
Condiment Tray
Jigger
Floated or Layered Cocktails
Sequencing

CHAPTER QUESTIONS

1. Which specific bar equipment has undergone the most significant change in the last two decades?

2. What is the meaning of the term "sequencing", when discussing the usefulness of the speedrack.

3. What is a glassrail, a bar mixer, a muddler?

4. What are the advantages of an automatic liquor dispensing system?

5. What tool is used in the preparation of a layered cocktail?

6. What do slush machines provide?

7. Which bar items are placed in the wells or jockey boxes?

8. Which bar products are more frequently stored in a walk-in refrigeration unit?

9. Why is a preventive maintenance program for bar equipment so crucial for the operator?

10. Give some examples of a combination working/preventive maintenance checklist.

11. What is the more common equipment in the underbar? in the backbar?

12. In addition to the standard cocktail/Martini glass, in which other type of glass can a Martini be served?

SUGGESTED READINGS

1. Plotkin, R. *Reducing Bar Costs–A Survival Plan for the 90s.* Tucson, AZ: P.S.D. Publishing, 1993.

2. Roy, A. *The Upstart Guide to Owning and Managing a Bar or Tavern.* Dover N.H.: Upstart Publishing, 1995.

chapter five

ALCOHOLIC BEVERAGE PRODUCTION

chapter outline

chapter objectives

Upon completion of this chapter you will be able to:

- State the three categories of alcoholic beverages.

- Name two examples of fermented beverages.

- Name two examples of distilled beverages.

- State three factors that affect fermentation.

- State two factors that affect distillation.

- Describe the role of yeast, sugar, and temperature on the fermentation process.

- State the role that proof and congeners play in the taste of a distilled spirit.

- Explain the difference in results from a column still and pot still.

INTRODUCTION

Managers of operations that serve alcoholic beverages need to know and understand the basics of alcoholic beverage production and classification. A knowledge of the products that they sell or serve is essential for several reasons:

1. Managers should know the differences (and similarities) between products so that stock can be purchased more effectively.
2. An understanding of production techniques will allow the manager to determine why one brand is more or less expensive than another.
3. Knowledge of the products is also important to best serve one's customers. Customers frequently have questions about drinks or would like suggestions. A properly trained manager can provide the information the customer is seeking.

This chapter begins with definitions of some of the terms that are important in beverage production. The definitions, along with some diagrams, will illustrate the relationship between the terms. Once the terms are spelled out a discussion of both fermentation and distillation will follow. Fermentation and distillation are the processes essential to the production of alcoholic beverages.

The chapter is not intended to be the definitive text on the topic. The intention is to provide the manager or future manager with the basics. A list of recommended literature at the end of Chapter 6 provides the reader with a source for those who wish to go into the topic more deeply.

Distilled spirits have been an integral part of most cultures of the world for many centuries. They have been held in high regard by both the people who make them and those who consume them. For example in the Russian language "vodka" means "the water of life." People leaving their European homelands to come to America brought whisky with them to help them survive the long journey and to serve as a medicine if any of their fellow passengers became ill on the passage.

BASIC DEFINITIONS

It is important to begin with definitions of the key terms. The technical definitions may surprise you because they may not conform to some commonly held ideas about the meanings of these words. Having defined the words they can then be freely used in the remainder of the text.

Alcoholic Beverage. A drinkable liquid containing ethyl alcohol [ethanol]. The concentration of ethanol ranges from 0.5 percent to 95 percent by volume. Federal and state taxes are charged on alcoholic beverages as low as 1 percent alcohol, while medicines and bitters with up to 40 percent alcohol are not taxed.

Fermented Beverages. Fermentation occurs when yeast is introduced into a liquid that contains fruits or grain containing sugar. The yeast converts the sugar into carbon dioxide and alcohol. Examples of fermented beverages are beer, wine, and sake.

Distilled Spirits are produced by the separation of alcohol from a fermented spirit in a still. Examples of distilled spirits are brandy, cognac, whisky, vodka, and tequila.

Compounded Spirit. A compounded spirit is a combination of a fermented beverage, a distilled spirit, and flavoring agents. Examples of some compounded spirits are gin, liqueurs, or cordials.

Congeners are the trace elements and components of the original fermented liquid that go through the distillation process with the alcohol. They provide flavor, body and color, and give the resulting spirit its distinctiveness.

Blending. Spirits are blended for a variety of reasons. One common reason is to overcome the natural variations in products and to help ensure consistency. Spirit producers make their beverages for a certain taste. Spirits will be blended with other batches of the same product from the same year or different years, and/or other products so that the producer can obtain the desired flavor.

Proof is one of the terms used to describe the strength of distilled spirits. Its origins come from the time before alcohol measuring devices. Equal parts of alcohol and gunpowder were mixed. Once ignited, if the mixture burned evenly it was 100 proof, or 50 percent alcohol. The bottling proof of spirit is often reduced by the addition of distilled water for either legal, marketing, or economic reasons.

The proof or percentage of alcohol of the spirit has an effect on the product. The higher the proof, the less congeners or flavor components in the product, resulting in less of the flavor of the original liquid. For example, a 151 proof rum is 75.5 percent alcohol and only 24.5 percent congeners, while an 80 proof rum is 40 percent alcohol and 60 percent congeners, resulting in a more flavorful product then the 151 proof rum.

Neutral Spirits. Spirits that are distilled from any material to 95 percent or higher of alcohol, 190 proof, are called neutral spirits. They contain very little of the character of the original product due to the high percentage of alcohol. Neutral spirits are blended with other spirits to raise the latter's alcohol percentage, or they are filtered through charcoal and sold as vodka.

THE FACTS ON FERMENTATION

Writings on alcoholic beverages go back until practically the beginning of recorded history. The first fermentation is believed to have happened by accident. The naturally occurring yeast that grows on the skin of most grapes got mixed with the grape juice when the grapes were crushed, or there might have been enough natural yeast in the air to cause the fermentation of the sugars in the liquid. The result was a wine, and once it was tasted, the process was repeated. It was not until the last 150 or so years that the process was understood scientifically. With this new understanding, the results could be methodically controlled by the producer.

Alcoholic fermentation is a chemical reaction that takes place in the absence of free air and which changes sugar into carbon dioxide and ethyl alcohol with the help of live yeast cells. The carbon dioxide generated in the process is normally released into the atmosphere, or it is kept in the bottle in the case of the secondary fermentation that occurs in the making of sparkling wines.

Fermentation is a very complex series of events. There are many strains of yeast, each having a slightly different effect on the final product. The atmosphere in many areas has a relatively large concentration of natural yeast, making it possible for fermentation to occur naturally. Most fermentation in the United States takes place with the use of added yeast, as the makers of beer and wine prefer a more controlled process. In Europe, the makers of beer and wine rely much more on naturally occurring yeast cultures. Many wine producers in Europe claim that the high quality of their products is due to the natural yeast.

There are several factors that have an effect on the fermentation process and the resulting beverage. The knowledge gained about the process in the last century and a half has allowed wine and beer makers to have much more control over the process and the outcomes. The following section explains some of the key factors affecting fermentation.

Characteristics of Yeast

The characteristics of the yeast will have an effect on the final product, and in order to produce a consistent product, care must be taken with the type of yeast used. A major American beer producer has a separate division that produces and ships yeast to each of its breweries on a weekly basis to ensure consistency. Different fermented beverages, beer, wine, and those produced to make distilled spirits, require different strains of yeast.

Temperature

Temperature affects the performance of different strains and types of yeast. They perform differently at various temperature ranges and conditions. White wines generally are fermented at lower temperatures, while red wines ferment best at higher temperatures.

Sugar

The amount and type of sugar also has an effect on the fermentation. Sugar feeds the yeast and causes the reaction to go on. The fermentation process will continue until all the sugar is consumed unless the level of alcohol rises to a level that kills the yeast. This accounts for the difference between dry (lack of sugar) and sweet wines. In dry wines all or most of the sugar is consumed by the yeast, leaving a beverage that is without sugar. Sweet wines are the result of the yeast being killed by the alcohol before it can consume all of the sugar. Different types and strains of yeast tolerate different levels of alcohol.

THE FACTS ON DISTILLATION

Distilled spirits are made by running a fermented beverage through the distillation process. The makeup of the original fermented beverage influences the characteristics of the distilled spirit. Distilled wine makes brandy, distilled beer makes whisky, etc.

Distillation is the process whereby the alcohol in a beverage is separated from the remainder of the fermented liquid. There must be alcohol in the original liquid for distillation to work. The distillation process is possible due to the lower boiling point of alcohol compared to water. The liquid containing the alcohol is heated to the temperature of 173°F—hot enough to cause the alcohol to vaporize but not the water in the beverage, turning the alcohol from a liquid into a gas. Once the alcohol is vaporized it is cooled, recondensed and captured in another container. Various flavors, coloring components or congeners of the original fermented liquid survive the distillation process.

The process of distillation is influenced by time and by the temperature of the liquids. The temperature that the fermented beverage is heated to influences the amount of alcohol and the amount of congeners that go through the process. A product that is distilled to 100 percent alcohol or 200 proof will not have any characteristics of the original fermented liquid. The product will be bitter and colorless.

There are two types of stills used in the manufacturing of distilled beverages—pot stills and column or Coffey stills.

Pot Still

The original type of still, and the one that produces the highest quality product, is the single-batch pot still. It is designed to process only one batch of fermented liquid at a time, and then it must be emptied and cleaned. It has two essential parts: the still and the worm condenser. The still is the large copper pot in which the fermented beverage is heated. The top of the still narrows into a long copper tube that is twisted into a coil. It is surrounded by cooled water where the alcohol vapor is collected. When cooled, the gases are recondensed and returned to the liquid state in the form of alcohol.

Modern pot stills are used to produce the highest quality and most expensive spirits in the world. The extra time and effort that it takes pays off in the quality of the final product. Some products are processed through the still more then once; for example, cognac is distilled twice, while Irish whiskey's smoothness can be attributed to its being processed three times through the pot still.

A diagram of an original pot still.

Column or Coffey Still

The running of a pot still is labor intensive and expensive. In 1826, a Scotsman invented a continuously running still that speeded up the production of spirits and lowered the price of distilled spirits, making them more accessible to the masses.

Fermented beverages are pumped into one end and distilled spirits come out of the other end. It does not have to be cleaned and emptied between batches, as does the pot still. The Coffey still is used for most whiskies, vodkas and gin. The following table demonstrates the types of stills used to make some of the more popular distilled spirits.

Some Spirits that are Made in the Two Types of Still

Coffey Still	Pot Still
Whisky	Scotch (single-malt)
Bourbon	Irish whiskey
Canadian	Tequila
Gin	Cognac
Vodka	
Brandy	

DISTILLED SPIRITS

Spirits generally fall into two categories, white and brown. The differences between the two are more than simply the color. The white spirits, vodka, gin, and rum, are generally lighter in flavor and are generally made to be mixed. Their lack of a distinctive flavor allows them to mix well with other beverages. The brown spirits, on the other hand, Scotch whisky, bourbon, Irish whiskey, and Canadian whisky, have a more distinctive flavor and are generally consumed straight or with only a splash of water or soda, or on the

A variety of distilled spirits in a store room.

rocks. People enjoy them for their distinct characteristics and prefer not to dilute the flavor with mixers.

Chapter 6 provides detailed information about the spirits available in the U.S. beverage trade.

SUMMARY

Bar managers need to be aware of the different production methods and classifications of alcoholic beverages. This knowledge will aid the manager in the purchasing of inventory for the bar, answering questions for guests, and understanding the difference in prices of the products that they serve and sell. This chapter gave an overview of the fermentation and distillation processes and for the different types of spirits. Classification of spirits and the production and classification of wine and beer will be covered in further detail in subsequent chapters.

To summarize what we have learned in this chapter: Fermentation is the process in which a liquid with sugar is converted to alcohol and carbon dioxide. Fermentation is the beginning of the process of making distilled spirits. The production of beer and wine has gone on for as long as recorded history. Surprisingly, it has only been in the past 150 years that the process has been fully understood scientifically. Advancements in the production of beer and wine have been considerable since the process has become better understood.

Distillation is the separation of the alcohol from the other components in a fermented beverage. The process of distillation produces liquors with a far higher percentage of alcohol than fermented beverages. There are several factors that affect the distilled spirit; the distillers control these factors to obtain the desired final results.

KEY TERMS

Alcoholic Beverages	Distillation	Column Still
Fermented Beverages	Neutral Spirit	Sour Mash
Yeast	Congeners	Sweet Mash
Distilled Spirits	Proof	Mash
Compounded Spirits	Vaporize	Malt
Still	Pot Still	

CHAPTER QUESTIONS

1. What crucial role does yeast play in the production of alcoholic beverages?
2. What is necessary for yeast to produce alcohol?

3. Name two examples of fermented beverages.
4. Which came first, fermented beverages of distilled spirits? Explain.
5. Name three examples of distilled spirits.
6. Name two examples of compounded spirits.
7. What is the relationship between proof and percentage of alcohol?
8. What is the relationship between proof and the character of the product?

chapter six

SPIRITS AND CORDIALS

chapter outline

chapter objectives

Upon completion of the chapter the student will be able to:

- Explain the shift in spirit consumption pattern in this country over the last few decades.

- Explain the production method of whisky.

- Describe the differences in production methods of Scotch, Irish, and American whiskies.

- Describe the differences between straight whisky and blended whisky.

- State the different way in which white spirits and brown spirits are consumed.

- State what gives gin its unique taste.

- Describe the difference between Puerto Rican and Jamaican rums.

- Explain the difference between brandy and cognac.

- Describe the different categories of liqueurs and give an example of each.

- Describe what differences in taste one would find between sour mash and sweet mash bourbon.

INTRODUCTION

Chapter five covered the basics of fermentation and distillation and beverage production. This chapter covers the details of specific spirits and cordials and is the first of the product knowledge chapters of the text. The emphasis of the chapter is to identify the factors that make spirits and cordials different and distinctive. Beverage managers need to know the differences as well as the similarities between the products they purchase and sell. An understanding of the specific details of the spirits allows managers to purchase more efficiently and stock the bar with products that better serve the needs of their guests.

Spirits fall into two main categories; brown and white. As discussed in the previous chapter, most spirits come out of the distillation process clear or very light colored. The color of the spirit comes primarily from aging in charred barrels.

CHANGING CONSUMPTION PATTERNS

The change in consumption patterns of alcohol in the United States is interesting. Since the mid-sixties the amount consumed per adult has declined. People are just drinking less for the reasons discussed in Chapter 1. This reduction in consumption has not been consistent across all lines of alcoholic beverages. Americans historically have preferred brown spirits over white spirits. However, consumption of brown spirits has declined as younger Americans prefer vodka- and gin-based drinks over the whisky their fathers and grandfathers favored. Brown spirits are full bodied with distinctive flavors. Drinkers of whisky primarily drink it straight or with a splash of water or soda so they can enjoy the flavor. To help combat the reduction in sales, distillers of brown spirits have developed marketing campaigns to attract 21–35 year olds to their products.

The lone success in the brown spirits market, showing an increase in consumption, is single malt scotch. Americans like the distinctive taste of single malt scotch and it has enjoyed growing popularity.

The shift in American drinking preferences has been to the lighter flavored spirits, vodka and gin, which are drunk in cocktails or mixed drinks, primarily with flavorful mixers such as juices. Vodka is distilled and filtered so the flavor of the ingredients it was made from is removed. Vodka, the national spirit of Russia, was not made in the U.S. until 1934. Production of this colorless spirit grew from 7,500 cases a year in 1934, to 40,000 cases in 1950, and 1.1 million cases in 1954. In 1967, vodka outsold gin; in 1976 it outsold whisky for the first time to become the number one selling spirit in our nation.

BROWN SPIRITS

Whisky

Beer and whisky have historically been produced in areas that are generally too cold or have too short a growing season to grow grapes. Generally these areas could not support the growth of grapes but could successfully grow grains, which are the basis of both beer and whisky.

Both Ireland and Scotland have developed and refined their own distinctive types of whisky. Although made with similar ingredients, they are remarkably different in taste. Immigrants from Europe brought their spirits with them to help withstand the long journey. Once settled in the new land, they imported their spirits from Europe.

The eighteenth century ushered in the production of whisky in America. It was first made in small family distilleries, mostly from rye and barley. Bourbon, or American whisky, was first distilled in Bourbon County, Kentucky, in 1789. Legally, bourbon can be made in any part of the United States, although most is produced in Kentucky and Indiana.

Production Factors that Affect Whiskies.   The characteristics of the various types of whiskies are influenced by several factors. Some of the factors or processes are simply carried out by tradition down the years, while others have become law and must be followed in order for the product to carry a certain name.

Grains.   The main grains used in whisky are rye, barley malt, and corn. The percentage of the ingredients dictates the product and designates the name on the label. For example, bourbon can be made with any grains as long as it is at least 51 percent corn. A whisky that is 75 percent corn or more is then called corn whisky.

Type of Wood Barrel Used.   Distilled beverages are generally colorless and bitter, and are often quite similar when they come out of the still. Aging in wood allows the spirits to absorb some of the tannin from the barrel and

Interior of a working distillery.

other coloring material from the wood container, making it less harsh and often sweeter than the original product. The type of wood barrel along with the type of processing has an effect on the final product. Generally oak is the predominant wood used. Variations in the final product can depend on whether the barrel is new or previously used. Some barrels are reused for the same product, and other barrels are used a second time for a different product. For example, tequila is generally aged in used bourbon barrels. This aging in a barrel that has been used previously for another product imparts a certain flavor that complements the whisky.

Some barrels are burned or charred inside prior to aging the product. The use of charred barrels happened by accident. The legend says that a barrel maker used a flame to heat the oak to help bend the wood to make barrels. On one batch of barrels he accidentally burned the wood without telling the whisky maker. The whisky maker used the barrels and found that the charred wood imparted a nice color to the whisky and improved the flavor, so they decided to continue the process. The difference between dark tequila and white tequila is that the dark tequila is aged in a charred barrel while the white is not. Some spirits are not aged at all. For example, gin and vodka are ready to drink directly from the still, while some scotches or cognacs may not be ready to drink until they have aged ten to twelve years.

The General Process for Making Whisky. Whiskies are made from the distillation of beer or a beer type liquid. Originally beer was used by distillers, but as the process was further refined special grain-based fermented beverages were used to better suit the final product.

Mash = A combination of the malt, grains, hot water, and yeast.

Grains = Any of the following used alone or in combination: corn, barley, rye, wheat.

Malt = A grain, usually barley, that is soaked in water and allowed to sprout.

Characteristics of Some of the Various Types of Whiskies.

Bourbon.   Bourbon must be made from at least 51 percent corn, but not more than 75 percent. It is aged a minimum of two years in charred oak barrels. *Distinctive characteristics:* Bourbon is generally made with sour mash. Most spirits are made with a fresh batch of yeast each time; this is considered "sweet mash." "Sour mash" bourbon is made with a portion of used yeast mixed with fresh yeast, providing a special flavor.

Scotch Whisky.   Scotch whisky is a product of Scotland and must be made there for it to bear the name. The product is made entirely from barley, preferably grown in Scotland. Scotch was originally produced as a single malt, and until 1853 all the product in the bottle came from the same batch. However, due to the inconsistencies between batches, and the strong flavor, producers began to blend the batches. The product was blended to make it lighter and increase its appeal. Blended scotches, which could be made from

Popular examples of brown spirits.

up to 150 different scotches and neutral spirits, have been the most popular for the general public, although there has been an upsurge in the popularity of single malt scotches since the 1980s. *Distinctive characteristics:* Scotch has a distinctive smoky flavor that comes from drying the malt with peat fires that are very smoky. The five regions of Scotland use different drying times and slight variations in the process, giving them distinctive products.

Irish Whiskey. Ireland prefers the spelling to be "whiskey" rather than the more common form of "whisky." Contrary to popular opinion, Irish whiskey is not made from potatoes. It is made from a blend of malted barley, corn, rye, and oats. *Distinctive characteristics:* Irish whiskey is known for its smoothness, which comes from its processing three times through a pot still. It is aged in seasoned, or used, barrels for a minimum of four years, though it is better when aged seven to eight years. It is known to be smooth with a medium body and a clean taste. It is best known in the United States for the popular cool-weather drink of Irish coffee. Interestingly, that drink originated at a bar in San Francisco, not in Ireland.

Canadian Whisky. Canadian whiskies are blended to be light and mellow. They must be aged a minimum of three years and are not allowed to be sold straight. Most Canadian whisky is six years old or older. The Canadian government is more lenient regarding regulations for the production of whisky than other governments. *Distinctive characteristics:* Drinkers appreciate the delicate flavor and light-bodied nature of the product. Canadian whiskies are usually made from a combination of corn, rye, barley malt, and wheat.

American Whisky. Residents of the United States did not start distilling whisky until almost 100 years after they distilled rum in New England. Whisky was first distilled in small family-owned operations, mostly on the Eastern seaboard. The growing nation needed new sources of revenue to fund the new government. They began taxing whisky, which caused a small rebellion. Distillers moved away from the Eastern seaboard to get away from tax collectors, and settled in Kentucky and southern Indiana, though in part for the excellent water.

Whisky production in the United States has grown considerably since its humble beginnings. There are presently three main categories of American whiskies: blends, straights, and light.

Straight Whisky. Approximately half of the American produced whisky is either straight or a blend of straight whiskies. Straight whiskies can be mixed with other straight whiskies and still keep the name of straight whisky. Once a straight whisky is blended with a neutral spirit or a light whisky, it is considered a blended whisky. The predominant grain used in the mash determines the designation of the label on the bottle.

Blended Whisky. The quality of blended whisky depends on the quality of the blender. Blended whisky is a combination of straight whiskies with grain spirits, light whiskies and neutral spirits. The result is a product that is lighter, better balanced and more consistent then most straight whiskies. Grain spirits are neutral spirits that have been aged in reused oak barrels to mellow and soften their flavor.

Light Whisky. Light whisky is distilled at a higher percentage of alcohol, resulting in a product that is less flavorful than other whiskies. The whisky is produced to be used in the blending process.

WHITE SPIRITS

White spirits are clear in color, generally have a less intense flavor, and are preferred mixed with juices rather than consumed straight or with a splash of water or soda. The taste of the spirits generally mixes well with an assortment

Vodka now comes in flavors for mixing.

of other beverages. They are generally not aged. The main white spirits are vodka, gin, and rum.

Vodka

Vodka translates from the Russian as literally the "water of life." It originated in Russia in the thirteenth century. The Smirnoff family were the premier distillers in Russia until the revolution of 1917. The formula and process made it to America in the 1930s with one of the cousins of the original family.

A neutral spirit, which eventually transformed the drinking habits of the nation, vodka was slow to catch on. When first introduced in this country, it was consumed almost exclusively by Russian, Polish, and Slavic immigrants who enjoyed it cold as straight shots. The consumption of vodka changed when a bar owner, faced with a large supply of ginger beer, experimented and found that mixing it with vodka made a drink, the Moscow Mule, that was quite good. As the popularity of the Moscow Mule grew, so did the number of different vodka drinks. Vodka mixes well with fruit juices, such as orange juice and cranberry juice.

Distinctive characteristics: Vodka was made from whatever products were the most abundant and the least expensive. The assortment of possible

Popular brands of white spirits that beverage operators should stock.

ingredients includes potatoes, grains, and corn. The ingredients used for fermentation do not have an effect on the final product because vodka is distilled to such a high proof and then filtered through charcoal, that none of the original flavor remains. Vodka does not need to be aged.

Gin

Gin was originally developed as a medicine by a Dutch doctor. He thought that the medicinal properties of juniper berries combined with pure alcohol would be a beneficial medicine. As word spread throughout Holland, an increasing number of Dutch citizens began to come down with the symptoms that the doctor's new medicine was supposed to cure.

Gin caught on in Europe and especially in England—British soldiers returning from the seventeenth-century wars on the continent brought home a taste for it. It was the first distilled spirit that was affordable for the common people, so it quickly spread in popularity throughout Britain and Europe.

Distinctive characteristics: Gin is made by re-distilling a neutral spirit, vodka, with the berries of a juniper bush. The juniper berries give the beverage a distinctive aromatic taste. The product is not aged. It is served in an assortment of cocktails and mixed drinks, ranging from martinis to gin and tonics.

Rum

Rum was the first spirit distilled in the United States. It has a somewhat colorful history that is rich in both fact and fiction. It is a product of sugarcane and is generally produced anywhere sugarcane is grown.

Rum played a central part in the slave trade. Rum distilled in New England was shipped to Africa and exchanged for Africans, who were turned into slaves. The slaves were brought to the West Indies and exchanged for molasses, which was brought to New England to make more rum.

Distinctive characteristics: There are two types of rums: light and full bodied. The difference between the two depends mostly on the method of fermentation and the distillation process used.

Light rums are commonly referred to as Puerto Rican Rums, although they are produced throughout the Caribbean. The rum is aged in used barrels that may or may not be charred. The rums that are aged the least are the lightest in flavor and body are labeled as white or silver. Rum that is aged a minimum of three years in the barrel so that it acquires a deeper color and mellower flavor is labeled as gold or amber. Caramel coloring is often used to balance the color from one batch to another.

Dark rums, more commonly referred to as Jamaican rums, are richer and more full bodied than light rums. They are aged more than light rums. Their strong, almost pungent flavor is generally appreciated more by the British than the Americans.

OTHER TYPES OF SPIRITS

Brandies—The Soul of Wine

Brandies are distilled from wine or fermented mash of fruit, and are produced anywhere in the world. The story goes that a Dutch shipmaster who previously had shipped many casks of wine between France and Holland came up with the idea of concentrating the wine to reduce space on the ship and therefore reduce shipping costs. His idea was to concentrate or distill the wine in France, ship it to Holland, and add the water back. When he arrived in Holland with his first shipment, his friends tasted it and thought it would be a waste to add water to the concentrated wine. Hence the beginning of the market for brandy.

Brandies are considered the soul of wine because wine is the base liquid used for distillation to make the product. When wine from anything other than grapes is used, such as plums, then the product must be named after the fruit used, such as plum brandy.

Cognac is brandy made in the Cognac region of France. It is recognized worldwide as the best brandy. The high quality is due to two factors: the special distillation process and the growing conditions. The chalky soil and climate of the Cognac area provide the environment for the grapes to grow their best and make cognac famous around the world.

 REMEMBER: ALL COGNACS ARE BRANDIES, BUT NOT ALL BRANDIES ARE COGNACS

Cognacs are labeled differently than other spirits. Different companies use different labeling systems to designate quality—while some companies use stars to indicate quality levels, other companies use letters to indicate quality.

The following is an explanation of one company's letter system:

E = Extra or Especial   P = Pale
S = Superior   V = Very
F = Fine   O = Old
X = Extra

For example a cognac labeled VS is aged four and a half years, while one labeled VSOP is seven to ten years old, and is considered VERY SUPERIOR OLD PALE. Some companies have abandoned letters or stars and use names instead.

Cognacs improve in wood for roughly 50 years, but aging that long is expensive because of evaporation and the tying up of capital for such a long period. The cognac improves from the contact with the wood. Once it is

With the advent of the new century, Cognacs are doing well in the U.S. market.

placed in the bottle the aging process ends. A product does not improve at all during the time it is sealed in the bottle. Cognac is most often consumed straight and is often savored after a meal.

Armagnac is the second most famous brandy. It is made from white grapes only, grown in soil that is less chalky than in the Cognac region. Armagnac is then aged in black oak rather than limousin oak, as for cognac. Generally, the same age requirements hold for armagnac as for cognac. The taste is drier, more pungent than cognac, and surprisingly smooth.

Ninety five percent of American brandy is produced in California. Approximately 20 percent is produced in pot stills. It is generally aged in white oak barrels.

Other Brandies

Kirsch from France, or Kirschwasser from Switzerland, are cherry brandies; Calvados from France is an apple brandy; Framboise from France is raspberry brandy; and Eau-de-vie de Poire from France is pear-flavored brandy.

Liqueurs and Cordials

The names for these products are interchangeable. They are by definition a distilled spirit steeped or re-distilled with fruits, flowers plants, juices, extracts, and are sweetened with 2.5 percent sugar. Most were originally used as medicinal remedies, love potions, aphrodisiacs, and general cure-alls.

Here are some examples of cognacs to be sipped & enjoyed.

Production Methods.   There are three ways to make liqueurs: infusion, maceration, and percolation. The flavoring agents used to make the beverage generally dictate the production method used.

Infusion is a cold process for delicate flavorings that are heat sensitive. The crushed fruits are soaked in water for up to one year.

Maceration [steeping] means soaking fruit in alcohol or brandy.

Percolation [or brewing] is another form of cold extraction. The flavoring agent is placed in the upper part of an apparatus, brandy or another spirit is then pumped over the leaves or herbs, allowed to drain, and then pumped through again. This process may be repeated for weeks or months.

Distillation is the only form of hot extraction and is used mostly for seeds and flowers, which can withstand the heat to take advantage of this quick method.

Categories of Liqueurs.   Liqueurs and cordials fall into three basic categories: herb and spice, seed and plant, and fruit. The following table lists some of the popular brands or types in each category.

Tequila

Tequila, also considered a spirit, is derived from the mescal plant that grows in Mexico. For a product to be called tequila it must come from or around the

To offer a wide variety of cordials, liqueurs, eau-de-vie and other exotic products is considered a good investment and can be a great marketing device.

Liqueurs go very nicely with coffee after a meal. Presenting liqueurs on carts helps promote their sales.

Liqueur/Cordial	Category	Flavor
Benedictine	Herb and Spice	27 herbs, spices, peels
Chartreuse	Herb and Spice	130 plants
Drambuie	Herb and Spice	Herbs, malt, grain whiskies, honey
Galiano	Herb and Spice	Herbs, spices, vanilla, anise
Amaretto	Seed and Plant	Almond and apricot pits
Bailey's Irish Cream	Seed and Plant	Whiskey, chocolate, cream
Kahlua	Seed and Plant	Coffee bean
Cointreau	Fruit	Peels of bitter and sweet oranges
Grand Marnier	Fruit	Bitter oranges with a cognac base
Midori	Fruit	Honey dew
Sloe Gin	Fruit	Sloe berry (a wild plum)

town of Tequila in the Guadalajara region of Mexico. Distilled beverages that do not come from the area around Tequila are simply called mescal.

The best mescal plant to make tequila from is the blue agave. Premium tequilas will have a high percentage of it, while super premium tequila will be 100 percent blue agave. Tequila is sold as either unaged white tequila, or gold tequila aged in charred barrels. There is no official government regula-

Tequila displayed in a bar, with glasses for shots or mixing.

tion for the length of time for aging gold tequila. The official designation of aged tequila is anejo, and it must be aged a minimum of one year to obtain that classification.

SUMMARY

Bar managers need to be aware of the different production methods and classifications of alcoholic beverages. This knowledge will aid the manager in the purchasing of inventory for the bar, answering questions for guests, understanding the different prices of the products that they serve and sell. This chapter gave an overview of the classification of the different types of spirits. The production and classifications of beer and wine will be covered in further detail in subsequent chapters.

Distilled spirits fall into two basic categories; white and brown spirits. Brown spirits have a more distinctive flavor and are generally served alone or with a splash or water or soda. White spirits have a less distinctive flavor and are generally mixed with juice and sodas. Brandies, cognacs, liqueurs, cordials, and tequila do not fall into either of the above categories but are important members of the spirits family.

KEY TERMS

Charred	Gin	Mixer
Brown Spirit	Rum	White Spirit
Bourbon	Cognac	Corn
Sweet Mash	Kirsch	Sour Mash
Malting	Blue Agave	Mashing
Fermentation	Liqueur	Distillation
Malted Barley	Infusion	Single Malt
Scotch Whisky	Percolation	Blended Whisky
Straight Whisky	Cordial	Irish Whiskey
Canadian Whisky	Maceration	Bouquet
Light Whisky	Distillation	Seasoned Barrel
Vodka	Armagnac	Neutral Spirit
Juniper Berries	Framboise	Tequila
Anejo	Brandy	

CHAPTER QUESTIONS

1. Where does the name bourbon come from?
2. What is the difference between bourbon and corn whisky? Are they not both made with corn?

3. How would you respond to a guest that says they prefer sour tasting drinks and understands that some bourbons are made with sour mash; please explain what sour mash means and if it indeed makes a "sour" bourbon?

4. What are the four main grains used in the making of whisky?

5. What two factors determine the label designation [i.e., bourbon, corn, rye, etc.] of American whiskies?

6. How would you explain the difference in flavor and cost between a blended scotch and a single malt scotch to a guest?

7. Explain what is meant by the phrase, "Aging makes a good whisky."

8. What are the three categories of American whiskies?

9. Can straight whisky be blended? If so, what can it be blended with and still maintain the title of straight whisky?

10. What is a blended whisky blended with to make it a blended whisky?

11. Name three factors that make scotch whisky distinctive, and two factors that make Irish whiskey different from other whiskies.

12. What is the difference in processing between a silver rum and a gold rum?

13. Both the words whisky and vodka translate literally into "water of life" in the native languages of the countries where they originated; why do you think they were given such an important name?

14. Both cognac and armagnac are French brandies; what are the differences?

15. Explain why it is not possible to have an American cognac?

16. What does anejo mean in regards to tequila?

17. What is the difference between tequila and mescal?

18. Explain the differences between the three production methods of cordials.

SUGGESTIONS FOR FURTHER READING

1. Bell, D. A. *Wine and Beverage Standards.* New York: Van Nostrand Reinhold, 1989

2. Grossman, H. S. *Grossman's Guide to Wines, Beers, and Spirits,* 7th ed. New York: Scribner's, 1983

3. Lipinski, R. A. and K. A. Lipinski. *Professional Guide to Alcoholic Beverages.* New York: Van Nostrand Reinhold, 1989.

chapter seven

WINE FUNDAMENTALS

chapter outline

chapter objectives

Upon completion of this chapter you will be able to:

- Discuss the origin and development of winemaking.

- Become familiar with the practices of suggestive selling.

- Become proficient with wine service techniques.

- Describe the role & responsibilities of a "Sommelier"
- List the leading grape varieties.
- Discuss the most popular red and white grapes.
- Identify wine regions of California, France, Italy, and Germany.
- Identify the other major wine producing nations.
- Read wine labels and discuss wine appelations and designations.
- Describe sparkling wine methods of production.
- Explain how food interacts with wine.
- Identify wine quality criteria and sensory characteristics.
- Discuss the three main evaluation criteria: The Visual, Olfactory, and Taste/Tactile.
- Discuss the role of wine in a bar and beverage operation.
- Be familiar with wine language and terminology.

THE ORIGINS OF WINE

Of all the alcoholic beverages, wine has certainly made the greatest impact on civilization. One of the finest American writers, Ernest Hemingway, wrote, "Wine is one of the most civilized things in the world and one of the natural things of the world that has been brought to the greatest perfection . . ." It has taken many centuries and continuous effort to bring wine to such perfection. The cultural impact of wine on American society is now being felt more than ever. Wine has become the ritual beverage at weddings and other festive occasions. Wine still holds religious significance for people gathering in churches and synagogues to worship their creator. The winemaking industry has also benefited the economies of the states of California, Washington, Oregon, Idaho, New York, and others.

The art and science of wine and winemaking is called enology, while the practice of cultivating the vine grape is called viticulture. Wine can be made with grains and various types of fruit; however, in the western hemisphere reference to wine alludes to the fermented juice from grapes.

People need to drink as much as they need to eat for survival. In fact, liquids are a greater requirement for sustaining life. It is often said that if a person becomes lost in a desert area he/she can survive for several weeks without food, but cannot live without liquids more than two or three days. Since the beginnings of civilization, humans have not been entirely satisfied with drinking the purest and unchanged nectar of nature—water—but felt the need to drink something with more flavor and taste. Early man experimented by mixing various essences with milk and extracting juice from berries and other fruits such as dates, figs, and pomegranates. Tropical plants, particularly the many varieties of cacti and palms, were the only source of liquids and food for those who adventurously crossed large desert lands. Rough ciders were made from every type of plant known, and countless concoctions were created by mixing water with essences of herbs, seeds and spices.

We often hear of archeologists uncovering petroglyphs and pictographs of ancient civilizations, long before recorded history, showing human forms holding cups in their hands in the process of drinking. We can only speculate as to what kind of beverage was in those cups since there is no definite evidence. One can assume that most probably the beverages were either a wine or a brew. In all probability, the first alcoholic beverage was discovered when someone realized that by leaving grape juice exposed to the outside air at the certain temperature, the liquid would "move" and ferment by the action of natural yeasts, allowing the grape sugar to convert into alcohol and carbon dioxide. Men and women became captivated by the happy feeling that came from drinking it. Soon, other means of obtaining alcohol, from whatever was available, were developed. Brews, pulques, and ciders were made out of grains, plants, and fruit. Fermented honey was mixed with liquids and made into a mead. Ciders were poured into open containers and allowed to stay in contact with the air until bubbles emerged on the surface.

Wine has been made since the beginning of civilization.

There are historical accounts of a brewing recipe, carved on a stone tablet, which dates back 7,000 years. More recently, a wine urn was uncovered in the Middle East and carbon-dated as more than 7,000 years old. Leonard H. Lesko, a professor of Egyptology at the University of California, Berkeley, includes in an attractive publication, pictures of Ancient Egyptian laborers in the process of harvesting and pressing the grapes (from King Khaemwaset, an eighteenth dynasty Theban tomb). In the same publication, Prof. Lesko presents evidence that a wine cellar was found next to King Tutankhamen's Wine tomb. Wine jars found in the burial place displayed well preserved capsules and seal impressions. The University of Pennsylvania Museum of Archeology and Anthropology displays remarkable ancient Egyptian remnants that are clearly related to preserving wine.

During the Greek Era, there is ample evidence of the popularity of wine, although Greek society was far more conservative than most ancient civilizations regarding wine consumption. The immortal Socrates was known to meet his pupils in a public place and share a cup of wine before teaching the wisdom of the ages. We have no written evidence from the great Greek philosopher; what we know of him comes from the equally great Plato. Plato reports a much stricter drinking standard. He wrote that no one should be allowed to drink wine before reaching the age of thirty, and that persons between eighteen and thirty should only be allowed a small taste. In his book "Vintage: The Story of Wine," Hugh Johnson, the world's best selling wine writer, quotes Plato's reply to those who questioned the very disciplinarian Greek view on wine and the drinking age: "One should not conduct fire to fire."

During the Roman Empire, the *Taberna Vinaria* (Wine Taverns) were the official meeting place of the Roman citizens. At the entrance, the Tabernas often displayed the sign, "IN VINO VERITAS" (in wine, the truth). The Romans firmly believed that the truth would rarely come out in abstemious circumstances.

One of the best known Roman historians, Pliny the Elder, wrote extensively on the methods used at the time to prevent wine turning into vinegar. Cedar and pine resins were often added to the wine, which was stored in large *amphoras* (clay jars) and covered with various materials, which in turn were topped with tarred pitch to prevent oxidation.

Grapes have grown for over fifty thousand years on the American continent. However, because we have so little information about the pre-Columbian civilizations, there is no evidence about winemaking and brewing practices until the advent of the Spaniards in the 1500s. Although there are conflicting interpretations of ancient records in all five continents, there is a common point of agreement in reporting a great flood in the old Chinese, Hindu, European, and American Indian accounts. The historical records of the Sumerian Kings are among the most ancient verifiable references. They report that "after the Great Flood the first King dynasty ruled at Kish." Kish was a prosperous place of trade and commerce located in the geographic region of the two main rivers of Western Asia, the Tigris and the Euphrates. From Kish, we have records of "wine trade." The Greek Historian Herodotus reports that the wines were brought by merchants to the banks of the great river and the wine was preserved in animal skin containers.

In our Western culture, the great flood is associated with the biblical flood. Genesis, chapter 9, verse 20 reads, "When the waters receded, Noah farmed the land and planted a vineyard. He made a juice of the grapes, fermented and drunk it and was inebriated in celebration to God." Contemporary writers Dave Balsiger and Charles E. Seller, Jr. (in their book, *In Search of Noah's Ark*) present archeological discoveries supported by scientific evidence that give credence to the Bible narration. These findings include wood fragments of the Ark itself, found on Mt. Ararat exactly where the Old Testament places them.

It is likely that grapes existed for thousands and perhaps millions of years before their juice was made into wine in any systematic way. Wine (from the Latin *vinum*), and other beverages (from the Latin *bibere*—to drink), evolved throughout the centuries and became so much a part of life that in some nations to drink them was considered a sign of rank and respectability. The higher the quality of the wine consumed, the greater was the esteem earned by the citizen in the community. An individual who consumed an inferior type of wine could hardly be trusted with a position of responsibility within society.

The popularity of wine has increased drastically in modern times. There is a type of wine for each occasion. Hearty wines that are particularly recommended with a meal to compliment and enhance the flavors of the food; lighter wines that are enjoyed during a reception, light snacks, or when friends or relatives are visiting; sweet, flowery wines that make a perfect dessert match; and sparkling wines that are a great choice for a festive occasion like a wedding or celebration. People drink wine for different reasons. Some like it as a stimulant, or as a tonic; others use it as a relaxant, or to help the digestion, for medicinal purposes, or as an aperitif. There are even those who mix wine with a soft drink to make the perfect thirst quencher. The French Medical Association reports that a glass of wine (particularly red wine), consumed with a meal on a daily basis, reduces the chances of cardiovascular diseases and actually prolongs life expectancy. Medical studies report that there are regions within certain nations where wine drinking citizens live 10 to 15 per cent longer than those who abstain from wine. This is often attributed to the fact that red wine (in particular), when consumed in moderation, significantly reduces the risk of heart disease by preventing plaque and fatty tissues from forming within the arterial walls. In many areas of France, Italy, and Spain parents give their children, from the age of three, one small glass of red wine everyday, usually during a meal.

Non-Alcoholic Wines

In the last two decades various non-alcoholic wines have been introduced into the market. The objective is to satisfy people's desire for the taste of wine without the "danger" of alcohol. The production methods are the same as for the alcoholic counterpart, except that the alcohol is removed by a chemical process. Today, many bar and beverage operations include one or two brands of non-alcoholic wine in their inventory. The federal government defines an alcoholic beverage as one containing between a minimum 0.5 per cent to a maximum 95 per cent of ethyl alcohol (or ethanol).

THE SELLING AND SERVING OF WINE

Suggestive Selling

Suggestive selling, if handled properly, can be rewarding for everyone. The operator and manager benefit from the increased sales. The bar staff and lounge servers earn higher tips since the customer's check will be higher. The bar or lounge patron will feel pleased by the special attention and will appreciate the guidance and suggestions provided about the various beverages. Often patrons perceive that the bartender or beverage server who takes time in guiding them through the selection is someone who truly cares about the profession and is genuinely concerned about providing quality service.

In order to provide effective suggestive selling, the bar staff should be thoroughly familiar with the product they serve. Bar employees should also use correct service techniques, beverage terminology, and understand the convivial aspect of service. Wine should be considered to be as important as any other alcoholic beverage that is handled in a bar operation. Training can be expensive for the beverage operator but it is indispensable. Smart training can be considered a long term investment that, in time, will certainly pay dividends. This is particularly true in a brand new operation. Frequently, new or inexperienced employees are willing to do their best, but if they are not properly trained in how to correctly present suggestive selling techniques, the results will not be satisfactory; both conviviality and procedural attributes are necessary if good results are desired.

Wine Service Techniques

Wine has experienced greater longevity than any other alcoholic beverage and it is produced in many countries in the world. Three decades ago, a well appointed wine list was mainly in the domain of upper scale restaurants. Today standard food-service operations also offer attractive and complete wine service. Many regard the service of wine to be as important as that of food. Time and care should be taken to become proficient in presenting, opening, and serving a bottle of wine. The handling of the bottle, the type of equipment, and the utensils may vary according to each operation but the essential steps remain the same. The following method is recommended:

1. In taking the wine order the server should abstain from making any type of comment about the quality of the guest's selection, the guest's pronunciation of the name brand, or any phrase that might be interpreted as inappropriate.

2. The bottle should be presented to the right of the host unopened, held from the bottom with an opened hand with the other hand holding the neck. It is proper to hold a serviette or napkin behind the bottle to create a frame for the bottle and the label, like a display case for a piece of artwork.

3. The label should be at the guest eye level and the waiter should again repeat the name and vintage of the wine. The host should be given ample time to read the label and make whatever comments he/she wishes, to other guests.

4. The bottle should never be subject to sudden motions or shaken, particularly with fine vintage reds. This is because sediments will have formed as a result of the natural process of aging.

5. The bottle should be rested on the bar counter or, if served in the lounge, on a side of the table (or a cart close by, if available). With the blade tool of the opener (corkscrew), the upper foil is scored under the lip of the neck. Novices find it easier to remove the entire foil. Such practice is incorrect. The cutting of the foil should be neat and quick, leaving a clean neck with no possibility of lead touching the wine.

6. The neck of the bottle and the exposed part of the cork should be cleaned thoroughly with the serviette. The opener is inserted in the cen-

Presenting the wine bottle.

The bottle should presented at the guest's eye level.

ter of the cork. Novices often place the opener in the side of the cork making it difficult for a clean, smooth pull. Remember, it is important that the bottle remain facing the host at all times.

7. The cork is placed on the table to the right of the host and a small amount of wine (approx. one ounce) is poured for the host to taste and approve. Dripping will be avoided by twisting the bottle after the pouring, with a quick, short movement of the wrist, and a wipe of the serviette.

8. The host should not be made to feel hurried when nosing, swirling, and tasting the wine before approving.

9. The other guests should be served, in a clockwise order, with ladies before gentlemen, with the host served last. One should consider general etiquette when pouring but a host, whether male or female, should always be poured last. Glasses should not be filled more than two thirds, whether serving sparkling wines in flutes or still wines; remember never to over-fill a glass.

10. When serving a white, rose, or blush (and red also if the guest requests it, particularly for a Beaujolais), the bottle should be placed in a wine bucket conveniently positioned table-side, or in an insulator type of cooler (without ice). The reds should be placed on the table, standing

The opener is inserted in the center of the cork.

The cork is placed to the right of the guest.

A small amount is poured for the host to taste and approve.

up. Depending on the table shape and size, where possible, it is recommended to position the bottle close to the host. The wine server, as much as possible, should *anticipate* the guest needs and pour the wine as needed during the meal, before the guests attempt to help themselves.

Novices often unintentionally violate the proper rules of wine service. The most frequent incorrect practices are (A) Failure to follow up consistently on wine service. It is embarassing to see guests reaching for the wine bucket and help themselves in pouring wine. (B) Neglecting to ensure that the wine bucket is half full with an equal amount of ice and water. If it contains only ice, the bottle cannot be inserted all the way to the bottom (C) Forgetting to wipe the bottle thoroughly when picking it up from the wine bucket. This causes unpleasant water spillages. (D) Leaving the glasses on the table even after patrons are done drinking wine. (E) Breaking the cork. (F) Neglecting to offer a second bottle after noticing that the first bottle is empty and the entree is yet to be served.

The Sommelier

Often referred to as "wine steward or stewardess" the sommelier is the member of the dining room staff in charge of the handling and service of wines. The sommelier has traditionally been male. Interestingly more females are showing interest in mastering this venerable craft. The sommelier's primary

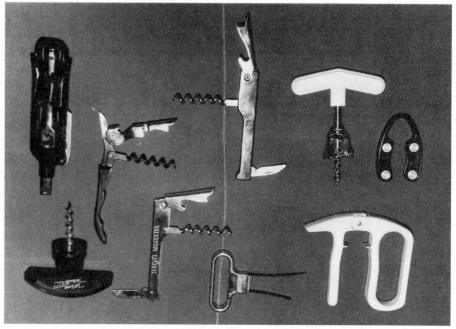

Bottle openers and tools for wine service.

The wine cellar. The sommelier's second home.

A sommelier carefully decants a 35 year old wine. The candle helps detect sediment.

responsibility is the service of wines but in some establishments he/she is also in charge of purchasing, receiving, storing, and maintaining an adequate stock of wine products.

The sommelier feels the same sense of pride whether carefully decanting a rare vintage or serving a bottle of common table wine. He/she is always ready to provide guidance and suggestions to guests about wine characteristics, appellations, vintages, wine districts, labels, and anything that may help the guest enjoy the dining experience.

The cellar is his/her second home, wine is the only nectar. Wine lists, bottle openers, wine buckets, and tasting cups are the tools of the trade. The key to the cellar is the most prized possession and the smile of a guest who truly enjoys a good wine, suggested by him/her is the greatest reward.

WINEMAKING STANDARDS AND FUNDAMENTALS

The bar and beverage professional is not required to be an expert in enology but it will certainly be helpful in providing quality service to know at least the basics of winemaking, plus the essentials on how to evaluate wine and assess wine quality criteria. Reading wine labels, understanding grape varieties, and knowing the wine regions is also important. According to a recent survey of the National Restaurant Association members, customers expectations are increasing. Today's patrons are more demanding and discriminating than in the past. The knowledge and skills of the bar and beverage professional of twenty-five years ago are no longer sufficient today. The beverage sector of the hospitality industry will have to be even more competitive in times to come. The successful bar manager, bartender, and beverage server must always be in the position of satisfying patrons ever changing demands and expectations.

What takes place during the process that takes the grape from the vine to the consumer's wine glass? The vine is allowed to grow in a soil that has been cleaned of weeds, plowed, and fertilized. Vines are pruned at the proper time, and with the blessing of a favorable climate, the grapes are allowed to grow and ripen until harvest time (typically, early or mid–September). The fruit is picked by manual or mechanical means. Sugar and acidity levels are tested to ensure that the picking time is a perfect one. The grapes are crushed and pressed resulting in a liquid called *must*. The must is then transferred to wooden barrels or large metal or cement tanks. Within a few days fermentation begins. Microorganisms and the natural (or added) yeast of the grape cause the sugar to convert into alcohol and carbon dioxide. Within a few weeks, fermentation ends and the must is now a wine. Before aging and bottling the new wine is cleared of unwanted particles and sediments by means

Crush at Winery

of *filtration* or more traditional procedures such as *racking,* in which the wine is transferred from one container to another, leaving behind the unwanted sediments. Before bottling and distribution, some wines are allowed to age for a number of years, but others for a brief time only.

The storing, the handling, and the serving of wine require special attention. Bottles of wine that requires aging should be maintained in a horizontal position so as to allow the liquid to stay in contact with the cork. A moist cork prevents air infiltration. All wines that are to be stored over a period of time, should be kept away from bright light and stored at the proper temperature. The ideal temperature for white, blush, and rosé wines is in the range of 50–55° F. (approximately 11–13° centigrade). Although red wine is recommended to be served at room temperature it should still be stored in a cool place. In general, red wines can handle higher storage temperature than whites without consequences. Conscientious winemakers of the past always ensured that wines were kept in cool places such as natural grottos.

Wine can be made from a blend of different grapes. For various reasons, a particular grape might lack certain characteristics. It might be too harsh or too dull; too acidic or too spicy. The skillful winemaker often blends one or more types of grape with the objective of obtaining the desired balance. Some blends may consist of several different grapes of which some may only contribute, say, 10 per cent of the blend. A good example is found in the popular blended reds from the Côtes du Rhone region in southern France.

LEADING WINE-GRAPE VARIETIES

Historians and viticulturists generally agree that *Vitis Vinifera* (the mother vine) has been in existence for hundreds of thousands and perhaps millions of years. Generally, wine scholars believe that the grapevine existed long before the advent of *man.* When referring to such a remote past, it is difficult to prove anything with certainty; however, it has been established that a wild vine known as *Vitis Silvestris* was growing in central eastern Europe approximately 50,000 years ago. Most of the grape varietals known today derive from these ancient mother vines. As a result of a variety of factors within viticultural evolution, grape varieties have multiplied throughout the centuries and there are now literally hundreds of them. As previously stated, some wines produced today are made out of the fermented juice of a single grape but there are also a large number of blended wines, which are the results of combining various percentages of different grapes. Dedicated winemakers are tireless in trying new blends and seeking the perfect balance. Perhaps more than any other area, it is here that the winemaker displays his/her artistry and creativity.

The grape is the deciding factor in giving the wine its identity and often, its name. When reading a wine label, (particularly of German wines) even experienced beverage professionals, can become perplexed and intimidated.

Depending on the country of origin, a typical label may include the name of the vineyard's proprietor, the wine merchant, the vintage year, the alcoholic content (per cent by volume), and most important, the type of wine, which is decided by the grape or, in the case of blends, the principal grape. Therefore if the label reads: "Robert Mondavi–Chardonnay–1995," the term "Chardonnay" means that, (a) the wine is made of 100 per cent Chardonnay grape or (b) the predominant grape (at least 75 per cent in the U.S.) of the blend is a Chardonnay. Along with Chardonnay, the most notable among the white grapes are Sauvignon Blanc, Chenin Blanc, Riesling, Pinot Blanc, Pinot Gris, Sémillon, Muscat, and Gewurztraminer. Other white grapes, that are extensively grown in Europe but not as prominently in the U.S. are: Muller-Thurgau, Viognier, Trebbiano (called Ugni Blanc or Saint Emilion, in France), Malvasia, Verdicchio, Viura, and Sylvaner.

Barrel Fermenting Chardonnay

The Palomino grape can be included in the "specialty grapes" classification since it is used mostly in the making of fortified wines. Spain's best known wine, Sherry, is made in the Jerez de la Frontera area and it is generally regarded, along with Portugal's Porto, as the world's finest fortified wine.

The principal red grapes are, Cabernet Sauvignon, Cabernet Franc, Pinot Noir, Merlot, Zinfandel, Gamay, Barbera, and Petite Syrah or Syrah (called Shiraz in Australia). Red grapes well known in Europe and often experimented with in the U.S. are, Cinsaut, Nebbiolo, Sangiovese, Spatburgunder, Trollinger, and Dolcetto. The Grenache, a light red grape, is responsible for some of the finest rosé wines, both in France and California. It is to be noted that blush and rosé wines are not only produced by a particular color grape but also by means of a specific winemaking method. Ironically, in the last two decades, America's best selling wine on a consistent basis, has been the White Zinfandel type, which is essentially a white wine displaying a gentle touch of pink color (blush), provided by the skins of red grapes. The color of a wine is in most cases determined by the grape skin pigment. Deep red grapes, from which skins have been removed, can produce fine white wines (see Pinot Noir/Champagne). Look to the inside of the back cover for an illustration of the different color of red wines.

Various shades of color can also be achieved by stopping the fermentation process at a certain time. Today winemakers can easily control fermentation thanks to methods that have been developed and perfected over the course of the past century. A method that is applied in most wine producing nations, is the use of Sulfur Dioxide (SO_2). Sulfur Dioxide limits the action of unwanted yeast, acts as an anti-oxidant, and favors the aerobic fermentation. Another efficient method is regulating the action of yeast by carefully monitoring and controlling the most crucial temperature zones. Other means of controlling fermentation are: the time method, the yeast strain method, the residual sugar adjustment method, and the thermovinification method.

Residual sugar is the sugar from the grape juice that is *not* consumed by the yeast. Therefore, the more residual sugar the sweeter the wine.

Malolactic fermentation is a bacterial fermentation that, unlike the typical fermentation process, is related only to the acids present in the must. Lactobacillus and other benevolent bacteria help the original malic acid transform into lactic acid and carbon dioxide. Because lactic acid is not as intense as malic acid the wine will be mellower in taste and will not contain the overly sharp acidity that could be regarded as an unpleasant taste

---

Wine alcoholic strength may vary from 7–14 per cent. Generally, fermentation stops when the alcohol level reaches 14 or 14½ per cent.

The following is a brief list of the most popular wine grapes and their most typical characteristics:

White Wine Grapes

Chardonnay. One of the most celebrated white wine grapes. As Cabernet is considered the king of red grapes, Chardonnay is unquestionably the queen of whites. Responsible (with Pinot Noir and Pinot Meuniere) for the great Champagne wines, it likes temperate and cool climates. In California, it has more acreage than any of the other prized white grapes. Chardonnay wines are elegant, dry, and crisp. They often, suggest hints of fruit such as apples, apricots, and peaches.

Chenin Blanc. Fruity, aromatic, and suavely acidic, this grape originates from the Loire River valley in France. California has been consistently producing excellent Chenin Blancs, which are known for versatility and for displaying

Barrel Shots

pleasantly aromatic and flowery characteristics. Definitely not classified as a dry wine, it can be medium dry or mildly sweet. The finest Chenin Blancs are matured in prime oak barrels thereby acquiring more character and consistency.

Riesling. A distinctly German grape, it is also widely cultivated in Alsace, France. Many ampelographers (grape specialists) consider this grape the most noble rival of the Chardonnay. Rieslings are known for their scented and delicate characteristics. Rieslings have done well in California where for some time they have been called White Riesling and Johannisberg Riesling. As a result of a recent legal dispute, the term "Johannisberg" will no longer appear on American wine labels.

Sauvignon Blanc. Sometime labeled as Fumé Blanc, this outstanding grape has been gaining ground in the American market. Full bodied and pleasantly complex, American Sauvignon Blancs are classified as dry or off-dry wines. Mildly cool coastal districts usually produce the drier type. This grape has an outstanding record of versatility, and for a long time it has been responsible for the superb "Noble Rot" (or *Pourriture Noble*) French dessert wines, such as Sauterne, Barsac, and Cerons. A Bordeaux, when blended with amounts of Sémillon, produces a distinctly dry wine such as Graves and Entre-Deux-Mers. The Sauvignon Blanc grape easily adapts to a variety of soils but prefers the chalky, gravelly type.

Clearing a Misconception. Contrary to a somewhat common belief, Chablis is not a single grape but a wine made with a blend of different grapes of which the most notable is the Chardonnay. The Chablis produced in small quantities in the Burgundy region of France ranks among the very finest. They feature on their labels various classifications of "crus" (selected crop), such as Grand Cru, Premiere Cru, Deuxieme Cru, Troisieme Cru (Grand, first, second, and third selected crop). Today various wine producing countries market large quantities of bulk white wines under a Chablis label. These Chablis-style wines are in general moderately priced. They can be acceptable table wines, but are often mediocre and even inferior. Look to the back inside coer for an illustration of the different color of white wines.

Red Wine Grapes

Cabernet Sauvignon. Deep red in color, robust, masculine, and blessed with complex and interesting aromas, the Cabernet Sauvignon is grown in most wine producing nations. This grape is responsible for some of the most prized Bordeaux wines such as the classic "Chateau Lafite-Rothschild," "Chateau Margaux," "Chateau Haut-Brion," and the other "Great Bordeauxs." In the U.S. it has for some time been the leader of the quality red wine production. Many wine experts agree that some of the world's finest Cabernet Sauvignons are now produced in California's Napa Valley and Sonoma regions. Wines made from this grape are known to age

Clusters of Cabernet Sauvignon grapes.

well. Cabernet Sauvignon often offer hints of cedar, grass, and herbs. They can also feature more or less distinct hints of fruit such as plums and berries and vegetables such as bell peppers.

Pinot Noir. If Cabernet Sauvignon put the region of Bordeaux, France, on the wine map, the Pinot Noir grape did the same for Burgundy. A great number of wine aficionados consider the Pinot Noir wine to be food's best companion, thanks to its all-around character and versatility. It is known that Pinot Noir can be paired to more foods than any other red wine. Not considered as potent and "big" as the Cabernets or Merlots this wine features a full body and a fine texture. Usually rich and interesting, it is produced in large quantities in the U.S. Although California has the largest acreage, Oregon's

Winery

Willamette Valley and Idaho's Snake River Valley (near Caldwell) vineyards have also been producing fine wines from this most versatile grape.

Merlot. A late entry to the American wine industry, Merlot has been, for sometime, under the shadow of more celebrated grapes. For a while it was used primarily for blending and softening heavier wines such as Cabernet Sauvignon. Today Merlot has acquired an identity of its own. Washington's Columbia Valley and many other U.S. wine growing regions, today produce some truly superior Merlots.

Zinfandel. Some grape specialists believe that Zinfandel is "the original American grape," while others claim it originated in Hungary and perhaps in Italy. Zinfandels can be light and mildly spicy but other varietals produce wines that are richer, more intense, and with lots of tannin. This grape is also responsible for the White Zinfandel (blush wine), today America's number one seller. For the past two decades a White Zinfandel (Sutter Home Wineries, Napa Valley, CA) has been consistently America's favorite wine.

In the U.S., rosé wines appear to have slightly declined in popularity. The Rhone region of southern France, produces the finest rosé wines (Tavel and Lirac). In U.S. volume bar and beverage operations, rosé wines are served through 3 or 5 gallons "bag in the box" automatic dispensing systems. Today, upper scale bar operations frequently offer wine servings that are poured from an individual bottle, stored inside a *Cuvinet* type of wine dispenser (see chapter 4 on bar equipment).

PRINCIPAL WINE COUNTRIES AND REGIONS

California

In the U.S., California is the leading state in wine production. Oregon, Washington, Idaho, New York, Texas, and many other states also feature various sizes and types of vineyard. Small but active and enterprising wineries and vineyards are now found even in states such as Nevada and Arizona, which are generally considered unsuitable (particularly in their southern sections) for wine production. When looking for quality, the most notable growing regions in California are in the northern section of the state, more precisely in the area north of San Francisco. Napa Valley, Sonoma, and Mendocino Counties are the best known areas. In terms of quantity or volume production, the San Joaquin Valley (often called Central Valley) is the leader. The Ernest & Julio Gallo Winery is the largest winemaker, being responsible for nearly one third of California's total production. Dedicated winemakers such as Robert Mondavi, still active as of this writing, Zelma Long, and the Fetzer family have brought winemaking to a magnificent, state-of-the-art level. Wine firms such as Jordan, Sterling, Simi, Sebastiani, Clos Du Bois, Kendall-Jackson, and Ferrari-Carano, have greatly contributed in establishing California wine areas as some of the finest on earth. The world's most recognized names in the winemaking tradition, eventually find themselves involved in wine related ventures either in Napa or Sonoma Valley. For example, over the last three decades two names of winemaking renown, Baron Philippe de Rothschild and Robert Mondavi (one representing the old heritage and the other, the new) joined forces in creating the truly superb "Opus One" wine. The winery is centrally located along the Napa's wine "strip." Other tireless winemakers are continuously experimenting in the creation of new products, by growing certain grapes that for various reasons, were not recommended a few decades ago, given California's soil, climate, and to an extent, the lack of centuries-old-experience required in successfully handling certain grapes. The development of the ancient Roman (now mostly Tuscan) Sangiovese grape is a good example.

Germany

German wines are easy to describe: mostly white, sweet, fragrant, unpretentious yet interesting, and low in alcoholic content as a result of the cool climate. There are red wines too, but in comparison to French, American and Italian counterparts, they are light and offer a much thinner body. Germany's wine regions are concentrated in the Central and South Western areas. There are four sections and eleven regions, of which the Mosel/Saar/Ruwer, the Rheingau, Rheinhessen, Rheinpfalz, and Franconia are the best known. German wine law states that the wine label must indicate one of the four sections of origin. The *Bereich* is the region of origin. The name of the *Grosslage* (collection of vineyards), which can be defined as a district within a region, does not appear on the label; however, the name of the larger region, such as those listed must be specified on the label. Note that some bottles of the very best German wine feature on their labels the name of the vineyard and the village (with an *"er"* added to the name of the village, for example, Opstein→ Opsteiner.)

Germany's wine production is regulated by the government. German authorities are very strict in enforcing quality and production criteria. There are various quality levels, from *Tafelwein* (table wine) to *QbA = Qualitatswein bestimmtes Anbaugebiete* (the first level of quality), to *QmP = Qualitatswein mit Pradikat* (Quality wine with special attributes, the second level of quality). Within this latter level, six grades are found, of which the last three are the most prized and costly. They are classified according to the "must weight" (grape sugar content) scale, Kabinett, Spätlese, Auslese, Beerenauslese, Trockenbeerenauslese, Eiswein. The last three categories are often referred to as "harvesting by picking the grape by the single, selected berry." The Eiswein (ice wine) is named from the frozen and shriveled state of the grapes. These last three categories include wines that are usually quite expensive and not always available on the American market.

In terms of climatic conditions, soil, and grape types, Germany may not be as fortunately placed as California or Italy for producing diversified wines. Many consider German wines to be limited to one type, and a good number of the wines are often not recommended to be paired with foods such as meats and seafood. However, everyone agrees that German winemakers have strived and succeeded in producing their wines in the best possible manner and on a consistent basis.

France

France and Italy are the leading wine producing countries in the world today. Unlike Germany, France's geographical distribution of vineyards is relatively uniform, with the possible exception of its northern section. Wine regions such as Bordeaux, Burgundy, Cognac, and Champagne are names known even to the novice. Bordeaux and Burgundy still produce the highest quality wines of France. Alsace, although not as well known as Bordeaux and

Burgundy, is believed by many to be responsible for some of the most authentic products in winemaking history. Alsace still practices traditional German wine-making customs. Consequently, a good portion of Alsatian wine production is of the German type, offering typical German wine attributes, being flowery, fragrant, and lovable. The renowned "Gewurztraminer" (Gewurtz = spice, spicy), which is now being produced extraordinarily successfully in California, originated from the German traminer grape. For historical and political reasons, it is no longer called Gewurztraminer in Germany but only in Alsace (France) and more recently in countries that have succeeded in producing this distinctive wine. The Loire, Rhone, Languedoc, and Provence are other French regions which include vineyards of great tradition and reputation.

Unlike the United States, where wine production is not as regulated as in some European countries, the French government imposes limitations and regulations on the types of grapes grown, the wine alcohol content, and the yield in hectoliters related to the size of the vineyard. Even the vineyard's method of management is regulated. The assurance of quality, given by the *Appelation d'Origine Controlée* (Appellation of Controlled Origin), is always included on the label of a wine that has earned such designation.

The most typical characteristics of the famous wines of Bordeaux, Burgundy, Loire, Alsace, Rhone, and Champagne, were discussed in the grape variety section earlier in the chapter.

A magnum of fine wine waiting to be enjoyed.

Italy

Various factors, such as a friendly Mediterranean climate, the physical configuration of the land, mountainous wind currents, a soil rich with minerals and nutrients, and several millennia of winemaking history, have ensured that the Italian peninsula possesses the ideal conditions for optimal wine production. Roman merchants had already developed, in Europe and on the Mediterranean coast, a vast wine trade over two thousand years ago. Wine was the institutional beverage of the Roman Empire. Hardly, a celebration, banquet, or event of significance was initiated without a wine libation. Rome was one of the ancient civilizations that worshiped a wine deity (Bacchus). History reports that during those times, spices and flavors wore often added to wines, a practice no longer used today. The Romans used resins and other additives to ensure wine preservation. The noted Roman historian Pliny the Elder wrote an entire book on the methods of preserving wine. Wine was traditionally stored in "Amphoras" (clay jars); however, during the second century A.D. the wooden barrel was introduced, making wine transportation an easier task.

Italy is formed of twenty regions, which in many ways can be regarded as twenty independent small nations. Each region speaks a distinct dialect, has its own heritage and traditions, its own cuisine, and its unique wines. The Marches (home of creatively bottled Verdicchio wine), for example, is an unknown region internationally as compared to Piedmont, Tuscany, Veneto, and Latium, and yet can often produce non-rated, inexpensive table wines of remarkably superior quality.

The Italian Government imposes certain restrictions on the wine trade in a similar manner to France. French wines that meet the criteria established by the government and are of the quality expected are identified on French wine labels as Appellation Controllee (Controlled Appelation). The equivalent Italian wine label will read D.O.C.—Denominations di Origine Controllata (Controlled Denomination of Origin). There is an even higher designation that includes wines that are considered truly superior, which reads: "D.O.C.G.— Denominazione di Origine Controllata and Garantita (Controlled and Guaranteed Denomination). Table wines (vini da tavola), although not displaying the D.O.C. designation, are generally of good quality.

Other Notable Wine Producing Nations

Spain and Portugal also enjoy fine winemaking traditions. Spain has been producing fine wines a few of which are now marketed in the U.S., Aragon, Catalonia, Jerez (producing sherry), Rioja, La Mancha, and Malaga are the best known wine growing regions. Duoro is the highest regarded wine area in Portugal, which is also known for the excellent Port wines. Sherries and Ports rank among the world's finest fortified wines. The cork used to seal wine bottles is taken from the bark of the cork tree, which is abundant in Portugal.

Switzerland, particularly the French section, includes numerous vineyards that are immaculately maintained and smartly managed. In general Swiss white wines are of good quality but they are difficult to find in the

The Best Known Wines of France, Germany, Italy, and California by Wine Region or Area of Origin

	Wines	Type	Regions
France			
	Arbois	W/P	Jura
	Bandol	R/W/P	Rhone, Provence
	Bellet	R/W/P	Rhone, Provence
	Bergerac	R/W	Dordogne
	Blanquette-de-Limoux	W	(Generic)
	Bonnezeaux	W	Loire
	Bourgueil	R	Loire
	Brouilly	R	Burgundy
	Cahors	R	(Generic)
	Cassis	P	Rhone, Provence
	Chardonnay	W	Burgundy
	Château Grillet	W	Rhone, Provence
	Château-Chalon	W	Jura
	Châteauneuf-du-Pape	R/W	Rhone, Provence
	Chenas	R	Burgundy
	Chinon	R	Loire
	Chiroubles	R	Burgundy
	Condrieu	W	Rhone, Provence
	Corbieres	R	(Generic)
	Cornas	R	Rhone, Provence
	Côte de Brouilly	R	Burgundy
	Côte Rôtie	R	Rhone, Provence
	Coteaux de l'Aubance	W	Loire
	Coteaux des Languedoc	R/W/P	Languedoc
	Coteaux du Layon	W	Loire
	Crémants	Sw	Alsace
	Crépy	W	Savoie
	Etoile	W/P	Jura
	Fitou	R	(Generic)
	Fleurie	R	Burgundy
	Fumé Blanc (Sauvignon Blanc)	W	Bordeaux, Loire
	Gamay Noir	R	Beaujolais
	Gaillac	R/W	(Generic)
	Gewurztraminer	W	Alsace
	Givry	R/W	Burgundy
	Hermitage	R/W	Rhone, Provence
	Julienas	R	Burgundy
	Jurancon	W	Pyrenees

P = Rose   R = Red   W = White   Sw = Sparkling

Wines	Type	Regions
La Palette		Rhone, Provence
Lirac	P	Rhone, Provence
Mercurey	R/W	Burgundy
Monbazillac	W	Dordogne
Montagny	W	Burgundy
Montlouis	W	Loire
Morgon	R	Burgundy
Moulin-a-Vent	R	Burgundy
Muscadet	W	Loire
Muscat	W	Alsace
Pinot Blanc	W	Alsace
Pinot Chardonnay	R	Burgundy
Pinot Gris	W	Alsace
Pouilly-Fuissé	W	Burgundy
Pouilly-Fumé (Blanc-Fumé-de Pouilly)	W	Loire
Quarts-de-Chaume	W	Loire
Quincy	W	Loire
Reuilly	W	Loire
Riesling	W	Alsace
Rully	R/W	Burgundy
Sancerre	W	Loire
Saumur	W	Loire
Saumur (Saumur-Champigny)	R	Loire
Savennieres	W	Loire
St. Amour	R	Burgundy
St. Nicolas-de-Bourgueil	R	Loire
St. Peray	W	Rhone, Provence
Sylvaner	W	Alsace
Syssel	W	Savoie
Tavel	P	Rhone, Provence
Vin de l'Orleanais	R	Loire
Vouvray	W	Loire
Germany		
Ayl	W	Mosel-Saar-Ruwer
Bad Durkheim	W/R	Rheinpfalz
Bernkastel	W	Mosel-Saar-Ruwer
Bingen	W	Rheinhessen
Bodenheim	W	Rheinhessen
Brauneberg	W	Mosel-Saar-Ruwer

(continued)

Wines	Type	Regions
Deidesheim	W/R	Rheinpfalz
Dhron	W	Mosel-Saar-Ruwer
Dienheim	W	Rheinhessen
Eitelsbach	W	Mosel-Saar-Ruwer
Eltville	W	Rheingau
Enkirch	W	Mosel-Saar-Ruwer
Erbach	W	Rheingau
Erden	W	Mosel-Saar-Ruwer
Escherndorf	W	Franken
Forst	W	Rheinpfalz
Geisenheim	W	Rheingau
Graach	W	Mosel-Saar-Ruwer
Hallgarten	W	Rheingau
Hattenheim	W	Rheingau
Hochheim	W	Rheingau
Johannisberg	W	Rheingau
Kallstadt	W/R	Rheinpfalz
Kasel (Casel)	W	Mosel-Saar-Ruwer
Kiedrich	W	Rheingau
Kinheim	W	Mosel-Saar-Ruwer
Kreuznach	W/R	Nahe
Krov (Crov)	W	Mosel-Saar-Ruwer
Maximin Grunhaus	W	Mosel-Saar-Ruwer
Mertesdorf	W	Mosel-Saar-Ruwer
Nackenheim	W	Rheinhessen
Neumagen	W	Mosel-Saar-Ruwer
Niederhaus	W	Nahe
Nierstein	W	Rheinhessen
Norheim	W	Nahe
Oberemmel	W	Mosel-Saar-Ruwer
Ockfen	W	Mosel-Saar-Ruwer
Oppenheim	W	Rheinhessen
Ostrich (Oestrich)	W	Rheingau
Piesport	W	Mosel-Saar-Ruwer
Randersacker	W	Franken
Rauenthal	W	Rheingau
Rudesheim	W	Rheingau
Ruppertsberg	W	Rheinpfalz
Serrig	W	Mosel-Saar-Ruwer
Traben-Trarbach	W	Mosel-Saar-Ruwer

Wines	Type	Regions
Trittenheim	W	Mosel-Saar-Ruwer
Ungstein	W	Rheinpfalz
Urzig	W	Mosel-Saar-Ruwer
Wachenheim	W	Rheinpfalz
Waldrach	W	Mosel-Saar-Ruwer
Walluf	W	Rheingau
Wehlen	W	Mosel-Saar-Ruwer
Wiltingen	W	Mosel-Saar-Ruwer
Winkel	W	Rheingau
Wintrich	W	Mosel-Saar-Ruwer
Worms	W	Rheinhessen
Zell	W	Mosel-Saar-Ruwer
Zeltingen	W	Mosel-Saar-Ruwer

Italy

Wines	Type	Regions
Aglianico del Vulture	R	Basilicata
Albana di Romagna	W	Emilia-Romagna
Alto Adige Cabernet	R	Trentino-Alto Adige
Amarone	R	Veneto
Asti	Sw	Piedmont
Barbareso	R	Piedmont
Barbera	R	Piedmont, Lombardy
Bardolino	R	Veneto
Barolo	R	Piedmont
Bonarda	R	Lombardy
Brachetto d'Acqui	R-Sr	Piedmont
Brunello di Montalcino	R	Tuscany
Cabenet	R	Northern Regions
Caldero	R	Italian Tyrol
Cannonau di Sardegna	R	Sardinia
Capri	W	Campania
Carema	R	Piedmont
Carignano del Sulcis	R	Sardinia
Carmignano	R	Tuscany
Chianti	R/W	Tuscany
Chianti Classico	R	Tuscany
Chianti Putto	R	Tuscany
Chiaretto (Chiarello)	W	Venetia
Cinque-Terre	R/W	Genoa
Ciro	R/W	Calabria
Colli Albani	W	Latium

(continued)

Wines	Type	Regions
Colli Berici	R/W/P	Vento
Colli Orientali Del Fruili	R/W	Friuli-Venezia Giulia
Collio Goriziano (Collio)	R/W	Friuli-Venizia Giulia
Cortese	W	Piedmont
Corvo	R/W	Sicily
Dolcetto	R	Piedmont
Donnaz	R	Valle d'Aosta
Donnici	R	Calabria
Enfer d'Arvier	R	Valle d'Aosta
Est! Est! Est!	W	Umbria, Latium
Etna	R/W/P	Sicily
Falero (Falernum)	R/W	Latium, Campania
Fiano di Avellino	W	Campania
Franciacorta Rosso & Pinot	R/W/Sw	Lombardy
Frascati	W/Sw	Rome, Latium
Freisa	R	Piedmont
Gabiano	W	Piedmont
Galestro	W	Tuscany
Gambellera	W/Sw	Vento
Gattinarra	R	Piedmont
Gewurztraminer	W	Northern Regions
Ghemme	R	Piedmont
Giro di Cagliari	R	Sardinia
Grave del Fruili	R/W	Friuli-Venezia Giulia
Greco di Bianco (Greco di Gerace)	W	Calabria
Greco di Tufo	W/Sw	Campania
Grignolino	R	Piedmont
Lacryma Christi	R/W/P	(Generic)
Lacryma Christi (Vesuvio)	W	Campania
Lago di Caldaro (Caldaro)	R	Trentino-Alto Adige
Lagrein Rosato	R/P	Venetia
Lambrusco	R/W/P	Northern Regions, Emilia-Romagna
Locorotondo	W/Sw	Apulia
Malvasia di Bosa	W	Sardinia
Malvasia di Cagliari	W	Sardinia
Marsala	B	Sicily
Merlot	R	Piedmont, Veneto
Monte Antico	W	Tuscany
Montepulciana d'Abruzzo	R/P	Abruzzi

Wines	Type	Regions
Moscadello di Montalcino	W/Sw	Tuscany
Moscato (di Cagliari, Saregna, Sorso-Sennori)	W/Sw	Sardinia
Moscato d'Asti	Sw	Piedmont
Nebbiolo	R	Piedmont
Orvieto	W	Umbria
Piave	R/W	Vento
Picolit	W	Friuli-Venezia Giulia
Pinot Bianco, Nero, Grigio	W	Vento
Pomino	R/W/B	Tuscany
Prosecco	W	Venetia
Recioto	R/W/Sw	Vento
Rosso di Montalcino	R	Tuscany
Sangiovese di Romagna	R	Emilia-Romagna
Santa Maddalena	R	Italian Tyrol
Sassicaia	R	Tuscany
Soave	W	Venetia, Vento
Spanna (Gattinara)	R	Piedmont
Taurasi	R	Campania
Terlano	W	Italian Tyrol, Lombardy
Tignanello	R	Tuscany
Torgiano (Lungarotti Rubesco, Torre di Giano)	R	Umbria
Torre Quarto	W	Apulia
Traminer	W	Northern Regions
Trebbiano	W	Emilia-Romagna
Trebbiano d'Abruzzi	W	Abruzzi
Trebbiano di Aprilia	W	Latium
Trentino	R/W	Trentino-Alto Adige
Val d'Arbia	W	Tuscany
Valpantena	R	Venetia
Valpolicella	R	Venetia
Valtellina	R	Italian Alps, Lombardy
Venegazzu	R/W/S	Vento
Verdicchio dei Castelli Jesi	W/Sw	The Marches, Adriatic
Verdicchio di Matelica	W/Sw	The Marches
Verdiso	W	Venetia
Verduzzo	W	Friuli-Venezia Giulia
Vernaccia di San Gimignano	W	Tuscany
Vernaccia di Serrapetrona	R/Sr	The Marches

(continued)

	Wines	Type	Regions
	Vin Santo		Tuscany
	Vino Nobile di Montepulciano	R	Tuscany
California			
	Barbera	R	Sonoma County, Santa Cruz
	Blanc de Noirs	Sw	Napa County
	Cabernet Sauvignon	R	Napa County, Livermore Valley
	Chardonnay	W	Livermore Valley, Napa County
	Chenin Blanc	W	Sonoma County, Napa County
	Fume Blanc	W	Sonoma County
	Gamay Beaujolais	R	Napa County, Santa Clara, Santa Cruz, San Benito
	Gewurztraminer	W	Napa County, Santa Clara, Santa Cruz, San Benito
	Grenache	P	Santa Clara, Santa Cruz, San Benito
	Grey Riesling	W	Livermore Valley, Santa Clara, Santa Cruz, San Benito
	Johannisberg Riesling	W	Napa County
	Merlot	R	Sonoma County, Marin
	Petite Sarah	R	Livermore Valley
	Pinot Noir	R	Napa County
	Sauvignon Blanc	W	Livermore Valley, Santa Clara, Santa Cruz, San Benito
	Semillon	W	Livermore Valley
	Sylvaner	W	Napa County
	Syrah	R	Santa Cruz
	Vin Gris de Grenache	P	Santa Cruz
	Vin Rose	P	Livermore Valley, Napa County
	Zinfandel	R	Livermore Valley, Napa County, Amador County

United States. Argentina is the world's fifth largest wine producer, although it is rarely found among the ratings of top quality-wine producing nations. China grows excellent grapes but very little wine is produced from them. Rice distillates and brews are still the Chinese favorites.

Although Greece and Hungary claim many centuries of winemaking tradition, they are still struggling to be internationally recognized. Chile, Argentina, Russia, Australia, Canada, Austria, Israel, and South Africa produce wines varying in quality from acceptable to excellent. Australia and South Africa are now competing in the U.S. market with wines that are regarded by many as unsur-

A bottle of French wine.

passed for their price/value relationship. Israeli wines were known for some time to be on heavy side, and often without a distinct character. This was partially due to the hot climate there. The development of Israel's cooler Golan Heights wine region in the past three decades deserves recognition for the versatile wines produced. Cabernet Sauvignon and Sauvignon Blanc are gaining ground there so much that some of them are imported into the United States and South America.

Grape, climate, soil, and the skills of the winemaker are the deciding factors in making quality wines. Not every region discussed here possesses the ideal soil and climate necessary for fine grapes and thus optimal winemaking. Healthy grapes need a number of favorable conditions, a minimum number of cold and frosty days, rain, and sun. Winemakers always hope for at least one hundred days of sunshine a year. Among the quality criteria mentioned the climate is the most uncertain.

The soil should have a certain amount of gravel to promote good drainage and at the same time allow the vine roots to reach deeper into the ground. In this manner, optimum benefit is derived from the available nutrients. Amounts of phosphate and potassium are necessary for the grape's healthy growth. The composition of soil and, in a brand new vineyard, the soil preparation itself, can be the deciding factor in the growing of healthy, and rich grapes. Countries such as Bulgaria, Ukraine, and Slovenia, although gifted with good soil and de-

A bottle of California wine.

cent climate, are not as fortunate in wine production as the more industrialized nations mentioned earlier. This is mainly due to the lack of the latest technology and equipment and sometimes, the scarcity of premium oak barrels for wine aging. However, they deserve praise for producing wines of improved quality compared to past decades. Today, most countries in the world are wine producers. Wine is made even in areas where, due to extreme climate, growing grapes would appear to be a task undertaken against difficult odds.

WINE CLASSIFICATIONS

Four distinct types of wines are recognized:

A) **Table wines,** which are by far the largest proportion of wine production. Alcohol contents vary, but are usually within the 8–14 per cent range.

B) **Sparkling wines,** of which Champagne is the best known, with the same alcoholic strength as the table wines.

C) **Fortified wines,** such as sherries and ports, which are "fortified" (or made stronger) so that their alcoholic content may reach the 24 per cent limit.

D) **Aromatized wines,** such as vermouth, that are normally within the 15–20 per cent alcohol range.

A bottle of wine from Oregon.

The quality of the wine depends on several factors of which the quality of the grapes and the skills of the winemakers are the most notable, although the soil and climate, also play an important role. Grapes are harvested and crushed, with the juice (called "must") undergoing a process of fermentation where sugar converts into ethyl alcohol and carbon dioxide (CO_2) by the action of yeast. Towards the end of this process the alcohol found in the wine "just born" is nearly 50 per cent of the natural sugar.

Some wines are bottled and introduced to the market while still young, while others are allowed to age so that during the process of maturing they acquire more character and consistency. A large quantity of the wines consumed today are blended for the purpose of obtaining maximum balance. White wine production is four to five times greater than that of red.

SPARKLING WINE METHODS

Sparkling wines have become increasingly popular in the last few decades. While France was once the only producer of fine sparkling wines (champagne), today Spain, Italy, and particularly California, are responsible for the making of some truly outstanding products. Three principle methods are

A bottle of wine from Italy.

adopted in making "bubbling" wines, (a) the Champenoise method (b) the Transfer method (c) the Charmat method. The first is the preferred one for quality, although in recent years the Transfer method has brought forward some surprisingly fine sparkling wines.

WINE LANGUAGE

BOTRYTIS CIRENEA

Also called "the noble rot," it is indeed a rot that ends up giving pleasant results. The grapes are allowed to stay on the vine longer than the usual harvesting time. A mold is permitted to attack the grapes causing the skin to shrink and most of the juice to be lost, but what remains is intense, concentrated, and high in sugar content. The end result is a fully textured, intensely sweet, thick wine. A perfect match with any dessert.

PHYLLOXERA

A plant louse insect, one of the most feared enemies of the vine. It attacks the roots and destroys vast portions of vineyards, causing devas-

A bottle of wine from Germany.

tating effects to the wine industry. Soil and viticulture experts have partially solved this problem by grafting U.S. rootstocks with vines from overseas. South American wine countries such as Chile are fortunate not to be plagued by this pest.

BODY

When discussing wine attributes such as "full body," we are referring to the concentration and consistency of solid matters in the wine. Body also alludes to the fullness and roundness of the wine. In general, red wines feature a "thicker" substance and "fuller" texture than whites. With few exceptions, white wines that possess a high degree of body and fullness are not desirable.

LEGS

In swirling a glass of wine for a few seconds, one will notice that a small amount of wine remains on the sides of the glass forming curved or straight flow patterns or rivulets. These are the "legs" (sometime called "tears"). Noticeable and pronounced legs may be indicative of alcoholic strength, viscosity and body. Glycerin and other wine components may add to the body and thickness of these rivulets.

VINTAGE

The term "vintage" (from the French *vendange*) indicates the year that the grapes matured and were harvested. Table wines generally do not feature a vintage year on their labels but they may still be of good quality. Contrary to common belief, red table wines can dramatically increase in character by aging.

CHAPTALIZATION

Some winemakers, according to specific needs, choose to add sugar to the grape must before or during fermentation. This is not only for the purpose of sweetening the wine, but also to increase alcoholic strength. The practice is called "chaptalization." The adding of sugar, or any other sweetening agent, is forbidden in several leading wine producing regions.

FOOD AND WINE PAIRING AND SENSORY PERCEPTION

It is generally believed that bar staff do not need to be as knowledgeable about food and wine pairing as the dining room sommelier and wine servers. However, many establishments across the U.S. and in other countries, bar patrons prefer to eat a meal or enjoy snacks while sitting at the bar counter or in the lounge. Bartenders and cocktail servers can benefit immensely by understanding the relationship between food and wine. In a modern restaurant, a patron might read the wine list while seated at the bar counter and ask the bartender to provide guidance or recommend a type of wine that would be suitable for his/her food selection. In general, the old adage still applies, "White wine is recommended with fish, seafood, and salads, while a red wine is the choice for red meats and spicy foods. A sweet wine will compliment most desserts." Today, as customers' expectations are rising, more professionalism, and therefore more elaborate comments, are expected from managers, bartenders, and beverage servers when asked about specific wine characteristics.

The conscientious bar manager, bartender, or beverage server should also consider that the patron is the ultimate authority, no matter what. It is a fact that a perfect wine-food match for one patron could be viewed as a poor one for another. Although there is an accepted medium, it is true that we all react differently to taste and olfactory sensations. It is generally believed that a commonly accepted sensory perception (For example: a distinct taste of tannin, or oak) will be agreed upon by about 75 per cent of patrons who enjoy wine. Bar staff should become familiar with at least the fundamentals of wine sensory standards since food and wine pairing knowledge will help create a better rapport between the server and the guest.

According to the National Restaurant Association, Americans who patronize bar and beverage operations spent approximately $9.5 billion in 1995. The projection for the turn of the century is nearly $12 billion. People spend considerably more money in beverage establishments than ever before. This is due largely to greater disposable income. However, it is also known that Americans go out more often, as compared to a few decades ago; and since the selection of beverages is greater than before, there are more options to experiment with. Patrons will request and enjoy new things, particularly if the bar staff provide proper guidance and employ suggestive selling. Increased wine sales will lead to a higher average check for the operator, a better average tip for the server, and ultimately, a more pleasant environment for the patron.

Organoleptic science identifies four basic tastes: salty, sweet, bitter, and sour. One more basic taste is in the process of being recognized: The taste of "fat." In comparison, the olfactory (nasal) sensation may include hundreds of perceptions. Chardonnays, for example, may offer subtle but pleasant hints of peaches and apples. Such "hints" before being detected by the palate, can be perceived by the nose in a far more diversified manner. Cabernet Sauvignons may suggest adjectives such as "weedy" or "grassy" and perhaps hints of cedar wood, olives, and/or bell peppers. Whatever the "hints," a good portion of them will first be discovered by inhaling the wine. Smelling or inhaling allows the perception of volatile sensations through the nostrils, which, in turn, signal the olfactory lobe in the brain and activate the sensorial memory cells.

Finally, it is the taste and the "mouth" of the wine that will enable the patron to enjoy the food with greater pleasure. Even people who don't drink wine with food on a consistent basis, agree to the following:

WINE CAN ENHANCE CERTAIN FLAVORS OF FOOD

WINE CAN OFFSET CERTAIN FLAVORS IN FOOD

WINE CAN COMPENSATE FOR LACK OF FLAVORS IN FOOD

WINE CAN BALANCE THE FLAVORS OF FOOD

FOOD CAN ENHANCE THE AROMA OR BOUQUET OF WINE

Although any alcoholic beverage is generally considered a "depressant," when consumed with food, wine can become a sensory "stimulant." Europeans are known to drink aperitifs before a meal in order to stimulate the appetite. Some fortified wines (vermouths, marsala, sherries) are great aperitifs. The drinking of aperitifs may cause one's salivary glands to secrete, thereby priming the palate and increasing the person's desire to savor food. An adequate amount of acetic acid in wine can provide the necessary astringent sensation so as to provoke a more hearty appetite.

Wine lovers are known to adopt certain basic principles when discussing food and wine pairing. Those principles may vary according to a person's experience, predisposition, palate, and so forth. There are people who choose a wine with high acidity so that the wine can "stand up" to foods that contain high acid levels (tomato, citrus condiments, lemon sauces). Others will match smoky, cured, brined, and salted foods with a slightly sweet, spicy wine. A fact to be considered is that people's habits and preferences change. So do taste buds. Thirty years ago no one dared pour balsamic vinegar over vanilla ice creams or fresh strawberries! On the same rationale, thirty years ago the favorite wine with chocolate was the Muscatel type. Some would prefer a glass of Porto or certain Portuguese and German wines; (The Blue Nun decades are still remembered. So are the Mateus and Lancers years). Who could have ever foreseen that winemakers would one day encourage drinkers to match Cabernet Sauvignon with dark chocolate?

An old rule that has always proved to be valid is to "ensure harmony" between wine and food. Such harmony is created by selecting a wine that is known to *possess characteristics and intensity corresponding to those found in the type of food chosen.* If one was to make a list of foods and, on the scale of one to one hundred, assign a number according to the scale of intensity in food flavor and taste, then, a roast of lamb dish with the proper condiments, a portion of Camembert or Roquefort cheese, or a spicy dish of barbecued beef, would for most people, rank high in the scale (somewhere in the eighties perhaps). At the same time, most people would probably rank low on the scale (around 20), a plain grilled breast of chicken, served with steamed plain vegetables. Considering the latter, the choice of a typical, light-natured Californian Sauvignon Blanc, would make a fine match and might actually enhance the colorless and bland taste of the chicken dish. How? By providing some character that is missing in the chicken dish (particularly the breast), but in such a mild manner as not to overpower it. However, the same light-natured wine would hardly be noticeable, if served with the spiced ribs, the lamb roast, or the strong flavored cheese. By applying the same rationale, serving a robust and complex French red Burgundy or a masculine and hearty Californian Cabernet Sauvignon with the same chicken dish, would in most people's opinion, overwhelm the mild taste of the chicken breast and plain vegetables. But most people would agree that the strong flavor, typical of a roast lamb dish would go head-to-head with a potent and powerful Californian Cabernet Sauvignon, or perhaps a well rounded and powerful Italian Super-Tuscan.

There are various types of tasting kits on the market that are of great help to wine novices. The kits include small jars containing natural or artificial concentrate that will reproduce some of the more common essences and flavors found in wine (tanning, oak, acetic acid and so forth). A few drops of concentrate over a small glass of water will enable the novice to form a sensory impression about such essences, enabling him/her to more easily identify them when drinking wine. This practice is often referred to as "Components Tasting."

Red wines, particularly, when young, are known to give a tart, astringent sensation felt usually around the gums. Tannin is the main reason for this sensation. An excessive amount can give the wine an unpleasant taste, while in proper measure it is actually beneficial as it allows wine to age well. A wine in which tannin is absent will taste dull. Tannin derives from the skins, stems and seeds of the grape.

It is often said that a particular wine tastes as if it is turning into vinegar. Excessive acetic acid is typically the reason, which can occur if the wine is overexposed to air because of a leaking cork or barrel (over-oxidation). On the average, a wine contains from 0.3 to 1.5 per cent acetic acid. Wine lovers tend to appreciate a generous amount of acid in the mouthfeel, while in general, wine novices can find it unpleasant.

A wine should be evaluated according to three distinct sensorial perceptions:

1. Visual (the appearance)
2. Olfactory (the "nose")
3. Taste/Tactile (the "palate," the feel in the mouth)

Of the three, due to the reasons mentioned earlier, the olfactory is by far the most significant. When evaluating various types of wine, as in a wine tasting session, it is recommended to sample the lighter wines before the heavier, the white before the reds, and the dry before the sweet. At the start of the new century the Internet's various websites offer attractive, informative, and up-to-date reports on wine news, wine tasting guides, food and wine pairing hints, wine publications, and wine buying guides.

FOOD & WINE PAIRING HINTS

Hors d'oeuvres	Light wines, dry or semi-dry with some acidity; Sauvignon Blanc, Beaujolais
Light snack	Blush wines and light sparkling wines are suggested.
Salads	Selections may vary according to the type of dressing. In most cases a blush (white Zinfandel) or a rosé are appropriate.
Pasta and starches	If the sauce is a light cream, a mild, dry white wine such as Frascati or Sauvignon Blanc would be required. If a red tomato sauce with meat or marinara is served, a light red wine, like Beaujolais is preferred. If the pasta dish is heavier (Lasagna, Cannelloni), a Chianti or a Pinot Noir are a good match.
Soups	A wine is not recommended with soups.
Beef	Definitely an earthy, aromatic, and complex Cabernet Sauvignon. Although better suited for

	duck and lamb, some Merlots can be a good choice as well.
Pork	There is more flexibility with pork than with beef and other red meats. A Chardonnay can be a fine match just as a Pinot Noir or Zinfandel could. When serving a well seasoned pork roast, a red wine more robust than Pinot Noir could be recommended.
Veal	A delicate white meat, it can be accompanied by a light but still full bodied white wine such as Pinot Grigio. If the sauce is zesty and spicy, a young Pinot Noir with some "bite" would be appropriate.
Lamb	Lamb is typical for its distinctive strong taste, definitely more pronounced than other meats. Dark and potent, a Californian Cabernet, a French red Burgundy or a Tuscan Brunello di Montalcino can make a fine match.
Chicken	Chicken is more versatile than most foods. It also offers more styles of preparation. A Chardonnay can be a proper match in most cases. If the chicken is fried, roasted, or served with heavy condiments, the wine should offer more body and texture. Again, a Pinot Noir can pair it well. If the chicken is barbecued a Gamay Beaujolais can be a good companion.
Fish & Seafood	As with chicken, one needs to exercise flexibility. In the case of a soft, delicate fish, a Sauvignon Blanc or a Riesling will do well. With seafood, any good quality dry white wine can be served.
Desserts	Sweet, flowery wines are preferred for most desserts. The Sauternes type and sweeter Chenin Blancs are good choices. Sparkling wines are in most cases a fine choice as well. Sometimes fortified wines (17–22 percent alcohol by volume) such as Port, Madeira, and Sherry are preferred.

KEY TERMS

Enology	Glycerine	Acetic Acid
Sommelier	Viscosity	Oxidation
Grape Variety	Varietal	Olfactory
Controlled Appelation	Racking	Blush
Pradikat	Malolactic Fermentation	Transfer Method

Chaptalization   Wine District   Charmat Method
Noble Rot   Texture   Champenois Method
Phylloxera   Residual sugar   Vintage
Legs   Organoleptic   Thermovinification
Body   Tannin

CHAPTER QUESTIONS

1. What were the first historical references to wine?
2. In defining an alcoholic beverage what is the minimum percentage of alcohol contained?
3. Which type of wine is commonly called "blush"?
4. In serving wine, should the glass be filled to the rim?
5. What are the principal methods used in making sparkling wine?
6. Beside California what other U.S. states are known to produce quality wines?
7. In food and wine pairing, a typical Cabernet Sauvignon is recommended to be served with which foods?
8. What is required from bar staff asked to assist patrons in selecting a wine?
9. What is the main difference in character between a Beaujolais and a Cabernet Sauvignon? Between a Chardonnay and a Chenin Blanc? What are Sauternes and Barsac known for?
10. In "wine language" what are the meanings of the following terms: a. Noble Rot b. Legs c. Chaptalization d. Phylloxera e. Racking?

SUGGESTED READINGS

1. Bell, D. *Wine and Beverage Standards.* New York: Van Nostrand Reinhold, 1989.
2. Kolpan, S., B. Smith & M. Weiss. *Exploring Wine.* New York: Culinary Institute America 1996.
3. Kotschevar, L., and V. Luciani. *Bar and Beverage Service.* Chicago: Education Foundation National Restaurant Association, 1996.

chapter eight

BEER

chapter outline

chapter objectives

Upon completion of this chapter you will be able to:

- Identify three demographic groups that consider beer as their preferred beverage.

- Name the top four domestic and imported beers sold in the U.S.

- Compare the general consumption of beer with the consumption of specialty beers.
- Describe the factors contributing to the growth of specialty beers.
- State the characteristics of those who prefer specialty beers.
- State the definition of beer.
- List four of the five major ingredients used to make beer and describe the effects they have on the taste of the beer.
- Describe the process of making ales by top fermentation and how they differ from beers made using bottom fermentation techniques.
- Name three types of ales and describe their characteristics.
- Explain the effect of prohibition on the beer industry in the first quarter of the twentieth century in America.
- Compare the general characteristics of top and bottom fermented beers.
- Describe the two meanings of the word 'lager'.
- Name three types of lager-style beers and describe their characteristics.
- Distinguish advantages and disadvantages of the three types of packaging used for beer.
- Explain the process of pasteurization and why it is used on beer.
- Describe the key factors in the storing and handling of the different forms of beer packages.
- Create a system to store beer best so it maintains its quality.
- State the importance of 'beer clean' glasses and explain the process.
- Explain the steps to properly pour a bottle of beer and assess the problems if those steps are not followed.
- Outline the proper storage and handling of keg beer.
- Explain the steps to properly pour a draft beer and assess the problems if those steps are not followed.

INTRODUCTION

Beverage managers need to have a basic knowledge of the types of beer so they can decide what to stock as well as communicate with their increasingly knowledgeable customers. The chapter will present the basics of beer without going into the details of how beers are made. The characteristics of the major styles of beers will be presented.

Table 1. Beer Consumer Profile in the U.S.

	Import	Craft/ Micro	Super Premium	Premium Regular	Premium Light	Below Premium Regular	Below Premium Light	Malt Liquor
			Breakdown by Beer Segment					
Gender								
Male	87%	84%	82%	89%	81%	89%	84%	90%
Female	13%	16%	18%	11%	19%	11%	16%	10%
Age								
21–27	35%	36%	32%	26%	29%	10%	18%	27%
28–34	26	26	24	24	25	15	20	20
35–44	21	20	19	24	20	29	24	30
45+	19	17	25	27	26	47	38	23
Income								
Less than $30,000	29%	28%	37%	41%	32%	44%	36%	67%
$30,000–$49,999	29	26	30	34	34	32	37	22
$50,000+	42	46	33	25	35	25	27	11
Race								
Caucasian	75%	90%	77%	76%	81%	82%	90%	22%
African-American	9	3	11	11	3	11	3	67
Hispanic-American	13	5	8	12	14	6	7	3

On average, 85% of all beer consumed in the U.S. is by men and 49% is consumed by adults legal age to 35. In addition, the 21–27 year old population prefers the profitable premium and above premium brands.

There has been an explosion in the number of types and brands of beer offered. The growth in the number of beers makes it difficult for bar managers to decide which types to stock given the limited storage space available. To do their jobs managers need to know the most popular brands of both important and domestic beers to aid them in deciding which brands to stock. Changes in beer consumption patterns need to be followed by those in the beverage industry. Beverage operation managers do not necessarily need to know how beer is made but they should understand how the various ingredients contribute to the quality and final flavor of the brew. The major types and sub-types of beers are presented so the future manager can know the differences between them.

All beer can be defined as either lager or ale style. Most beer consumers are aware of the general characteristics of the two types of beers. Lagers are smoother and often thought to be more elegant; while ales are more hearty, full-bodied, and robust. However, there are beers in both categories that seem to bend the distinction. Bocks and Double Bocks are dark and malty beers that are more ale-like even though they are actually lagers; weizen or wheat beers are light in color and dry, markedly different than the majority of other ales.

Lagers appeal to a wider market and make up about 90 per cent of all beers sold, while ales appeal to a market of beer drinkers who prefer more distinctive types of beer.

BEER CONSUMPTION IN THE UNITED STATES

The demographics, or vital statistics, of beer drinkers are important to those in the beverage industry. Beverage operation managers can compare the demographics of their target market with the demographics of their drinkers to determine which products to feature.

The Most Popular Beers Sold in the United States

Table 2. Leading Beer Brands *1997 Market Share*

	Shipments (Barrels in Millions)	Market Share
1 Budweiser	36.3	18.7%
2 Bud Light	22.1	11.4%
3 Miller Lite	16.0	8.3%
4 Coors Light	13.6	7.0%
5 Busch	8.0	4.1%
6 Natural Light	7.0	3.6%
7 Miller Genuine Draft	5.7	2.9%
8 Miller High Life	5.0	2.6%
9 Busch Light	4.7	2.4%
10 Milwaukee's Best	3.9	2.0%

America's top ten selling brands again led total U.S. beer sales and represent 63% of total sales. Miller Brewing Company and Anheuser-Busch Companies produce nine of the top ten brands.

The Specialty and Microbrew Market

With the general decline in alcohol consumption nationwide, beer is one product that is increasing in sales as well as increasing in the number of products offered. According to the 1995 Impact Databank beer market review, overall beer consumption in the U.S. has declined three percent since 1985, while the specialty beer segment grew 50 per cent by 1994. New breweries are

The new beer trend: Specialty brews.

popping up almost weekly, and existing breweries are expanding the products they offer to take advantage of the growing market. Beer industry experts credit the phenomenal growth of the specialty/microbrew category to several factors. Factors contributing to the growth in microbreweries/specialty beers include:

1. The ability of breweries to produce a great variety of new and distinctive beers.
2. They appeal to people other than the normal beer drinker.
3. They appeal to a more affluent market.
4. They appeal to a group that enjoys experimenting with new brands.

The market segment that prefers specialty beers/microbrews tends to be young, college educated, with above average incomes, and to drink more than the average beer drinker. Specialty beers have moved beer from a blue collar to a white collar beverage. Although they only make up about 10 per cent of beer drinkers in the country they are making an impact on bars and restaurants.

The new beer trend: Specialty brews.

Table 3. U.S. Specialty/Microbrew Market (Production in Barrels 1990–1994)

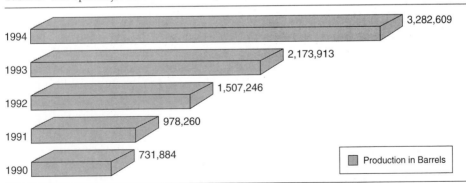

Year	Production in Barrels
1994	3,282,609
1993	2,173,913
1992	1,507,246
1991	978,260
1990	731,884

Source: 1995 Impact Databank Beer Market Review.

WHAT IS BEER, AND HOW DO THE INGREDIENTS INFLUENCE THE TASTE?

Making a fine beer is similar to making a quality food item; the final product depends on the ingredients and the skill of the brewer. There are many factors that have to be taken into account in the production of a fine beer, but the process of making both the major types of beer is essentially the same; the differences come in the ingredients and temperatures of both fermentation and storing.

A Definition

> Beer is defined as a beverage fermented from grains and water. Beer is also the generic name for all fermented beverages made from malted grains, hops, and water, and falls into two main categories: ales or top fermented types, and lagers, or pilsner, or bottom fermented types.

Brief History

Making beer has been going on since earliest recorded history. According to *Grossman's Guide to Wines, Beers, & Spirits,* the Egyptians made beer from corn and the Greeks learned the art of making beer from the Egyptians. Throughout history there is some record of the production and consumption of beer by most nations and their peoples. The Bavarian Purity Order of 1516, which is still followed in Germany, Norway, and Switzerland, states that beer can only be made from barley, water, yeast, and hops.

Ale was the first type of beer. The ability to ferment beer at warm temperatures allowed the production of ale to flourish long before the invention of commercial refrigeration. In Britain home brewing was done by the female of the house, along with the baking of the bread, so it is no wonder that the yeast to make ale is similar to bread yeast.

The pilgrims held ale in such high esteem they brought it with them on the trip to the New World. Running low on ale was one of the reasons cited for stopping at Plymouth Rock instead of journeying to warmer climates south. Beer became a staple of the Puritan diet, both providing much needed nutrients and also being considered safer to drink then water.

For most of history, beer was brewed for near immediate consumption. The brew would not keep much longer then that. Pasteurization helped prevent spoilage and reduced the effect of the yeast that remained from the fermentation process. Pasteurization also allowed brewers to grow from local operations to national companies. The next invention that aided in the growth of large brewery companies was the use of glass bottles to ship the brew in.

Prior to Prohibition, there were over 2,000 breweries in the United States producing a wide range of styles of beers. Prohibition caused the demise of all except the major beer companies. After Prohibition and World War II, breweries produced lager-style beers to quench the thirst of the growing American public. Large breweries dominated the beer scene, and still do. More recently the American public began to desire more flavorful beers. Regional breweries begin to pop up to produce ale-style beers to serve the diversity in tastes. Brewpubs, or bars producing their own beer, also opened to satisfy this need. Major American breweries expanded, and are still expanding, their offerings to meet the growing diversity of public taste. There is now a great assortment of beers for the enthusiast to enjoy.

The Ingredients Used to Make Beer

There are four or five basic ingredients used to produce beer: water, barley, hops, yeast, and for some lager style beers, adjunct grains.

Water:　　The most important and often most publicized ingredient in the brewing process is water. This makes sense seeing that water makes up 85–95 per cent of beer by weight. Although the source of the water, hence it's mention often in advertising, is important, breweries that use

Beer and other beverages have had throughout history the power to bring people together.

Hops:	The primary flavoring ingredient and often considered the spice of the beer. Hops contribute to the overall character, and serve as a natural preservative.
Yeast:	The most crucial and carefully selected ingredient used in process of making beer is this special microscopic plant. Fermentation produces many by-products that affects the character of the beer.
Malt:	Barley grain is germinated, or sprouted, causing a chemical change in the grain allowing the starch to be converted into sugar that is necessary for fermentation. The malt is then processed, roasted to various degrees, to contribute the flavor and color the brewer desires in the beer.
Adjunct Grains:	Barley is the most common grain used to make beer. Grains, generally corn and rice, other than barley used to make beers are called adjunct grains. American lager-style beers use rice and corn to reduce the cost of the beer as well as lighten the flavor, color, and body of the beer producing a beverage that is preferred by many American beer drinkers.

city water supplies run their water through multiple stages of filtration to remove any undesirable flavors or minerals.

 REMEMBER, LIFE IS TOO SHORT TO DRINK BAD BEER!

BEER TYPES

Beer or malted beverages fall into two main categories: *ales* or *top fermented types,* and *lagers* or *bottom fermented types.*

Ales, or Top Fermented Beers

American ales have descended from the British colonists. They have been around for a very long time and have generally fought a losing battle in popularity against lagers for most of the twentieth century. Ales are a more distinctive flavored beer and were generally produced and consumed in Europe. The recent explosion in the American specialty beer market has led to the production of ale-style beers by smaller brewing companies nationwide to satisfy the growing thirst for distinctively flavored brews.

The old style process of **top fermentation** is used in the making of ales. The fermentation, takes place at warmer temperatures for a relatively short period of time producing beers that are darker in color, higher in alcohol, fuller bodied in taste, and more distinctly flavored. Ales are best stored at 40–45°F and generally require more time in the bottle to allow them to develop full flavor. Some of the grains used in the production of ales are roasted, changing the flavor and giving a darker color. Ales are generally served warmer than lager style beers. Ale is more vinous in nature than other brewed beverages, possesses a greater percentage of alcohol (4-5 per cent by weight) than a lager, is more aromatic and full bodied, and has a more pronounced hop flavor and tartness.

There are a variety of different types of ales produced including:

Bitter Ale. Bitter ale is the best known British ale. It is copper colored, more heavily hopped, and has a greater proportion of hops added, than regular ales.

Examples of Bitter Ales; Fuller's E.S.B, Brakspear Henley Ale.

Stout and Porter. **Porter** originated in Britain about 1722 to satisfy the public demand for a brew that was like an equal blend from casks of ale and beer. It was named after the working class profession of the London porter who preferred this style of beer. Porter is made with colored malt and is a dark or chocolate brown, heavy-bodied, malty-flavored brew with a slightly sweet taste and a less pronounced hop flavor than ale. It is usually about 5 per cent alcohol by weight. It is no longer widely produced in Britain but continues to grow in popularity in the United States.

Examples of Porters; Samuel Smith Taddy Porter, Samuel Adams Honey Porter.

Stouts grew out of the demand for a "stouter" porter. Consumers liked the porter but many wanted a beverage that was even more full-bodied. The beer became a type of its own. Stouts have a dark color (some are almost black), a rich malty flavor usually combined with a rather strong bitter hop taste, and a high alcohol content (5–6.5 per cent by weight). Stout usually has a medium carbonation and is best served at temperatures above 45°F. Stout is a heavy beer that is often mixed with a lager or lighter ale to make a "Black and Tan."

Example of Stouts; Guinness Extra Stout, Samuel Smith Oatmeal Stout, Samuel Adams Cream Stout.

Wheat Beer [Weissbier]. Wheat beer (or white beer, or German weissbier) uses up to 60 per cent of wheat in the malt, the remainder being barley. Wheat beer was first made in Britain, but its major markets developed on the continent of Europe, especially in Germany and Belgium. It has a distinctive yeasty or bready aroma and a complex as well as unique spicy flavor. It is fruity in flavor and aroma, and often has fruit such as cherries or raspberries added.

There are two distinct styles, each with its following. Some prefer the Hefe-weizen (or Hefe Weiss, as it is sometimes called), a wheat beer with the yeast left in the bottle, a great source of vitamins, nourishment, and flavor. Others prefer the filtered version called Kristall-klar, which is more like a lager. The Kristall-klar is frequently served with a twist of lemon, which tends to cut the head and lessen some of the sharpness of flavor, making it more like a lager.

Examples of Wheat Beers; EKU Hefe Weiss, Edelweiss Hefetrub Dunkle, Pinkus Weizen.

Lagers, or Bottom Fermented Beers

The term **lager** has two meanings in the beer context. One use of the term describes a style of beers that is golden in color with a light and medium body. It is the type of beer produced by the major American beer companies. The other meaning of the term lager is derived from a German word that means to store or stock. Lager-style beers are stored for several weeks or months to allow them to mellow prior to packaging. The aging of a better lager will last for several months, but all too many domestic products see little more than a week of storage time, so great is the rush to the marketplace. Lagers are fermented in a cooled tank with a strain of yeast that falls to the bottom of the tank, hence the term **"bottom fermented"** beer. The longer the beer is aged, the more "complete" will be the flavor, and the resultant brew will have more body and a longer shelf life.

There are a number of types of larger beers, each with its own individual flavor:

Light Lagers.   Light lagers are pale in color, light in body, are fairly high in carbonation. They generally have a soft, mellow, dry taste. They are

Table 5. Ales, or Top Fermented Beers

Beer Style	Color	Taste	Examples of Brands
Bitter Ale	Copper	Heavily Hopped	Fuller's London Pride
Stout	Dark, almost black	Full-bodied, rich, malty, strong bitter hop taste	Guinness Extra Stout
Porter	Dark	Malty, slightly sweet, less pronounced hop flavor than ale.	Samuel Adams' Honey Sierra Nevada
Wheat beer	Light, sometimes cloudy if unfiltered	Complex taste and unique spicy flavor	Paulaner Hefe-Weizen
Scottish Ale		A strong brew, with higher alcohol than most, generally less hoppy than most English ales, with a slight touch of smoke from the peat fire used to roast the malt	McEwan's Scotch Ale
Pale Ale		More hop flavor than bitter	Bass Ale Sierra Nevada

best served cold, at around 40–45°. The taste of light lagers arises from the malt having more influence on aroma and taste than the hops. American lager beers use corn or rice as an **adjunct**, or addition to the barley malt. The appearance of many domestic beers is becoming paler in both color and flavor; the rice and corn adjuncts work to lighten both the color and flavor as well as being less expensive than barley.

Pilsner. Pilsner, or Pilsener is a beer made in the style of Pilsen, Czechoslovakia, light in color, with a prominent hop flavor, and a dry and clean finish. This is the style, minus the prominent hop flavor, that most American beers are modeled on.

Dark Lagers. The Munich type, or **dark lager,** Munchner or Bavarian, has a dark-brown color, and is full-bodied with a sweet and slight hop taste. It is more aromatic and creamy than light lagers. The color of a true dark lager comes from the addition of roasted barley. The alcohol content in these lagers approaches 5 per cent by weight.

Bock Beer. Bock is believed to have originated in the once-famous beer capital of Einbeck. A heavy dark beer with a slightly sweet malt flavor and strong hop background, bock is generally brewed in the winter for consumption in the spring. True bock derives its color malting process and may have as much as 10 per cent alcohol by weight. **Double Bocks** or doppelbocks are stronger, with an alcohol content of 7.5–13.2 per cent. Their names generally end in -ator, and have a billy goat on the label.

Specialty Lagers

Steam Beer. Steam beer is an American invention that originated on the West Coast of the United States as a direct result of the desire for malt beverages and the extreme shortage of ice. It is a lager beer made by bottom fermentation but at the higher fermenting temperatures of an ale. Steam beer is made today by only one West Coast firm, Anchor Brewing, and the product is both bottled and served from kegs. Steam beer has a golden-brown color, sharp hoppy taste, full body, and a lingering malt finish.

Malt Liquor. In America, as in most of the rest of the world, the term malt liquor is loosely defined with no legal or universally accepted meaning. In general, malt liquor has higher alcohol and warmer fermentation temperatures. An average American malt liquor has 4.5–5 per cent alcohol (compared to 3.6–3.8 per cent for lagers.) In many American states and in some foreign countries, a brew cannot be called beer or ale if its alcoholic content exceeds specified limits. Malt liquor is one of the allowed terms that is often hung on higher-alcohol brews, particularly imports, just to satisfy local labeling laws. The name is somewhat misleading since the beer is not as malty as other beers and is not a liquor. There are many good malt liquors, and they come in a wide variety of styles and flavors. The first American malt liquor was Colt .45, developed by the Altes Brewery in Detroit.

Lights, Ices, and Drys.   Light beer, an American specialty, is a low calorie version of a pilsner-style beer. They are brewed to have 100 or fewer calories, compared to 135 to 170 calories for regular beers and an alcohol content that ranges from 2.3–3.6 per cent by weight. **Dry beer** is a light beer with less sweetness than most other lagers and little or no aftertaste. **Ice beers** are golden in color with a smooth taste, medium body with an alcohol content of 4.4 per cent by weight.

Non-alcoholic Beer.   There has been a growth in the popularity of non-alcoholic beer in the last five to ten years. This reflects consumers' desires for a healthier lifestyle and the trend toward reduced consumption. Improved technology that allows the nonalcoholic brews to retain more of their original flavor with the alcohol removed has also contributed to the growth in this segment. Beer classified as nonalcohol beer contains less than 0.5 percent of alcohol by volume.

Many brewing companies are now offering non-alcoholic beers.

Table 6. Lagers, or Bottom Fermented Beers

Beer Style	Color	Taste
Light Lager	Pale	Soft, mellow, dry taste
Pilsner	Light	Prominent hops, dry clean finish
Dark Lager	Dark brown	Full-bodied, with a sweet and slight hop taste
Bock	Dark	Slightly sweet malt flavor with a prominent hop flavor
Steam	Deep brown colored	Aromatic odor, tangy bitter taste, with a dry finish
Ice	Golden to amber	Smooth taste
Light	Golden	Lower in calories than other lager-style beers.
Dry	Golden	Less sweetness, with little if any after taste.

PACKAGING

Beer is packaged in an assortment of sizes of containers. The three main types of containers are bottles, cans, and stainless steel kegs.

Bottles. Brewers use both colored and clear glass for beer packaging. Colored (green or brown) is preferred because light is harmful to beer. The most common size of bottle was 12 ounces, but with the growth of both the European and micro-brewery segments of the market imperial pints, 22 ounces are becoming more popular. Although there is no difference in taste between bottled and canned beer, bottles are the leading choice for individual portions served on the premises.

Cans. Beer sold in cans is mostly for off-premises sales. With only a few exceptions most brewers use 12 ounce cans. Canned beer both chills faster than bottled beer and loses it chill faster. Cans weigh less, are easier to stack and do not break.

Kegs or Draft Beer. Most beer packaged in kegs is sold to on-premises accounts. The most common keg size used for American beers is called a half barrel and is 15.5 gallons. Beer is also packaged in quarter barrels at 7.75 gallons. Draft is the most profitable way to serve beer in a beverage operation, often costing about half the cost per ounce of beer from bottles or cans.

PASTEURIZATION

Many brands and types of beer are pasteurized, that is, heated to kill any of the yeast that made it through the fermentation process. The beer is pasteurized once it is packaged. The exception is draft beer, which, because of the size of the keg, would require too much heat to complete pasteurization. Some customers prefer draft beer over pasteurized beer because they feel the heating ruins the flavor of the beer. Recent advances in filtering technology have allowed brewers to filter the beer using superfine filter capable of removing the yeast cells. These beers are marketed as "Genuine Draft."

THE STORAGE, HANDLING, SERVING, AND POURING OF BEER

Beer is a big part of an operation's business. The serving of a good glass of beer reflects well on the operation, encourages customers to return, and produces a good profit. Care must be taken in the storage, handling, serving, and pouring of beer to ensure a good quality product that customers will enjoy.

Beer is a perishable product and has the shortest shelf life of any alcoholic beverage. Both cleanliness and refrigeration are the keys to maintaining the quality of beer. It is imperative that beer is kept cold, or at least not hot, and rotated on a regular basis.

Canned and Bottled Beer

Storage. Although beer improves in quality with age in the lagering vats, it does not improve while in the package. The fresher the beer the better it will taste and the more the guest will appreciate it. It is important that your inventory of beer is turned over in the same way as the other perishable products your business sells. The best rotation system is FIFO, or first in, first out. When your inventory is received it is placed to the back or the bottom of the storage area, while the existing inventory is placed on the top or in the front. This is done to ensure the older products get served before the newer products.

It is important for packaged beer, especially bottles, to be stored in a dark place. Most glass bottles used for beer are colored either brown or green to reduce direct light effecting the beer. Beer that is left in direct light for too long can acquire undesirable flavors and aroma. The beer is said to be "skunky" because its odor resembles that of a skunk. While canned beer is protected from the sun, care should be taken not to allow it to be stored in direct sunlight causing it to overheat, also leading to a skunky or bruised beer.

Temperature. Canned and bottled beers need to be stored at a temperature between 40 and 70°F. As storage temperatures increase, especially approaching 100°F, the aroma and flavor of the beer diminishes rapidly. At temperatures much lower than 40 the beer may freeze causing the solids to separate from the liquids destroying the taste of the beer. It is also important that package beer is kept dry. Dampness can weaken paper cases and holders making them hard to handle and the bottles or cans dirty and unsightly.

Serving. The flavors and aromas of beer are best if the beer is served at 40°F. Storage coolers should be set at 36–38 degrees to allow for the slight warming that will occur to the beer when being served at room temperature. Care should be taken not to shake or agitate the beer too much when opening a container. Beer that is agitated will tend to gush out causing a mess and short changing the customer.

"Beer Clean" Glasses

Beer, either packaged or from draft, should always be served in a "beer clean" glass. A glass that is beer clean will produce a high quality product. Care must be taken by the bartender to ensure the cleanliness of the glass. Although the glass may look clean, it may have a film, odors, or bacteria, that will interfere with the guest's enjoyment.

Odors. There may be odors left on the glass by detergents, less than clean bar towels, sanitizers, or stale air, which will interfere with the taste of the beer.

Film. A film or residue can be left on the glass by soap, detergents or sanitizers, food or other items left in the wash water, or smoke.

Bacteria. A glass that looks clean to the eye could have bacteria on it that could spread illness as well as interfere with the natural flavor of the beer.

Steps to "Beer Clean" Glasses

It is best to use a three sink set-up. The first sink is for washing, the second for rinsing, and the third for sanitizing. It is essential that you use both detergents and sanitizers designed for cleaning beer glasses.

The steps in the process are:

1. Empty the glass into a open drain and rinse in water to remove any remaining beer from the glass.
2. Wash the glass is a sink with warm water and detergent designed for beer glasses.
3. Use a three spindled bristle brush in the sink to thoroughly clean all of the surfaces of the glass.
4. Rinse the glass in a sink containing fresh and clean water. Make sure the entire inside surface is rinsed.

Once the glass has been washed there are a few things that must be done to ensure the glass remains beer clean:

1. Allow the glass to air dry. Do not use a towel!
2. Store glasses up-side down in an area free of odors, grease or dust.
3. Do not store glasses on a smooth surface, use a surface that will allow for air circulation.
4. Do not chill glasses in a cooler that stores food or other items with odors.
5. Do not allow glasses to freeze. Chill glasses only to 36–40 degrees.

Pouring.　The final step in ensuring a quality beverage experience for your guest is the physical pouring of the beer. The beer should be poured to produce a head, or collar, of foam. The collar of foam allows the beer to develop its full aroma and flavor. For best results open the bottle or can in front of the guest. First ask if they would like to open the bottle or can or would prefer you to open it for them.

Steps to properly pour bottled beer:

1. Place the neck of the bottle or the lip of the can over the edge of the beer clean glass.
2. Quickly raise the bottom of the bottle or can to a high angle.
3. The glass will quickly fill with a fine head of foam.
4. Lower the bottle as the glass fills and allows the head to rise to the top.

Draft Beer

Draft beer is not pasteurized and so is perishable. Special care must be taken in its storage and handing; it needs to be kept cold, 36°F–38°F, at all times. Storage temperatures much above 45°F may cause the beer to begin fermentation again leading to a deterioration of flavor.

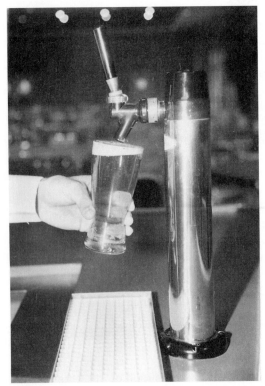

When pouring draft beer, the glass should be tilted slightly.

Storage. Be sure to rotate the kegs. Make sure the oldest beer is served first. Like packaged beer, draft beer is best when served fresh. The kegs should be placed in the cooler immediately upon delivery. Keep the amount of time the kegs remains outside the cooler as short as possible.

Temperature. Ideally the cooler for draft beer should be used only for draft beer. The frequent opening of the cooler could raise the temperature of the beer to an unsafe level causing quality problems. The beer may also pick up some of the odors of the food giving the beer an "off" flavor. The temperature of the cooler should be checked on a regular basis.

Pouring. A glass of beer should be visually appealing as well as tasty. Pouring the beer with a proper collar of foam is the key to a good glass of beer. The collar of foam, or head, allows the beer to release its flavor and increases the customer's enjoyment of the product.

The steps to properly pour draft beer:

1. Be sure to start with a 'beer clean' glass.
2. Place the glass, at an angle, one inch below the faucet.

The beer head or collar of foam should be of approximately ¾ to 1 inch.

3. Open the faucet, all the way, quickly. Do not let the faucet touch the glass while dispensing the beer.
4. Allow the beer to pour into the center of the glass until the glass is about half full slowly bringing the glass from the angle to an upright position.
5. Close the faucet quickly once a ¾"–1" head has reached the top of the glass.

Draft beer is the most profitable item most beverage operations serve. The quality of a glass draft beer depends on the cleanliness of system, cleanliness of the glass, proper storage temperature of the kegs, and correct pressure. Draft beer can be simply drawn directly from kegs or be drawn a distance from the kegs through lines. Regardless of the system, the equipment and lines must be kept clean to ensure a consistently good glass of beer for customers. Most beer suppliers will demonstrate the procedures to properly clean and maintain the draft system.

SUMMARY

The growth in the number of beers on the market is one of the phenomena of the beverage industry. Knowledge of the many varieties and types is crucial for food and beverage managers responsible for deciding which products to stock in their operation. While managers may not need to know the specifics of how beer is made they should know the factors that differentiate the various beer products on the markets.

Research has been done on the demographics of the typical American beer drinker. He is a male between the ages of 21 and 49 years old, with little or no college and an income under $50,000 a year. The average drinker of specialty or microbrew beers in the U.S. are different than the people who prefer to drink domestic beers. They are generally younger, college educated, with above average incomes, and make up only about 20 per cent or the beer drinkers in America.

KEY TERMS

Microbrew, Microbeer	Porter	Malt Liquor
Specialty Beer	Stout	Dry Beer
Beer	Wheat Beer [Weissbier]	Ice Beer
Hops	Lager	Imperial Pint
Yeast	Bottom Fermentation	Pasteurization
Malt	Pilsner	FIFO
Adjunct Grains	Dark Lager	"Beer Clean" Glasses
Ales	Bock	Draft Beer
Top Fermentation	Steam Beer	

CHAPTER QUESTIONS

1. List three of the groups in the U.S. who consider beer to be their preferred beverage. What do they have in common? What value is this information to beverage-operation managers?
2. How do the customers that prefer microbrewery/specialty beers compare with those who say they prefer regular beer as their drink of choice?
3. Explain how the general consumption of beer compares with the consumption of specialty beers.
4. What are the four ingredients found in beers and what do they contribute to the overall quality of the finished product? What is the fifth ingredient found in some, but not all, beers?
5. What are the general characteristics of top and bottom fermented beers?
6. The major American beers fall into which category of beers?
7. What effect did Prohibition have on the beer industry in America?
8. Name one advantage and one disadvantage of each of the three types of packages used for beer.
9. Is all beer pasteurized? Which types are, which types are not? Why would beer be pasteurized?
10. What is meant by "beer clean" glasses? Why are they important?
11. List the key factors in the storage and handling of beer in a beverage operation.
12. Explain the steps in properly pouring a glass of draft beer.

SUGGESTED READINGS

1. Baron, S. *Brewed in America: A History of Beer and Ale in the United States.* Boston, MA: Little Brown & Company, 1962.
2. Bell, D. *Wine and Beverage Standards,* New York: Van Nostrand Reinhold, 1989.
3. Jackson, M. *Michael Jackson's Beer Companion.* Philadelphia, PA: Running Press, 1993.
4. LaFrance, P. *Beer Basics; A quick and easy guide,* New York; John Wiley & Sons, 1995.
5. Lipinski, R. and K. Lipinski. *Professional Guide to Alcoholic Beverages,* New York: Van Nostrand Reinhold, 1989.

chapter nine

MIXOLOGY
AND THE BARTENDER

chapter objectives

Upon completion of this chapter you will be able to:

- Be familiar with the principal methods of dispensing liquor.

- Identify the four mixing methods.

- Discuss the proper amount of ice and drink level, standard portions, and variations of drinks.

- Be familiar with the necessary ingredients to mix the thirty most popular cocktails.

- Discuss the bar beverage manager's responsibilities and the six fundamental management functions.

- Discuss basic bartenders duties, lounge and cocktail service.

INTRODUCTION

Mixology is the science of making drinks; the skills of the bartender. A bar manager needs to understand what goes on behind the bar but does not need to know his/her mixology to the degree that the bartender does. The manager should know what goes on behind the bar so that he/she can assist the bartender at busy times; in addition the manager should watch the bar personnel to ensure that the job is done correctly, and make adjustments when needed. This chapter is not intended to replace any of the fine books on the market that cover the making and mixing of drinks, and their recipes. Its purpose is to acquaint bar managers with the basics of what they need to know to manage and control a bar and the beverage operation. For more detail on this topic the reader is advised to consult the books listed under Suggestions for Further Reading towards the end of the chapter.

HISTORY OF MIXOLOGY

The mixing of one or more spirits, beer or wines, with one or more non-alcoholic beverages is an American invention. Prior to the mixing of cocktails with ice, spirits were generally consumed straight at room temperature.

METHODS OF DISPENSING SPIRITS

There are three methods used in bars to dispense spirits when guests order a drink; free pouring, measured pour, and electronic or mechanical dispensing. No method is the best for all situations, management must weigh the advantages and disadvantages of each method, the type of bar, and customer preferences when deciding which to implement in their bar operation.

Free Pouring

Free pouring is the dispensing of alcohol directly from the bottle. The method is the faster because it allows bartenders to dispense the alcohol with one hand while dispensing the mixer with the other hand. The method works because most alcohol pours at a similar rate so bartenders can use a counting method to determine how much they pour. The fact that it is also the most popular with guests weighs heavily with many bar operators.

Advantages. Customers generally prefer drinks that are free poured over those dispensed in other ways. They feel that the bartender is overpouring the alcohol, not realizing that bar staff can just as easily underpour a drink when free pouring. The speed of dispensing is a reason given by many bars for using the method. Busy bars are afraid that they will lose business if they do not prepare the customer's drinks fast enough, so they are willing to give up the control aspect in favor of speedy service.

Disadvantages. The lack of any measuring device reduces the control of the spirits poured by this method. Bartenders often have the opportunity

Bartenders free pouring alcohol directly from the bottle.

to "go into business for themselves" by overpouring drinks of guests in exchange for healthy tips. In this scenario the bartender and the customer make out at the expense of bar management. In addition, the lack of measurement of the spirits could lead to reduced consistency in the taste of the drinks.

Measured Pouring

There are two methods used for measured pouring. The most common is the use of a shot glass or jigger to measure the amount of alcohol used in the drink. The method uses a process called the "hingeing method." The jigger is held on top of the glass, filled with alcohol, then tipped in a hingeing motion to transfer the alcohol to the glass. The second form of measured pouring is by using a calibrated measurer on the top of the bottle. The pourer has a mechanism that dispenses a pre-selected amount of alcohol when used properly.

Advantages. Both measured pouring methods allow for more control of the spirits poured then free pouring. Although the control aspect of these methods are not fool-proof they are an improvement over free pouring. They also help the bartender produce more consistent drinks.

Disadvantages. The use of a shot glass or jigger slows down the bartender by forcing the use of two hands to dispense the alcohol rather than one

Pouring alcohol into a jigger makes a correct measure.

as in the free pouring method. There is also the possibility of carry-over from one product to another when the jigger is used to make several drinks in a row with different spirits.

Electronic/Mechanical Liquor Dispensing

It is interesting to note that the gasoline we use in our automobiles sells for at least $1.25 a gallon and is dispensed through a $10,000 pump, whereas alcohol that sells for up to $175 a gallon is most likely either free poured or simply measured with a $2 jigger. Electronic/mechanical dispensing works in several ways. One system simply measures out a known volume of a spirit and dispenses it through a gun-like apparatus. The other type system does the same and, in addition, rings up the drink through the cash register or POS [point of sales] terminal. Although this latter type of dispensing offers greater control and consistency over drinks for the business owner, it is generally the least preferred by guests. Guests do not seem to trust drinks that come out of a machine. However, if a bar's customers have nothing better to do than watch the bartender pour their drinks the bar's management has more to worry about.

Advantages. The control aspect of this method is the greatest advantage cited by both manufacturers and bar owners. Spirits are dispensed accurately,

Electronically pouring a pre-set amount of alcohol.

and either tallied or rang into the cash register or POS terminal. This is the only method of dispensing spirits that does not rely on the bartender to record the sale of a drink, and is of great help in the control of theft (which we will learn more about in Chapter 15). The convenience of dispensing the spirit out of a gun speeds up service and helps the bartender increase his productivity.

Disadvantages.   Although bar customers are said not to prefer drinks that come out of a machine, how many customers actually see the bartender pouring the drinks? Apart from the few guests that sit at the bar, most customers do not see their drink being prepared. The machines are expensive to purchase and maintain, although most manufacturers claim that the outlay can be recovered in reduced costs in a short period of time.

Summary Comment on Deciding on a Liquor Dispensing Method

Bar owners and operators must choose the method of dispensing drinks that best suits their bar. Consideration must be given to customer reactions and cost control concerns. It is important to please one's customers but not at the expenses of one's business. Speed of service is another vital factor to consider.

MIXING METHODS

There are four basic drink-mixing methods used to make the majority of drinks. They vary depending on the ingredients used in the drink. The simple mixes, the combining of two or more liquids that mix together easily, require only a simple stir, while the more exotic drinks, made from ice cream and or fruits require mechanical mixing to combine the ingredients into a smooth drink that is easy and pleasant to drink.

Build Method

The most basic mixing method is the build method. It is used for the most common type of drinks, highballs. A *highball* is the combination of one *spirit* and one mixer. The original mixer was ginger ale but highballs have developed to include soft drinks or juice mixers. The point that distinguishes a drink made by the build method from drinks made by other methods is that the drink is made and served in the same glass. Highballs are best *made to order*, as the guest requests them, rather than in batches. A drink made to order and served immediately ensures that the guest receives it at its peak of quality.
The steps in making a drink with the build method:

1. The glass is filled with the proper amount of ice (given in the recipe and measured as a portion of the glass, ½, ¾ etc.)
2. Measure the spirit and add to glass

3. Add the mixer: to fill the glass to ½ inch from the top
4. Add the garnish: if called for
5. Give the drink a quick stir with the stir stick, serve with a smile!

Stir Method

The stir method is used for drinks that are served *up*, or *neat*, meaning without ice. Some guests prefer to enjoy their drink without the presence of ice, which melts and dilutes the taste. Although they do not want ice in their drink they may still prefer to have the drink chilled. Care must be taken when stirring the spirit with the ice. Too aggressive stirring will break down the ice causing it to melt faster and dilute the drink. The stir method is used to make drinks made of two or more spirits, wines and spirits, such as martinis, and Manhattans served up. (If the guest prefers the drink served on the rocks, make it using the build method explained earlier.) The stir method was made famous by James Bond, who preferred his martini, "stirred, not shaken."

Cocktails served up, or neat, are normally served in a stemmed glass. The stemmed glass has a bowl suspended off the table with a stem and a pedestal. The stem allows the guest to pick up and enjoy the drink without

Bartender briefly stirring the cocktail using the bar spoon.

touching the bowl and thus warming the drink. The drink will stay cold, and be more enjoyable to guest if the glass is chilled prior to serving a drink in it.

The steps in making a drink with the stir method:

1. Place a scoop of ice in the mixing cup
2. Measure the spirit and the other ingredients, except the garnish
3. Stir the drink to expose the liquid to the ice
4. Strain the drink into a glass
5. Garnish as needed, serve with a smile!

Shake/Mix Method

The shake method is used for drinks with ingredients that require more vigorous mixing to be combined properly. Ingredients like eggs and cream require quite a bit of mechanical action or agitation to combine them. Some operations by-pass the shake method and blend drinks in a mechanical drink mixer as a way to save time.

The steps in making a drink with the Shake Method.

1. Place a scoop of ice in the mixing glass
2. Measure the ingredients for the drink [except the garnish] into the mixing glass
3. Place the stainless steel mixing cup over the glass
4. Shake 10–15 times
5. Remove the mixing cup, strain the drink into the chilled glass
6. Add the garnish and serve with a smile!

Blend Method

The blend method is used for drinks with ingredients that need to be pureed or broken up. Fresh or frozen fruits, ice creams, or ice in frozen drinks, etc. add much to drinks and need to be blended to be smooth enough to drink.

Table 1. A Summary of the Four Mixing Methods

Mixing Method	Unique Characteristics	Types of Drinks
Build	The drink is made and served in the same glass	Highballs
Stir	Use to chill drinks for guests who order them up, or neat	Drinks with two or more spirits, and/or a spirit and a wine
Shake	For ingredients that require more vigorous mixing	Specialty drinks
Blend	For ingredients that need to be pureed or broken down to blend	Frozen drinks and/or drinks made with fruits

The cups of the blender are big enough for the bartender to make several drinks at the same time if needed.

MIXED DRINKS AS A SPECIES

Someone has given mixed drinks classifications similar to those found in the world of biology. The notion was probably derived from the definition of mixology as the science of making drinks. Mixed drinks are classified into families arising from similarities in the way they are made and served.

The Four Components of a Drink

Drinks are made up of components. There are four components to a drink. The quality of the drink is only as good as the quality of its components. Care must be taken by the management of an operation to provide the quality their guests expect. The size of portions of ingredients used in drinks reflect only a small increase in the cost per drink whether higher or lower quality spirits are used. However customers will resent being charged top dollar for a drink made with less than top-shelf ingredients.

Base Ingredient. The base ingredient is generally the primary spirit used in the drink. It is the ingredient that gives the drink its characteristic taste and flavor.

Modifying Ingredient. The modifying ingredient is either the *mixer,* a non-alcoholic beverage such as juice or soda used in the drink, or the secondary spirit. The modifying ingredient compliments the base ingredient. There are several options available for the bar manager in the selection of mixers.

Accent. The accent is an optional ingredient that may be found in drinks. It adds minor flavor to the drink.

Garnish. A knowledge of the proper garnish to be used in a drink is a key skill for bartenders. Customers judge items they purchase by what they think they are worth compared to what they paid for them. The use of garnishes often allows the customer to believe that the drink is worth more than it is. Garnishes often make a drink more visually appealing and appetizing with only a small amount of work and cost to the bar.

The garnish can serve several purposes in a drink. It can be used strictly for show, a paper umbrella in a Polynesian drink, or it can be an important component of the drink, the lime wedge in a vodka and tonic. Most drinks do not have specific garnishes; this allows the bartender to demonstrate creativity. Some drinks have classic garnishes, a celery stalk in a Bloody Mary, or an olive in a martini. Some garnishes determine the name of the drink; a martini

A typical garnish box filled with lemon twists, oranges, cherries, limes, olives, and lemons.

served with an onion rather than an olive is called a "Gibson." Upscale bars and restaurants generally charge more for their drinks and use more elaborate garnishes.

The garnish is an important component of the drink and care must be taken to safeguard its quality. Nothing can ruin a fine drink faster than a garnish that is wilted or not at its highest quality. Bartenders need to be careful to only cut enough garnishes for the shift.

Table 2. Examples of Some Common Garnishes for Drinks

Garnish	Drink
Pearl Onions	Gibson
Orange Flags	Old Fashioned, Sour
Green Olives	Martini, Dry Manhattan, Dry Rob Roy
Lemon Twist	Martini, Perfect Manhattan, Rob Roy
Lime Wedge [squeezed]	Tonic drinks, Cubra Libre
Maraschino Cherry	Manhattan, Rob Roy
Salt Rim	Salty Dog, Margarita
Whipped Cream	Hot drinks, Ice Cream drinks

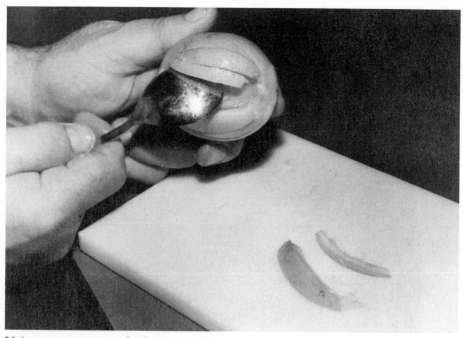

Using a spoon to make lemon twists.

Ingredient Amounts

The ratio of the ingredients of the drink to one another affects the quality and consistency of the drink. Customers will quickly become dissatisfied with a bar that fails to serve a good consistent drink.

Base Ingredient. The base ingredient of a drink goes in second after the ice in a drink that is built. It is measured by the jigger. The size of the jigger is determined by the management of the bar and sometimes varies. A bar may use one size jigger for happy hour and another size for regular service at the bar.

Ice. Ice is not considered an ingredient of the drink, its cost is not used to determine the cost of the drink, but it has a dramatic affect on the taste, consistency, and enjoyment. Ice chills the other ingredients making them more thirst quenching and easier to drink. The ice also takes up a sizable portion of the glass, affecting the amount of mixer added and the overtaste of the final drink. Ice is measured by the portion of the glass, filled, three quartered filled, half filled, or one quartered filled.

Modifying Ingredient. The modifying ingredient is added after the ice and spirit of a built drink. It is generally not measured, but fills the area left by the rest of ingredients. It is important that the bartender accurately measures the other ingredients for the consistency of the drink.

The correct way to ice a glass.

The incorrect way to ice a glass. The glass can chip leaving glass fragments in the ice. A dangerous thing to experience by the patron.

Ice is a food product. It should not be contaminated. Bottles or container should not be kept cold by placing it on the same ice that will be served to the patron.

Accent.   The accent, if used, is measured in drops or dashes. The ingredients used as accents: tabasco hot sauce, worcestershire sauce, or grenadine have intense flavor or colors that complement the other ingredients and would overpower them if used in too high a concentration.

Garnish.   The garnish is added as the last ingredient and generally by the piece. A green olive or a twist for a martini, a lime wedge for vodka or gin and tonic, etc.

DRINK MAKING METHODS AND PROCEDURES

Factors Affecting How Customers Judge Drinks

Bartenders and managers need to be aware of the factors in the preparation of the drink that will affect how the customer judges the drink. Customers seek a well-made consistently tasting drink. The bar that satisfies its guest in that will gain repeat business, while the one that does not will lose its customers elsewhere.

Amount of Ice

The importance of ice in the quality and consistency of a mixed drink was mentioned earlier. Ice also has an effect on how strong the alcohol taste is in the drink. A drink can taste "weak in alcohol" for two reasons. Perhaps the bartender has intentionally underpoured the alcohol in the drink for one of several reasons, or he may have neglected to put enough ice in the glass resulting in a drink that has too much mixer. Customers will often judge the drink by this strength, or taste, of alcohol.

Drink Level

A glass that is filled too high or too low will either make it difficult for the bartender or the server to serve the drink, or will possibly upset the guest. The glass should be filled to about ½ inch [the thickness of a finger] from the top. This will allow the glass to be moved without spilling. A glass that is not filled enough will cause the guest to feel short changed. A drink glass that is not properly filled will also throw off the ratio of spirit to mixer and thus the taste of the drink.

The glass in the middle has the right amount of ice. The amount of ice in both the right and the left glasses is incorrect.

Hints for Bartenders

The goal of the bartender must be to work as quickly and accurately as possible to produce consistent quality drinks. Customers will be upset, and possibly not return, if it takes too long to get a drink, or the drink is prepared incorrectly, or is inconsistent. Accuracy is also crucial in controlling the costs of the operation. For example, if your bartender mistakenly makes a vodka and tonic when the guest ordered a gin and tonic, the customer does not realize the mistake until the drink is tasted. Once tasted the drink cannot be served to another guest and it must be discarded, negatively affecting the economics of the operation.

The majority of the drinks that bartenders prepare are made when ordered and in single batches. Bar staff should not prepare a large number of gin and tonics in anticipation of a rush in business at the bar. Many drinks deteriorate in quality once prepared and should be served as soon as possible. Bartenders are often faced with multiple orders or large groups of guests, which forces them to make several drinks at the same time. There is a suggested order to making drinks so that they maintain their quality and reach the guests at their peak.

When faced with multiple drinks in an order it is best to start preparing them in the following order:

1. Machine-blended drinks
2. One or multiple liquor drinks, made without mixers
3. Glasses of wine
4. Drinks made with juices and non-carbonated mixers
5. Coffee drinks and hand-shaken drinks
6. Drinks with carbonated mixers
7. Open bottles of beer
8. Draft beers

The drinks can blend while the bartender is preparing the remainder of the order.

The liquors will not deteriorate while the remainder of the order is being prepared.

The wine will not reduce in quality while the remainder of the order is being prepared.

Juices and non-carbonated mixers are very stable.

Although the coffee may cool down a little, these drinks are more stable than those made with carbonated mixers.

Carbonated mixers could lose their "fizz" reducing the quality of the drink.

Bottles of beer should remain chilled as long as possible for maximum quality.

The carbonation in draft beer systems is not very stable and declines quickly.

STANDARD PORTIONS/VARIATIONS OF DRINKS

The manager or owner of the bar sets the standard size of the jigger or amount of liquor served in a drink. This is the amount served in a drink when a customer orders. Due to personal preference a customer may desire a drink made with other proportions of alcohol to mixer. It is important for a bar manager and bartender to know the ratio of alcohol to mixer in the various drinks their customers consume so they can monitor their consumption. Following is a list of variations commonly requested in bars:

Table 3. Standard Portions/Ratios of Drinks

Drink	General size of glass	Amount of liquor/liqueur	Ratio liquor to mixer
Standard Highball	9 oz. Glass w/ ice	1 oz.	1:2
Tall Highball	10 or 12 oz. w/ ice	1 oz.	1:4
Double Tall Highball	10 or 12 oz. w/ ice	2 oz.	1:2
Short Highball	7 oz. rocks glass w/ ice	1 oz.	1:1
Double Highball	9 oz. glass w/ ice	2 oz.	2:1

RECIPES OF THE THIRTY MOST POPULAR COCKTAILS

In general, the term "drink" applies to all beverages that are mixed. However, to avoid confusion, beverage operators usually refer to a drink as a spirit mixed with a soda (Gin & Tonic, Rum & Coke, Scotch & Soda). A cocktail is a mixture of one or more spirits with a cordial (or liqueur), a fruit juice, a soda and sometimes a food item (Bouillon, Cream of Milk). With a few exceptions drinks do not require a garnish while many cocktails are usually served with one or more garnishes such as a cherry, a slice of orange, an olive, a lemon peel, a lime or lemon wedge, an onion, a pineapple wedge, etc.

The following is a list of some of the most popular cocktails (the main spirit used in the mixing of each cocktail is given in parentheses):

Black Russian (Vodka)
Ingredients and Mixing Method: 1½ oz Vodka, ¾ oz Coffee Liqueur, pour over ice cubes into old fashioned glass.

Bloody Mary (Vodka)
Ingredients and Mixing Method: 1½ oz Vodka, 3 oz Tomato Juice, 1 dash Lemon Juice, ½ tsp Worcestershire Sauce, 2–3 drops Tabasco Sauce, Salt and Pepper to taste, shake with ice and strain into old-fashioned glass over ice cubes. A wedge of lime may be added.

Greyhound (Vodka/Gin)
Ingredients and Mixing Method: 1½ oz gin, add grapefruit juice to fill, pour into highball glass over ice cubes. Stir well. (Gin can be substituted for vodka).

Harvey Wallbanger (Vodka)

Ingredients and Mixing Method: 1 oz Vodka, 4 oz Orange Juice, ½ oz Galliano. Pour vodka and orange juice into Collins glass filled with ice cubes. Stir and float Galliano on top.

Long Island Tea (Vodka)

Ingredients and Mixing Method: ½ oz Vodka, ½ oz Gin, ½ oz Light Rum, ½ oz Tequila, Juice of ½ Lemon, 1 dash Cola. Combine ingredients and pour over ice in highball glass. Add cola for color and garnish with slice of lemon.

Screwdriver (Vodka)

Ingredients and Mixing Method: 1½ oz Vodka, 5 oz Orange Juice, pour into highball glass over ice cubes. Stir well.

White Russian (Vodka)

Ingredients and Mixing Method: 1½ oz Vodka, ½ oz Coffee Liqueur, Milk or Cream, pour over ice cubes into old-fashioned glass.

Irish Coffee (Irish Whiskey)

Ingredients and Mixing Method: 1½ oz Irish Whiskey, Hot Black Coffee, Sugar, Whipped Cream. Rim cup with sugar, pour in whiskey, fill to ½ inch of top with coffee and add whipped cream on top.

Manhattan (Bourbon)

Ingredients and Mixing Method: ½ oz Sweet Vermouth, 2 oz Blended Whisky, stir with ice and strain into cocktail martini glass. Serve with a cherry.

Whisky Sour (Whisky)

Ingredients and Mixing Method: Juice of ½ Lemon, ½ tsp. Powdered Sugar, 2 oz Blended Whisky. Shake with ice and strain into sour glass. Decorate with half slice of lemon, add cherry.

Dry Martini (5-to-1) (Gin)

Ingredients and Mixing Method: 1⅔ oz Gin, ⅓ oz Dry Vermouth. Stir vermouth and gin over ice cubes in mixing glass. Strain into cocktail glass. Serve with a twist of lemon peel or olive, if desired.

Gin Fizz (Gin)

Ingredients and Mixing Method: Juice of ½ Lemon, 1 tsp. Powdered Sugar, 2 oz Gin, Club Soda. Shake with ice and strain into highball glass with two ice cubes. Fill with club soda and stir.

Tom Collins (Gin)

Ingredients and Mixing Method: Juice of ½ Lemon, 1 tsp. Powdered Sugar, 2 oz sweet and sour Collins Mix, 1½ oz Gin. Cherry, Orange, or Lime with tooth pick on top to garnish. Shake with ice and strain into sour glass. Add several ice cubes, fill with carbonated water, and stir. Serve with a straw.

Jamaica Me Crazy (Rum)
Ingredients and Mixing Method: 1.5 oz Dark Rum, ½ oz Spiced Rum, ¼ oz Blue Curacao, 2 oz Cream of Coconut, 1 oz Pineapple Juice, 1 oz Tropicana Orange Juice, 1 oz Margarita Mix, 2 × 8 oz Scoops of Crushed Ice. Blend thoroughly. Pour into specialty glass. Garnish with pineapple flag.

Pina Colada (Rum)
Ingredients and Mixing Method: 1.5 oz Light Rum, 3 oz Light Coconut Milk, 3 oz Pineapple Juice. Put all ingredients into an electric blender with 2 cups of crushed ice. Blend at a high speed for a short length of time. Strain into a Collins Glass and serve with a straw.

Strawberry Daiquiri (Rum)
Ingredients and Mixing Method: 1½ oz Spiced Rum, 1¾ Sweet & Sour Mix, 3 oz Frozen Strawberries. Blend all ingredients with a scoop of crushed ice.

Brandy Alexander (Brandy)
Ingredients and Mixing Method: ¾ oz Creme de Cacoa (brown), ¾ oz Brandy, 1 oz Heavy Cream. Mix well with crushed ice. Serve in martini glass or Coupette glass, unless requested on the rocks. Top with Nutmeg.

Frozen Margarita (Tequila)
Ingredients and Mixing Method: 1 oz Tequila, ½ oz Triple Sec, 1 oz Lemon or Lime Juice. Blend ingredients at low speed for 5 seconds with 1 cup of crushed ice, then at high speed until firm. Pour into cocktail glass and garnish with a slice of lemon or lime.

Margarita (Tequila)
Ingredients and Mixing Method: 1½ oz Tequila, ½ oz Triple Sec, 1 oz Lemon or Lime juice. Rub martini glass with rind of lemon or lime, alp rim in salt, shake ingredients with ice and strain into the salt rimmed glass.

Tequila Sunrise (Tequila)
Ingredients and Mixing Method: 2 oz Tequila, 4 oz Orange Juice, ¾ oz Grenadine. Stir tequila and orange juice with ice and strain into highball glass. Add ice cubes, pour in grenadine slowly and allow to settle before drinking.

Rob Roy (Scotch)
Ingredients and Mixing Method: 2 oz Scotch, ½ oz Sweet Vermouth (red), Dash of Bitters. Serve in martini cocktail glass unless requested on the rocks. Stir with ice and strain into cocktail glass.

Rusty Nail (Scotch)
Ingredients and Mixing Method: 1½ oz Scotch, ¾ oz Drambuie. Serve in a rock glass with ice cubes, float Drambuie on top.

Shirley Temple (Non–Alcoholic)

Ingredients and Mixing Method: 7 oz Ginger Ale, 1 oz Grenadine, 1 Lemon Slice, 1 Cherry. Pour ginger ale over ice, sprinkle grenadine syrup over it. Garnish with lemon or cherry.

Grasshopper

Ingredients and Mixing Method: ¾ oz Creme de Menthe (green), ¾ oz Creme de Cocoa (white), 1 oz Heavy Cream. Shake well with cracked ice and strain into a cocktail martini glass.

Stinger

Ingredients and Mixing Method: 2 oz Brandy, 1 oz Creme de Menthe (white). Shake well with ice and strain into cocktail glass.

Kir

Ingredients and Mixing Method: 5 oz White Wine, ½ oz Creme de Cassis. Pour wine into wine glass. Add Creme de Cassis, a twist of lemon, and stir.

Kir Royale

Ingredients and Mixing Method: 5 oz Champagne, ½ oz Creme de Cassis. Serve in champagne, tulip, or flute glass.

Dubonnet Highball

Ingredients and Mixing Method: 2 oz of Dubonnet into highball glass with two ice cubes. Fill with ginger ale, add a twist of lemon peel, and stir.

While it is important that bartenders be well trained, it is virtually impossible for a bartender to be familiar with all cocktail recipes; some bartenders' guides list over a thousand of them. Therefore, with the aim of ensuring consistency among bartenders THERE SHOULD BE A REFERENCE for staff to consult when needed. Management should provide a cocktail guide of choice or establish a file containing standardized cocktail recipes.

BEHIND THE BAR PROCEDURES—BARTENDERS' DUTIES

Bars expect their bartenders to perform many different tasks when behind the bar. The size of the bar, the size of the staff, and the type of operation affect the duties that bartenders perform. The following is a list of some skills and attributes required of a good bartender:

1. The bartender should ask the guest if they would like a refill when there is only about a quarter of the drink remaining.
2. A bartender should not gossip about guests or enter into conversations between guests when not invited.

3. The bartender should at least acknowledge all guests when seated at the bar if he/she cannot serve them immediately.
4. The bartender should remain calm at all times.
5. A good bartender will always greet guests with a smile and be polite and cordial.
6. The bartender should not spend too much time talking to regulars and ignoring new customers to the bar. Remember, yesterday's newcomer is today's regular.
7. A good bartender will be well versed in the drinks as well as the products served so he/she can recommend drinks to customers if asked.
8. A bartender should be ethical and unobtrusive in all dealings with customers and servers.
9. The bartender should follow the rules of the establishment that employs him/her.
10. Care should be taken by the bartender to enter all drinks sales into the cash register.
11. Guests should be served in a prompt and efficient manner at all times.
12. The bartender should take care in properly stocking the bar and preparing garnishes to ensure they do not run out during a business period.
13. A good bartender will only serve the highest quality products to their guests.

The bartender is serving with a smile, therefore his guests are also enjoying themselves.

(This list has been adapted from one provided in *The Professional Guide to Bartending; An Encyclopedia of American Mixology*, [2nd Edition] by R. Plotkin, P.S.D. Publishing Company, Tucson, AZ, 1998.)

A MANAGER'S DUTIES AND RESPONSIBILITIES

A manager's duties and responsibilities may vary according to the type of operation. Owners or executives may decide to appoint a manager with full authority, while others prefer to be consulted before a major decision is made. In either case, the manager is the person of trust and the catalyst behind every activity. The success of the operation may very well depend on his/her capability in handling certain responsibilities. In a small beverage operation the manager has to supply all the technical and administrative know-how needed, while in larger corporate settings, he/she is supported and aided by other departments, purchasing, human resources, payroll, accounting, auditing, etc. In general we can summarize the responsibilities as follows:

Planning

Prepares monthly forecast of revenue and expenses by considering past sales records and other factors.

Plans and administers for staff vacation, leave of absence, substitutes, promotions, payroll, payroll updates, terminations, and hiring.

Prepares schedules and maintains a calendar book complete with deadlines to be met.

Discusses bar menus with bartenders and cocktail servers on issues like: sales mix, changes, low and high margin beverage items, specialty drinks, customer feedback.

Plans training of new employees, and providing incentives and motivation for existing personnel.

Organizing

Maintains up-to-date job descriptions and job specifications.

Prepares all beverage requisitions, keeps neat record of all revenues, expenses, accounts receivables, accounts payables (in some operations).

Defines clearly all staff responsibilities, to each other and to the patrons. Enforces staff adherence to opening and closing checklists.

Coordinating

Conducts daily or weekly roll calls (according to needs) and meetings with bar and lounge employees for the purpose of giving information, building team effort, solving problems, etc.

Observes guest reactions and gathers feedback to determine priorities and alternatives on meeting guest satisfaction.

Supervising

Corrects immediately any deviation from established service standards.

Follows up training of new employees, checks progress, provides assistance to current employees in need of additional training.

Maintains order and discipline by enforcing established house rules, particularly those pertaining to personal conduct, grooming, personal hygiene, and cooperation.

Strives to establish team work and group pride, and encourages collective efforts.

Becomes familiar with labor laws and all legal aspects of labor issues.

Controlling

Reviews daily, weekly, and monthly results compared to what was forecasted and makes adjustments where they are most needed.

Verifies that the income statement matches with the total of guest checks, and ensures that all beverage items are properly recorded on guest checks.

Service manager instructing bartenders and servers before service.

Takes all necessary measures to prevent in-house theft and employees illegal practices.

Monitors drinks portion control and waste.

Some establishments may offer uncommon garnishes such as cucumber dill, fresh spearmint, stick cinnamon, kiwi slices, pieces of tropical fruit, etc.

Standard condiment items include: Tabasco bitters, Worcestershire sauce, sugar–superfine and cube, salt–table and coarse, and certain ground spices like nutmeg, cinnamon, pepper, and celery salt.

Each station set-up should include selected condiments and bar food. Everything must be in its designated place.

A basic stock of non-alcoholic beverages should be issued and set up in each station at the beginning of the shift or function. Issues may vary according to the anticipated demand. Additional issues should be made as needed.

Non-alcoholic beverages are separated into carbonated mixes, juices, and other liquids for mixing. Common carbonated mixes are Coke, Seven Up, club soda, tonic water, ginger ale, root beer, Dr. Pepper, and various colas.

Common pre-mixes are: Collins Mix, Sweet and Sour, Margarita Mix, Pina Colada Mix, Rose's Water.

Fresh fruit juices, milk, cream, and any perishable product must be requisitioned from the kitchen for each shift or function if scheduled. Since these

The supervisor is filling out a daily requisition in order to bring the stock up to par.

Table 4. An Example of Daily Requisition and Maintenance of Proper Bar Stock Amounts

Standard Bar Foods:		Amount
Citrus Fruits	Lemon twists wedges and slices	
	Lime wedges	
	Orange slices	
	Cherries	
Cocktail Onions		
Olives		
Celery stalks		

foods do not store well, it is *important* not to requisition more than necessary for the needs of each particular shift or function. Dairy products should be returned to the kitchen at the end of the day. All other bar food such as spices, sugar, salt, celery salt, various condiments, Angostura bitters, Tabasco, and Worcestershire sauce should be returned to the proper storage area.

BEFORE-THE-SHIFT SET-UP CHECKLIST

Bar Product/Equipment/Utensils

Wine, House White
Wine, House Red
Wine, House Rosé
Wine, House Blush
Wine, Bottle (according to establishment inventory list)
Bourbon
Canadian
Scotch
Blend
Brandy
Cognac
Armagnac
Tequila
Gin
Vodka
Rum
Cordials (according to establishment inventory list)
Beers, Domestic and Imported (according to establishment inventory list)

Specialty Beers
Blender
Mixing Glass
Strainer
Can/Bottle Opener
Shaker
Muddler
Bar Mat
Bar Spoon
Bottle Pourers
Measuring Jigger
Bar Towels
Cutting Board
Fruit Knife
Cocktail Trays
Cocktail Napkins
Corkscrew, Pocket
Corkscrew, Bench
Stir Sticks, box
Frilly Pix, box
Bucket, 5 gal
Wine Cooler
Wine Bucket, Plastic

COCKTAIL SERVICES STANDARDS

Techniques

Be ready with a suggestion for the guest who is *undecided*.

Repeat the order back to the guest after the guest orders.

If more than one guest is seated at the table, take the order from left to right.

Never substitute a brand without asking.

When another server's guest requests service, supply it if possible. If it is not possible, let the other server know. *Do not* say: "It's not my station."

The server should pay close attention to special requests, such as water on the side, brand names, garnishes, etc.

Upgrading: suggest one of our call brands. If a guest orders scotch, suggest Chivas or Dewars; for gin, suggest Beefeaters or Tanqueray; for bourbon, Makers, etc.

Avoid writing while guest is speaking. Constant eye contact assures the guest you are listening to what is being said.

Inquire how the guest will pay: cash, comp (comp is a complimentary drink which can only be given by managers), etc.

All servers carry on their trays a dampened bar cloth to clean the tables. Do not use cocktail napkins to wipe off the tables.

Do not clean ashtrays in front of guests.

Always replace a dirty ashtray with a clean one.

Drink Preparation and Transport

Check the drink appearance before serving.

Check for spillage on the side of the glass, clean glassware, and consistent drink garnishes.

Always use a tray to carry drinks, empty glasses, ashtrays, and any serviceware item.

Placing the Order with the Bartender

Do not order if someone is receiving service in front of you. Begin with "Order, please." Wait for the bartender to acknowledge you. The bartender will signal you with a response.

Prior to placing your order, inform bartender as to which type of transaction the order will be.

Always specify your order by the brand the guest specified. Indicate that you are finished ordering by declaring "out."

Recommended Drink Order Sequence

(This may vary according to establishment. Listed here is one of the most common sequences)

Bourbon
Vodka
Scotch
Gin
Rum
Brandy
Tequila
Cordials and Liqueurs; Blended Drinks
Wines
Beers, Domestic
Beers, Imported
Sodas
Juices

Banquet service staff ready for guests to arrive.

The cocktail server must always use a tray, even for one single glass.

Serving Drinks to the Guest

Always place a napkin under the glass directly in front of each guest. Do not place a napkin under a wine bottle.

Glasses should only be handled by the base, never by the rim.

Pick up all the empty glasses. Never put fingers inside the glasses as you remove them.

Always use a tray.

Whenever possible, servers should move clockwise around the table.

When serving beer, set the glass on the table, proceed to slowly pour half the contents of the bottle into the glass and then try to create a "head" by pouring the remainder of the bottle into the glass.

After the drinks are served, pick up all the empty glasses you can, clean the table, and leave clean ashtrays.

Three Minute Rule: return to the table within three minutes after you have served drinks, to ensure drinks and garnishes are correct and the service satisfactory.

Keep serving areas clean: empty ashtrays, change napkins, visit all tables, take orders, etc.

Cocktail server serving guests.

Cocktail Server Duties

1. Take all beverage orders in your assigned station and place orders with bartender verbally. *Be sure to specify the type of transaction* (whether the order is a comp or cash).
2. Serve beverages to guests in a timely manner. Present guest with ticket and collect money at time of delivery not after they are done.
3. Stock cocktail station with all materials needed to serve food and beverages before, and at the end of, each shift.
4. Keep management informed of any situations or problems that occur while on your shift, you are the eyes and ears of the bar and lounge.
5. Make sure to "card" all guests who appear younger than 30 years old and who wish to consume alcoholic beverages. Minors (anyone under the age of 21) are not allowed in the bar/lounge.
6. When taking orders from guests try to "upsell" premium brands to customers. If a guest asks for a vodka tonic offer Absolut or any premium brand name.
7. Be familiar with all the types and brands of alcohol the bar sells. Be able to answer any questions and to recommend different drinks and beers.
8. Know all prices of appetizers, drinks, and beers sold at the bar.
9. Be efficient when taking orders and serving them. Always check a second round of drinks with prior guests before returning to the bar and ordering.
10. Always count back change to the guest to make sure you are accurate; if you are wrong you'll be cheating the guest or yourself out of money.
11. Greet guests and treat them as if they are in your own home. If they feel comfortable they will want to come back again.
12. Be sure to garnish all drinks properly; if you are not sure which garnish to use ask the bartender.
13. When placing orders at the bar be specific as to which type of beverage it is, and if it is a brand name, e.g., Absolut tonic, tell the bartender.
14. When placing an order with the bartender begin by saying "order please," then order your cocktails first and beers last.
15. Always roam your assigned station, do not hang out at the bar unnecessarily.
16. Smile, make sure to have a good time, then your guests will too!

KEY TERMS

Free pouring	Build Mixer	Double Tall
Measured pouring	Stir Method	Double Tall Highball
Jigger	Shake Method	Spirit Highball

Electronic/mechanical dispensing	Basic Ingredient	Cocktail
Hingeing Method	Modifying Ingredient	Short
Made to order	Accent	Double
Up, or neat	Garnish	Tall Highball
Stemmed glass		

CHAPTER QUESTIONS

1. Your bartender gets an order from a server from one table for the following: one pitcher of beer, two coffee and brandies, a gin and tonic, one martini up, another on the rocks, a frozen margarita, and a glass of chardonnay. List the drinks in the proper order they should be prepared in to ensure maximum quality for the guest.

2. Rank the alcohol potency of the drink variations from high to low. Explain why it is important to communicate this to your bartenders.

3. If the goal of the bar is to maximize profit, why is it really uncommon to see a bar with an electronic liquor dispensing (ELD) system? What factors should bar owners weigh when making the decision to purchase an ELD?

4. You have two bartenders working for you: one is very accurate but slow, while the other is very fast but tends to make mistakes about five percent of the time. Which bartender would you prefer working for you? Does your choice depend on the type and amount of business of the bar?

SUGGESTIONS FOR FURTHER READING

For a comprehensive book of drink recipes.
1. Plotkin, R. *The Bartender's Companion; A Complete Guide to Drink Recipes.* Tucson, AZ: P.S.D. Publishing Company, 1988.

For a great overview on bartending procedures:
2. Plotkin, R. *The Professional Guide to Bartending; An Encyclopedia of American Mixology,* 2nd Edition. Tucson, AZ: P.S.D. Publishing Company, 1988.

chapter ten

STAFFING CONCERNS

chapter outline

Chapter Objectives
Staffing: The Most Demanding of Management Functions
Staffing Concerns
Key Terms
Chapter Questions

chapter objectives

Reading this chapter will enable you to:

- Define and discuss staffing as a primary management concerns.

- Become familiar with organizational charts and organization structure.

- Describe the roles of the various positions within a beverage operation.

- Identify and discuss current issues facing labor availability and quality in the beverage industry.

- Discuss recruiting and hiring methods.

- Understand the responsibilities of the person conducting the interview.

- Become familiar with federal laws affecting the hiring process.

- Apply the proper labor laws and learn what managers should do to avoid terminations that can later be considered violations to labor laws.

STAFFING: THE MOST DEMANDING
OF MANAGEMENT FUNCTIONS

Staffing is the process of recruiting and hiring an adequate number of employees to meet operational needs. Every bar and beverage operator, whether an independent owner of a small local bar or a human resource director of a large hotel, agrees that, of all management functions, staffing has become the most challenging and demanding one. Careful and competent staffing can be the key to the success of the operation. The interior decor, the furnishings, the equipment, and the appointments of a bar can be attractive and well planned but if the staff does not respond in meeting management objectives and, most importantly, in exceeding patrons' expectations and meeting their ever changing demands, in the long run the operation will not succeed.

Bar employees can positively or adversely affect beverage revenue and profitability, more directly than employees of any other sector of the hospitality industry. Staffing has become a very competitive issue. The workforce is changing and with it many of the traditional sources of employees. The search for a productive, cost-efficient employee requires dedication and knowledge of many labor-related areas on the part of the recruiter.

Understanding the history and the mechanics of recruiting methods is essential. Is using employee referrals, posting work vacancies, and other methods of **internal staffing** more reliable than **outside recruiting?** In terms of hiring productive dedicated employees what are the historical proportions of personnel hired through newspaper advertising and employment agencies compared to other outside sources?

Avoiding high personnel turnover and finding employees who perform their tasks with enthusiasm and reliability on a daily basis, has become a most challenging task.

Organization Chart

As in most businesses, a bar and beverage operation conforms to a specific model and plan of organization. This human resource model is best described by the Organization Chart. This is a drawing or diagram that displays the various departments and their level (or layers) of staffing. It also includes the relationships between the various departments. The "chain of command" chart (often referred to as such) of local bar operation may include only two levels. The owner/working manager and two employees. But a large beverage operation, such as one that is part of a major hotel, may require five or more levels.

Bar Staff Responsibilities

The organization charts display the various departments and how they are interdependent on each other. It also shows the beverage department "chain of command." Although these terms may suggest military connotations, they are very appropriate considering that the beverage department hierarchy is set up along the lines of an army organization. Just as a private reports to the sergeant who in turn reports to the captain and so on, the barback reports to the bartender who's immediate supervisor is the bar manager. The bar manager is under the supervision of the Food and Beverage (F & B) Director who reports to the property General Manager. Such a hierarchy is necessary for the effective functioning of the organization. Without it there would be chaos and confusion. Each member of the hierarchy has a distinct set of responsibilities included in a "job description."

The positions of F&B director (or even larger properties, V.P. of F&B), bar manager, and sometimes that of head bartender are considered management positions. In most cases, they are salaried positions whereas bartenders, cocktail servers, barbacks, and bar runners are compensated an hourly basis. The food and beverage director is the person responsible for the overall administration of the beverage department. He/she is ultimately responsible for overseeing all the department activities such as purchasing, staffing, controlling, and other management functions. Decision making skills are vital in this position. The organizational layers can be summarized in three categories, **Entry Level/Apprentice Positions** such as barbacks and runners, **Skilled/Professional Positions** such as bartenders, and **Managerial/Supervisory Positions** such as the management and upper management layers described earlier.

The manager and the bar staff team preparing for the shift.

The central, most visible person in the bar & beverage organization is the bartender. Today over half a million bartenders provide beverage service in nearly 160,000 bar and beverage operations across the country. Barbacks, bar helpers and/or bar runners assist the bartender in advance preparation duties and during the shift according to needs.

Barbacks who prove over a period of time to be reliable employees and learn the necessary skills of mixology are customarily promoted to a bartender position.

In some operations the **wine steward** or **sommelier** is included in the beverage department payroll, although he/she may work mostly in a dining room among waitstaff. The primary responsibility of the sommelier is the service of wine and the management of the wine cellar. The sommelier profession is more extensively discussed in Chapter 7.

The primary responsibility of the **cocktail server** is to provide beverage service in a lounge or in some cases, in the dining room. The attitude, personality, and service skills of a cocktail server can significantly add to the success of the beverage operation.

STAFFING CONCERNS

The basic functions of management (Planning, Organizing, Directing, Staffing, Controlling) are the same in every business but the manner in which they are executed may vary according to the nature of the business. General Motors Corp. would apply staffing guidelines differently than a food and beverage operation. In a bar the competent manager takes into consideration not only the abilities of the employee to perform certain procedural tasks but, above all, to handle people. The old adage, "Hire Convivial and Teach Procedural," has never been as valid. Staffing a beverage operation is not as easy as it might seem. So much has to be taken into consideration as composed to the staffing requirements of other businesses. Applicants for a position in a bar have to possess certain personal and convivial characteristics that, for example, are not required in applicants seeking work on a vehicle assembly line. It all begins with determining the needs of the operation and the execution of the recruiting process.

Trained employees can be expensive for the operator to hire but they are indispensable; well trained human resources can be the most important asset for a business. At times, even a well-planned and executed training program does not give satisfactory results. Human attributes, unlike mechanical working procedures, are not easy to direct. Generally speaking, technical skills are easier to learn and follow than interpersonal skills. There comes a time when it is very difficult, or almost impossible to teach someone how to display a pleasant, positive attitude on a consistent basis. Just as it may be a difficult task to teach a certain individual how to smile. Anyone *can* smile, but here we refer to staff members offering guests a genuine sincere smile, typical of a person who takes pride in his/her profession and consequently feels enthusi-

Employees being trained on policy and procedures that will enable them to be more effective on the job.

asm and personal satisfaction when serving people. Simply stated, there are people who do not possess the disposition of conviviality. It is not in them no matter how hard they try. They might be reliable, dedicated employees, but not feeling the born desire to serve others, they'll perform their tasks mechanically. Personalized service cannot be given in a mechanical, detached manner. It has to include a warm, naturally friendly touch and it requires a personal commitment to the profession.

A recent survey conducted by the UNLV Hospitality Research and Development Center in Las Vegas, Nevada, reports that a large number of bar employees admitted that they entered the profession because it was an easy one to find, it required little training, and making tips offered a certain attraction. Others said that performing the duties of a bartender is something that they would do only when waiting for something better to come along. In most cases, these employees' work performance is a mediocre or an inconsistent one. They could not possibly provide the patron with a superior and consistent quality of service since the inner desire to do so is not there in the first place.

An additional concern is society's perception of professions such as that of food server or bartender. In some parts of the country these are still considered menial jobs and often not fully legitimate professions. In reality, to be of service to people is an honorable tradition and a profession that can become rewarding in many aspects. Mixology and bartending are crafts that take considerable time to learn and master. Bar and beverage operators, when hiring a novice, should, from the very beginning, seek to instill pride and encouragement for having chosen that profession. Bar employees should be made to feel that being a professional, capable bartender is considered a personal accomplishment.

Competent operators know that by establishing a motivating environment good results are usually obtained. There comes a time when the **empowerment** (allowing employees to make decisions on how to best serve guests) leads the employee to feel fulfilled and professionally satisfied. The wise operator also knows that faithful, productive employees should be given incentives and occasional rewards for their efforts and dedication to the job.

Screening and Interviewing

When screening and interviewing, the wise manager has to pay special attention to whether the applicant possesses the necessary convivial attributes. Although it may be tempting for the manager to give more consideration to applicants who have previous relevant experience, it is strongly recommended not to disqualify applicants who possess no experience but appear to be motivated and enthusiastic about the job. Obviously these individuals will have to be trained. Training is costly for the employer but in the long run it will be well worth it. Once properly trained, employees who are motivated

A manager interviewing an applicant for a bartender position; the success of the operation begins with smart recruiting.

and eager to do a good job, will outperform others who are more experienced, who handle their duties adequately, but have little desire to take an extra step or go out of their way to please a customer.

The staffing process includes five stages:

Screening
Interviewing
Evaluating
Selecting
Hiring

Before interviewing the wise manager always prepares a set of questions relevant to each position that the individual is applying for. The questions should be carefully worded so that the manager can easily discern the applicant's predisposition for that particular job. There are some questions that should absolutely be avoided. In particular, the interviewer should stay away from making comments and asking questions about:

The individual's present or former marital status including questions about present or former spouses, children, and family related inquiries.

Religion, religious affiliations, personal beliefs, and political preferences.

Race and race related questions or comments, ethnic background, and country of origin.

Age and health conditions.

Credit rating, debts, and military and police record.

Workers compensation claims/on-the-job injuries.

Union affiliations and attitude towards labor unions.

Litigation history (i.e. any lawsuits filed against previous employers and why).

It is recommended that the manager conducting the interview create a relaxed, comfortable atmosphere and allow the applicant ample time to talk about himself/herself. Individuals who are nervous and made to feel pressured while being interviewed may not feel confident enough to complete the interview satisfactorily. It is not recommended to sit behind a desk, to stand up, or walk when interviewing. The best practice is to sit close to the applicant, maintain eye contact, adopt a relaxed tone of voice and occasionally smile, so as to make the applicant feel he/she is in a comfortable environment. It is essential for the interviewer to listen attentively and not interrupt the applicant. If the candidate is not a very talkative person, it is suggested not to apply pressure.

The following questions are recommended for the manager or operator when interviewing for bar staff positions: (the example given here is from an interview for a bartender opening)

1. What were your work responsibilities in your previous job? Did you have any problem in applying them? Do you remember a particularly pleasant or unpleasant incident from your previous job?

2. If you are hired as a bartender, what are you expecting your duties to be? What should be the duties and responsibilities of your bar helper?

3. How do you rate yourself on camaraderie? Do you work well with others? Do you have any problems following instructions from your supervisors? Relating to your fellow bartenders? Getting along with other staff members?

4. If you caught a fellow bartender stealing or attempting illegal practices, what would you do?

5. What are your goals and objectives as a professional? What do see yourself doing two and four years from now?

6. How do you rate yourself in product knowledge? Mixing cocktails, identifying characteristics of spirits, cordials, wine, and beer? How do you rate yourself in handling a customer who is upset because of poor service or for other reasons?

7. How do you rate yourself on organization? And in "timing" when working a busy bar?

8. Are you aware of increasing customer expectations about quality of service? And of patrons' increasing concerns about cleanliness and sanitary standards of establishments?

9. If your supervisor asks you to train an inexperienced employee, would you be willing to do it?

10. What prompted you to apply for this position?

Once the interview is completed, it is proper to comment on how soon he/she will be notified about the hiring decision, offer a sincere handshake, and escort the applicant to the exit.

Hints for the Interviewer

An average interview session may last from fifteen minutes up to one hour. This, plus the time spent in verifying previous employment and references, may not be sufficient for the manager to discern accurately the applicant's suitability for the job. Oftentimes individuals who handle themselves superbly during the interview, do not perform satisfactorily on the job. Conversely, there are applicants who do not appear particularly outstanding during an interview but once on the job they prove to be reliable, dedicated, and enthusiastic employees. Future headaches for both the employer and employee, can be avoided by the interviewer who cares about making the extra effort and searches for more "insight" during the interview session.

While speaking or listening to the applicant, the interviewer should, as unobtrusively as possible, pay attention to the person's body language. It is usually a good sign to see the applicant sit or stand with the correct posture,

The smile, pleasant attitude and posture of the applicant makes a positive impression on the interviewer.

appearing confident, showing assertiveness, and a relaxed, positive disposition. On the contrary, it is definitely a negative sign if an applicant displays an overly timid and introvert disposition; rubs the hands nervously, scratches his/her nails and squeezes the fingers. Other negative traits include the tapping of shoes on the floor, a tense, apprehensive look throughout the body, and the inability to maintain eye contact. The interviewer should consider that bar patrons will look favorably on a bartender or any member of the beverage staff, who displays a positive, assertive, and pleasant *disposition.*

As stated earlier, the interviewer should avoid asking questions about the applicant's personal health. However he/she should realize that there are no laws against taking a good look at the physical appearance of the applicant. This should be done very discretely and in an unobtrusive manner. Without any intention of violating the laws affecting the hiring of personnel (see section on Federal Laws), the interviewer should bear in mind that bartenders, cocktail servers, barbacks, and other bar personnel, stand for most of the duration of their working shift. It is in the best interest of the applicant that he/she be in good health, have strong legs and ankles, and be able to wear comfortable shoes. Poor health can affect employee appearance, and decrease stamina and vitality. It will also greatly affect the employee's overall disposition. Employees who are ill and insist on working can be edgy and abrupt when serving customers. The "rush hour" period can be very physically demanding. Nothing less than a good, healthy condition, will allow bartenders the required coordination and timing to handle the stress typical of rush hour.

The same rationale is valid when discussing professional appearance. Bar employees who display a clean, attractive uniform, and are properly groomed, will not only make a good impression on management but, ultimately more crucial, on patrons. If the applicant, during the interview, does not seem to care about neatness and appearance, they most likely will not care when working.

Another suggestion for the person handling the recruitment of employees is that special emphasis should be placed on the attitude and motivation displayed by the applicant. The ability to work well with others should also be considered crucial. In this regard a recent survey of hospitality employees' terminations is informative. The survey reports that only 10 per cent of the employees let go were terminated due to poor work performance; 90 per cent were discharged mostly for reasons of negative attitude and lack of motivation.

An even more recent survey on employee turnover reports that over 75 per cent of employees who quit their jobs admit that the reasons for leaving were not related to wages, compensation, or unsatisfactory working conditions but in most cases because of personality clashes with fellow employees and/or supervisors.

At the dawn of a new century, most business owners agree that "staffing" has become the most challenging and demanding task in the hospitality industry.

Federal Laws to Be Considered When Hiring

The wise manager always considers the legal aspects of hiring. Not only for the purpose of avoiding labor grievances and lawsuits but also for a genuine concern for equality among people and out of respect for others.

There are federal, state, and local laws that affect the hiring of personnel. Some of them have been in effect for decades, others have been introduced recently. The ones that are of most concern for bar and beverage operators are the following:

FAIR LABOR STANDARDS ACT
The Fair Labor Standards Act is one of the oldest federal employment laws. It was introduced in 1938. The act protects workers from the age of 40–70 from discharge for the reason of age. It also establishes rules governing working teenagers and union activities.

EQUAL PAY ACT
Introduced in 1963, the Equal Pay Act establishes that employers provide equal wage compensation for male and female workers when performing the same type of work.

CIVIL RIGHTS ACT

A controversial bill for a long time, the Civil Rights Act was introduced in 1964. Similar in many aspects to the 1972 Equal Opportunity Employment Act, it prohibits discrimination against job applicants and employees already on the work force, in matters of a person's color, race, sex, and country of origin.

This act settled many previous disputes between labor organizations and some bar and beverage operators who favored the hiring of only male or only female bartenders.

VIETNAM ERA VETERANS READJUSTMENT

Introduced in 1974, this act seeks to protect veterans of the Vietnam war against workplace discrimination.

PRIVACY ACT

A 1974 act, it is intended to prevent employers from asking interviewees and employees questions that may be considered discriminatory and may constitute invasion of personal privacy.

IMMIGRATION REFORM AND CONTROL ACT

The I.R.C.A. of 1986 establishes that it is illegal to hire aliens not authorized to work in the U.S. It makes it mandatory for employers to verify that job applicants provide proof of permanent residency ("Green" Card) or proof of citizenship. The Act includes a "grandfather clause" stating that aliens hired before November 1986 can be allowed to remain on the job.

AMERICANS WITH DISABILITIES ACT

The most recent of the federal laws, the Americans with Disabilities Act (1990), forbids discrimination against the disabled and established that employers must provide proper facilities and suitable working conditions for disabled individuals.

CIVIL RIGHTS ACT (2)–SEXUAL HARASSMENT

In 1980 the Equal Employment Opportunity Commission (EEOC) was introduced. One of the main responsibilities of this commission is to expand the section of the Civil Rights Act concerning sexual harassment. Sexual harassment has been defined as follows:

> Unwelcome sexual advances, requests for sexual favors, and other verbal or other physical conduct of sexual nature . . . when:

1. Submission to such conduct is made either explicitly or implicitly a term or condition of a person's employment; or
2. Submission to or rejection of such conduct . . . is used as the basis of an employment decision affecting such person; or

3. Such conduct has the purpose or effect of unreasonably interfering with a person's work performance or creating an intimidating, hostile, or offensive working environment.

There are other laws of concern to the beverage operator apart from those listed above. Management should always reviewed local and state laws of public health, and Fire Code. Other laws include the requirement of training employees in performing the Heimlich Maneuver to assist choking victims; the enforcement of no smoking signs in certain areas; health card and vaccination requirements; and the TAM, TIPS, and AA or Serving Alcohol Responsibly certifications.

Employee Turnover

As the century turns, the vast majority of hospitality operators agree that one of the biggest challenges they are facing is keeping employees for any period of time. Staff turnover will definitely be one of the major issues in years to come, particularly since the labor pool of loyal, steady employees appears to decrease gradually. Employers complain that turnover is reaching alarming proportions. Some recent reports list a good number of bar beverage estab-

To help avoid employee turnover, the establishment is offering a more comfortable working environment and providing incentives such as the employee of the month award.

lishments in which hourly paid employee turnover reaches the 200 per cent per year mark. In comparison, salaried employees, such as managers and directors, are still within the 25–30 per cent per year range of twenty years ago.

Labor Procedures and Terminations

If the hiring of bar and beverage staff requires special attention, the firing should be handled even more carefully. Taking disciplinary actions such as warnings, suspensions, and terminations can be a difficult task for the manager. Disciplinary measures should not be taken with a punitive intention but by way of corrective action.

Local bartender and beverage employee unions exist in most major cities across America. A "Collective Bargaining Agreement" is a labor contract between the employer and the union representing the work force. A beverage operation that has agreed to accept a union contract must adhere to the terms established by such contract. These terms regulate work categories, pay scales, yearly pay increases, scheduling guidelines, minimum and maximum daily and/or weekly hours, vacation time, overtime compensation, grievance procedures, sick leave, suspensions, terminations, and so forth. A union contract cannot take away management's right to manage but it can certainly limit it. Some union contracts regulate the specific working duties performed by the employees. For example, a labor contract may restrict the bartender from performing certain duties that should only be handled by barbacks or bar helpers (replenishing ice bins, stocking beer, washing glasses, etc.).

The elimination of cross-work and multiple-working responsibilities is one of the areas in which union leaders concentrate on most when preparing a contract to be signed by the employer. While cross-work can decrease the number of employees needed in the operation, union leaders would rather see the employer hire and retain a greater number of employees. This means higher payroll costs for the employer but also more membership dues for the union.

At times managers become disappointed with the work performance of certain employees and make plans for their replacement. If the employee who is performing poorly has just started the job, the recommended practice for the manager is to talk to the employee, make him/her aware of the problem and use encouraging phrases. In most cases employees respond positively and good results are obtained. If there is little or no response, before making disciplinary decisions or issuing a termination notice, the manager should familiarize himself/herself with national labor laws' probation periods and if applicable, with the "trial periods" allowed by local union collective bargaining agreements. If the employee has been with the company for some time, the termination may become a delicate, and even difficult, task to handle. The firing of an employee, who is a member of a local union, without "just cause" may entail costly and unpleasant legal implications for the employer. Often, even in an establishment not bound by a union contract, a termination that is proved to be unconstitutional and issued not in full accordance with labor laws, could lead to the reinstatement of the employee with back pay.

A typical bartenders' union contract requires that an employee who is performing poorly be warned verbally and in writing a specific number of times before further disciplinary action can be taken. In most cases a termination has to be preceded by a suspension. In a grievance dispute the employer must provide evidence that the employee was given sufficient time and opportunities to correct the problem. Terminations that are issued hurriedly and that are for reasons that do not include "willful misconduct" are considered a violation of labor laws.

KEY TERMS

Organization Chart	Willful Misconduct	Fair Labor Standard Act
Recruitment	Collective Bargaining	Internal Recruiting
Screening	Agreement	Just Cause
Sexual Harassment	Privacy Act	Rush Hour
Warning Notice	Equal Pay Act	
Outside Recruiting		

CHAPTER QUESTIONS

1. Of all the management functions why is staffing considered the most demanding?
2. What is an organization chart and what is its purpose?
3. In the chain of command system, is the Food and Beverage Director above or below the bar manager?
4. What are the general duties and responsibilities of management?
5. What are the staffing concerns of beverage operators today?
6. What should the manager take into consideration when interviewing an applicant?
7. Which are some of the questions the interviewer should avoid? What are the most common recruiting methods?
8. In brief what is the content of the Privacy Act? The Fair Labor Standards Act? The Equal Pay Act?
9. Can a manager fire a bar employee without "just cause"?
10. What is a Collective Bargaining Agreement?

chapter eleven

PROMOTING RESPONSIBLE DRINKING AND ALCOHOL AWARENESS

chapter outline

Chapter Objectives
Introduction
Overview
Importance to Customers
Differing Viewpoints
Goal of a System to Promote Responsible Drinking
The SERVSAFE Responsible Alcohol Service Program
Other Programs to Promote Responsible Drinking and Alcohol Awareness
Summary
Key Terms
Chapter Questions

chapter objectives

Upon completion of this chapter you will be able to:

- Discuss the importance of promoting responsible drinking to customers.
- State the different viewpoints between owners and managers and bartenders and servers toward promoting responsible drinking.

- Name the causes of the shifting in consumer's consumption patterns of alcoholic beverages.

- Define third party liability and dramshop laws and how they effect the beverage industry.

- List the goals of a system to promote responsible drinking in a beverage operation.

- List the key points of the Servsafe Responsible Alcohol Service Program.

- Describe the behavioral signs of the various levels of intoxication.

- List the various ways to deal with intoxicated guests.

INTRODUCTION

A growing number of bars and beverage operations are training their staff in a system of increased alcohol awareness with the aim of promoting responsible drinking by their patrons. The driving force behind the growth in these programs is a combination of increasing liquor liability insurance rates and the public's concern over the safe consumption of alcohol. The introduction of a system to educate bar staff in this respect shows that the owner is being proactive rather than reactive when it comes to the safety of their guests and the community.

Managers need to be aware of the advantages and disadvantages of programs to promote responsible drinking and raise alcohol awareness. This chapter will discuss the need for a program. The viewpoints of both the servers and the owners/managers will be examined to illustrate how the two groups, differing views of the system can and will affect its implementation.

OVERVIEW

Alcohol is an integral part of our culture and intertwined into most of our lives. It is usually a part of many of life's special events. Champagne is used to usher in the New Year, toast newlyweds, and honor achievements. Alcohol is a valuable addition to the profit of food and beverage operations. People enjoy having a drink after work or with a meal. The problem lies in the effect that alcohol consumption has on some people. There is a dark side to alcohol and alcohol consumption. Some people can drink alcohol without a problem, while others have trouble stopping drinking once they have begun. Seventy people are killed daily in the U.S., over 25,000 annually, in alcohol related accidents. Unfortunately, the majority of those killed or injured are innocent bystanders.

Studies show that approximately 37 per cent of alcohol is consumed in bar or food service establishments. Bars and restaurants need to take a proactive approach to this problem by training their staff in the awareness of responsible alcohol service. The food and beverage sector realizes that self

Throughout history drunkenness has caused problems.

regulation is better than government-imposed programs. The hospitality industry needs to establish its own policies on alcohol to reduce or eliminate the need for further government regulation.

Americans are becoming increasingly aware of the number of alcohol-related traffic accidents and fatalities. Alcohol-related traffic fatalities remain the leading cause of death for young adults between the ages of 16 and 24. The cost of the law suits resulting from these accidents is continuing to rise, forcing bars and beverage operations to rethink the way they do business. State and local authorities are increasing the penalties for driving under the influence of alcohol and decreasing the amount of alcohol in a person's blood that classifies them as legally drunk. National organizations such as Mothers Against Drunk Driving (MADD) and Students Against Drunk Driving (SADD) have worked hard to increase the public's awareness of the problem and lobbied for stiffer penalties.

The increased severity of laws and regulations pertaining to driving while under the influence has caused a shift in people's consumption patterns. The increased awareness of the problems caused by alcohol has brought about this shift in the laws and regulations. The majority of states have laws that specify that if a person has a Blood Alcohol Content (BAC) of 0.10 per cent they are legally intoxicated. Intoxicated must be defined by an objective measure rather than by something subjective like behavior. This puts servers of alcohol at a disadvantage because they do not have the opportunity to check the guest's BAC when deciding whether to serve them the next drink; they must rely on more subjective and less accurate methods such as observation.

The overall rate of consumption of alcohol by the American public has declined steadily since about 1967. There has also been a shift in where people consume alcoholic beverages; an increase in people purchasing alcohol at off-premise operations, such as grocery or liquor stores, to consume at home, and a decrease in purchase at bars and restaurants. The tougher laws seem to be working, alcohol-related traffic accidents and fatalities have decreased in the 1990s.

The beverage industry has decided to try to curb the problem themselves before the government passes new and stricter regulations. Several major beer companies have developed and advertised campaigns to promote responsible drinking and raise alcohol awareness. Anheuser Busch has developed several programs such as, "Let's Control Underage Drinking Before it Starts," Miller Brewing Company has adopted a program titled, "Know When to Say When" and runs a number of commercials showing consumers the proper and improper times to consume alcohol.

IMPORTANCE TO CUSTOMERS

People go out to a restaurant or bar for a number of reasons. These reasons were discussed in Chapter 1. They may be meeting friends, out for entertainment, looking to meet someone new, etc. Whatever the reason they are look-

People patronize bars and lounges not just to consume alcoholic beverages but to relax, meet old friends, and make new ones.

ing for a place to have a good time. The problem lies in the fact that different people's definition of what constitutes a good time differs dramatically.

What spoils a good time for very many people is having to be around somebody or a group of people who have consumed too much alcohol. Most customers do not care to frequent an establishment where they have to duck from flying chairs or use a rest room that has been damaged by another patron. Although, a system to promote responsible drinking does not prevent customers from getting drunk it does have the potential to reduce drunkenness significantly. A bar that gains the reputation of being proactive rather than reactive on responsible drinking will generally be well thought of by its guests. Customers will know that they can come to that location and be reasonably assured that they will be relatively free from some of the problems described earlier.

DIFFERING VIEWPOINTS

The differing viewpoints of the customer, server, and owner/manager of the beverage operation to any program must be considered. Each group will look at a proposed program from a different vantage point. For the program to be effective the perspectives of all three groups must be taken on board.

The Problem

The problem, then, in promoting a program like this in a bar is in reconciling the viewpoints of the parties involved. Each group has a different agenda and a different stake in the operation of the bar. The variance in the reasons they are there and what they hope to get out of the experience has the potential to cause problems.

Another factor that complicates the issue is that different people exhibit different behaviors when intoxicated or under the influence of alcohol. For the program to work the servers of alcohol must determine which of their customers are intoxicated and which are not, and act accordingly. They are at an disadvantage because their decision must be based on observations rather than on the use of scientific methods, such as the blood or chemical breathalyzer tests that law enforcement officers use.

The View of the Bartenders and Servers

The key to a program for promoting responsible drinking is the server of the drink. The bartenders and the servers are on the front line of the bar's attempt to control the abuse of alcohol at the location. The management can spend many hours and dollars on training their staff, but since they do not follow the servers to the tables when they are waiting on customers they have very little control over whether or not the server is using the procedures recommended in the program.

Servers and bartenders have several legitimate concerns on the matter. Their concerns must be understood and addressed by the owner/manager of the bar if they expect the program to work successfully. The major complaint of servers is that they feel that a tough responsibility has shifted from the law enforcement community to them. Determining if a guest is intoxicated or not is difficult and very often a judgment call. Alcohol affects different people at different rates causing people to exhibit a variety of types of behaviors. Most operations have a difficult enough time training servers to be good at serving, let alone training them to determine the level of intoxication of the guest and when to cut off service. The guidelines for the program to promote responsible drinking are straight forward but may not work in all situations. They will prove to be less effective in an operation where customers can get drinks from several places rather than from one. It is difficult for servers to track a customer's behavior and consumption rate if he is being served by two bartenders and three servers.

Servers are also concerned that if they refuse, service guests could very well become violent. Belligerence and untruly behavior are both very common symptoms of intoxication. Generally guests do not easily accept the suggestion that they have had too much to drink and they cannot be served any more. Drinking is mistakenly considered a sign of maturity in our culture. Some people are insulted when they are refused service and may act violently.

Servers and bartenders are generally leery of refusing or cutting off service to a guest out of the fear that the guest may not leave them a tip or

A patron looking intoxicated. Management will soon cut him off.

gratuity for their service. (A common ploy used by bartenders to boost tips is to purposely overpour drinks to regular customers in exchange for a bigger tip.) The issue is a legitimate concern for employees who are generally paid below minimum wage and rely heavily on their tips as a form of compensation.

The Advantages to Bartenders and Servers

Although there are several important concerns for bartenders and servers there also are several very compelling reasons for them to participate and actively use the program. The working conditions of the bar improve dramatically. Guests are generally much easier and more fun to work with when they are sober rather than intoxicated. Sober guests are less likely to cause fights or damage to the bar. Once a bar gains a reputation for promoting responsible drinking and increased alcohol awareness while discouraging guests from becoming intoxicated, the type of clientele that the bar will attract often changes. It will most likely discourage those looking to get drunk and cause trouble and replace them with people who appreciate a place where they can enjoy the evening without the problems that a bunch of intoxicated people cause.

The View of the Owner and Manager

The owners and managers of beverage operations look at the situation from an understandably different perspective than that of the servers and bartenders. Their compensation is based on the sales and profits of the operation, not the gratuity left by the guests. The owner/manager of the operation will suffer most as the result of a *third-party liability or dramshop law suit.* This is the largest financial risk to an operator of a beverage operation. Third-party liability occurs when an intoxicated customer of a bar leaves the bar and causes injury to someone. The family or the injured party may first sue the intoxicated person who caused the damage; if they are unable to collect from them because of a lack of money, they may well sue the bar. It is a civil violation if an individual brings suit against you for injuries caused by an intoxicated guest of your operation. Some states have dramshop laws that hold an establishment liable when one of its intoxicated guests causes injury to another person. Dramshop laws make it illegal for a bar to serve an intoxicated person. This notion of third-party liability is the basis for many alcohol-related lawsuits.

Some owners/managers look at the situation from a shortsighted perspective. They feel that if they limit the amount of alcohol the guest consumes they will lose money due to reduced sales; this is in fact true. Reducing the number of intoxicated people in a bar will reduce both sales and profits but more importantly it will also reduce the number of potentially dangerous people behind the wheel and the number of alcohol-related fatalities and law suits. The average cost of an alcohol-related law suit is between one and two million dollars. This is a large cost to any operation and one that is not easily covered by the increased drink sales.

The Advantages to the Owner/Manager

There are several advantages to the manager/owner of a beverage operation of instituting the program. Alcohol-related accidents receive much publicity and cause some people to look unfavorably on operations that serve alcoholic beverages. A bar manager/owner can receive favorable publicity as a good community citizen if he/she can be proactive in training staff in the procedures of controlling the level of alcohol consumption of its guests.

Good publicity is welcome but many operators make such decisions based solely on how they effect the profit of the operation. The most obvious advantages to the manager/owner are the multiple opportunities arising to reduce the operational costs of the bar. Many insurance companies reduce the cost of liability insurance policies for beverage operations that have trained their staff in a program to promote responsible drinking. In addition, fewer intoxicated guests in an operation will most likely reduce the amount of damage as a result of fights or malicious damage in the bar. As the reputation of the bar grows, the crowd of problem drinkers will move to other bars and be replaced, most likely, by more responsible drinkers.

The Importance of Understanding the Servers Viewpoint

The server is the key to the success of the program. The manager/owner of the operation must take into account the servers' concern if they expect the program to work. The most effective way to ensure success is for the manager/owner to be consistent in their support of the program and the servers' decisions. If a server's decision to cut off service to a guest is repeatedly overturned by the manager/owner, the server will figure that it is not worth the time and effort to cut off service to a guest and continue to serve. The manager/owner must look past the person being a good friend or regular customer and abide by the decision of the server.

The financial repercussions of cutting off a guest must also be considered by the manager/owner. A possible policy to compensate the server from the manager's account for loss of tips from a guest that they cut off might encourage servers to be more vigilant. The few dollars that it may cause the bar for each guest or party cut off would not even come close to the cost of a law suit.

Ongoing training is the key to the success of the program. Thorough training is essential to orientate the employees to the value of the program and is needed at all regularly scheduled employee meetings to reinforce the material. Employees need an opportunity to discuss the parts that are working and those that are not working with others. Practicing the techniques on one another is a good way to reinforce the components.

GOAL OF A SYSTEM TO PROMOTE RESPONSIBLE DRINKING

The goal of the various systems to promote responsible drinking is simply to monitor the consumption of alcohol by guests so as to reduce the possibility of them becoming intoxicated. The program does not guarantee that guests will not become intoxicated. It provides a system for servers to identify the various levels of intoxication and the proper steps to prevent guests from becoming drunk and needing service cut off to them. The interaction of the bartenders and servers of an operation makes it relatively easy to institute the program. Communication of guests' condition from one employee to another can be simple and effective. The ideal situation would be for servers to err on the side of cutting off service too soon rather than too late.

The goals of the program are assisted by the fact that a majority of people are limiting their consumption of alcohol for any of a number of reasons, such as health concerns, changes in lifestyle, and the tightening of laws regarding drinking and driving.

THE SERVSAFE RESPONSIBLE ALCOHOL SERVICE PROGRAM

There are several programs on the market to train servers on the responsible service of alcohol and intervention. The SERVSAFE Responsible Alcohol Service Program of the Education Foundation of the National Restaurant Association will be illustrated to demonstrate an example of one of the programs. Later in the chapter there are notes on some of the other programs. The use of the SERVSAFE Responsible Alcohol Service Program here is by no means an endorsement of the program over any one of the other programs.

Overview of the Program

The program consists of a manager's course book, server's study guide, a video available to reinforce the book material, and a test for people who have completed the course. Students who successfully pass the test will receive a certificate that is proof of alcohol service training, now mandatory in many areas.

The Program

The program is broken down into the following sections:

1. The Law and Your Responsibility
2. How Alcohol Affects Your Body
3. Managing the Responsible Service of Alcohol
4. Responsible Alcohol Service Policies
5. Other Activities

A group of servers who have just received their SERVSAFE certification and are ready to apply the principles they have learned.

1. The Law and Your Responsibility.   The servers of alcohol as well as the manager/owner of a beverage operation must be aware of the laws regarding the service of alcohol; and the production, export, import, and sale of alcohol.

The alcohol industry is one of the most regulated industries in the U.S. Establishments that sell and serve alcohol must be aware of both the legal obligations of the liquor code and the possible liabilities imposed by the civil court system. The laws pertaining to the serving of alcohol rest on two premises.

LIQUOR LICENSES ARE A PRIVILEGE NOT A RIGHT
AND
THE CONSUMPTION OF ALCOHOL IS A PRIVILEGE NOT A RIGHT

Owners/managers, bartenders and servers must be aware of those two facts and understand the laws that pertain to each.

2. How Alcohol Affects Your Body.   Servers of alcohol need to understand the effects that alcohol has on the human body and how these effects can vary between different individuals. These points are crucial for the server who must monitor the level of intoxication of a guest when deciding whether to continue service or cut it off.

The key components of the section are:

Equivalencies of Drinks. Knowing how much alcohol is in each drink will help the server greatly in determining the level of intoxication of the guest.

The rule of thumb is as follows, each of these drinks contains approximately ½ oz of alcohol 12 oz beer = 4 oz wine = 1.25 oz 80-proof alcohol = 1.0 oz 100 proof alcohol = 1 drink

Alcohol's Path Through the Body. The amount of alcohol in the body is measured by Blood Alcohol Content (BAC). Alcohol is absorbed in the blood primarily through the small intestine and is metabolized at the rate of one drink per hour.

Know Your Limit. Servers must be aware of the limits of consumption of their guests. The limits are general and differ most by the size of the person.

Safe limits of alcohol consumption:

The First Hour	Number of Drinks
Small person	1–2
Medium person	2–3
Large person	3–4

Subsequent hours
One drink per hour, regardless of body size

Factors Affecting Absorption. There are several factors that affect the rate of alcohol absorption into the body:

Positive	Negative	Both
[slows down absorption]	*[speeds up absorption]*	
Food—fatty and high protein	Carbonation	Amount of alcohol consumed and time spent drinking
Water	Stress, depression, dieting, and fatigue	Body size, type, and gender
	Drugs and medication	
	Tolerance	
	Altitude	

Behavior Signs of Alcohol Absorption:
Relaxed Inhibitions
Impaired Judgments
Slowed Reaction Times
Impaired Motor Coordination

A server is looking for behavior signs to ensure the patron is fine to serve another drink.

3. Managing the Responsible Service of Alcohol. Managers need to be able to manage the responsible service of alcohol. This can be a difficult task with customers coming to their establishment to have a good time. Management has the key role in the responsible service of alcohol in their operation.

The key points in the section are:

Assessing Your Operation. Managers need to determine the type of business and clientele they wish to have so that they can develop policies that will ensure the safety of their liquor license and will be welcome and accommodating to their guests.

The Needs of Different Businesses. Different types of bars attract different types of clientele. Managers must be aware of the potential problems associated with their type of operation.

Managing Your Employees. Managers must hire the proper employees and train them in the procedures to promote responsible drinking. Training must be ongoing for the process to work and remain effective.

Establishing Written Policies. Clear, easy to understand written policies are needed to make management's expectations of employees clear to all the staff. Once policies are established and implemented they must be followed by all levels of the staff and management, with no exceptions for regulars or friends.

Promotions and Advertising.   There must be a shift in emphasis from the consumption of alcohol to other activities in promotions and advertising. Promote special events, food specials, and entertainment rather than the over consumption of alcohol.

Guest Awareness.   The guest is most able to control his/her own behavior. Simple reminders to guests through point-of-sale material is effective and helpful.

4. Responsible Alcohol Service Policies.   The bar must have formal policies to promote responsible drinking. The employees, as well as management, must be aware of the policies for the system to work.
The key points in the section are:

The Importance and Proper Procedures for Checking IDs.   There are severe legal penalties for serving minors. Staff must be made aware of the importance and proper procedure for checking guests IDs.

Monitoring the Guests.   When a guest enters the operation the server needs to monitor them for future reference. The three keys to monitoring are:

S Size up: note the guest's size and body type
I Interview: talk with the guest to gain valuable clues about various factors
R Evaluate the guest as to their condition and as either being green, yellow, or red level.

Dealing with Guests at the Various Levels.   Guests in the different levels of intoxication need to be treated in different ways.
Guests in the Green Level
Offer hospitable customer service of food and alcohol.
Guests in the Yellow Level
Begin to slow down the service of alcohol, increase the service of food, and non-alcoholic drinks.
Prevent guests from reaching the red level.
Guests in the Red Level
Discontinue the service of alcohol.

5. Other Activities in the Program.   *Role Play Exercises:* The manager's book contains several role-playing exercises in which the staff can act out situations that may occur in the running of the bar. The exercises help prepare them for situations and include a discussion section so that the group can talk about the situation and the proper way to handle it.

OTHER PROGRAMS TO PROMOTE RESPONSIBLE DRINKING AND ALCOHOL AWARENESS

Traffic Light System—Education Foundation of the American Hotel and Motel Association

Similar to the SERVSAFE program, training materials for both managers and servers, and a video to supplement the material.

TAM—Techniques of Alcohol Management

A one day seminar for employers and employees developed by the Michigan Licensed Beverage Association.

TIPS—Training for Intervention Procedures by Servers of Alcohol

A one day seminar for servers and bartenders containing the critical elements for server intervention; designed by Morris Chafez, founding director of the National Institute on Alcohol Abuse and Alcoholism.

SUMMARY

Alcohol is an integral part of our society and most of our celebrations. People enjoy relaxing or complementing their meal with an alcoholic beverage. Unfortunately, some people are enable to control the amount of alcohol that they consume and this results in traffic accidents and fatalities. Even though only 37 per cent of the alcohol consumed in this country is consumed at commercial bars or restaurants the food and beverage industry has come under fire for the problems of alcohol. Since the pressure on the hospitality industry to be more responsible does not appear to be letting up, the industry must take an active role in confronting the problem.

Restaurants and beverage operations can train their staff in procedures to promote responsible drinking and alcohol awareness. For the programs to be effective management must be aware of the server's concerns in regard to instituting the procedures. There are obvious, and maybe less obvious, concerns of both manager/owner and bartenders and servers toward the issues concerned.

KEY TERMS

Off-premise	BAC	Cut Off Service
Proactive	On-premise	Dramshop
Intoxicated	Reactive	Legal Code
Third-Party (Civil) Liability		

CHAPTER QUESTIONS

1. Why is it important to promote responsible drinking to the customers of a bar or lounge?
2. Please explain the different viewpoints between owners and managers and bartenders and servers toward promoting responsible drinking. What are the causes of the conflict?
3. Name the causes of the shifting in consumer's consumption patterns of alcoholic beverages. What would you suggest would be the best way for the beverage industry to compensate for the shifting patterns?
4. Define third party liability and dramshop laws and explain how they effect the beverage industry.
5. List the goals of a system to promote responsible drinking in a beverage operation. Explain why each is important.
6. List the key points of the Servsafe Responsible Alcohol Service Program. Discuss why it is important to implement in an operation that serves alcohol to the public.
7. Describe the behavioral signs of the various levels of intoxication.
8. List the various ways to deal with intoxicated guests. List what should and should not be done when dealing with intoxicated guests.

chapter twelve

LEGAL FACTORS IN BEVERAGE SERVICE

chapter outline

chapter objectives

Upon completion of the chapter the student will be able to:

- State three problems that helped usher in Prohibition.

- Describe the different levels of alcohol regulation in the United States.

- Trace the development of liquor laws in history.

- Define both dramshop laws and third-party liability laws and explain how they effect the operation of a bar.

- Identify the three parties in a third-party liability lawsuit.

- Differentiate between on-premise and off-premise beverage operations.

- Describe the difference between license and closed states.

- State the purpose of local option laws.

- Differentiate between local laws and state liquor laws.

- Name ten items possibly controlled by state governments affecting operations that sell alcohol.

- List three items federal laws cover in the sale of alcohol.

- Differentiate between areas of federal control and areas of state control in regards to alcoholic beverages.

INTRODUCTION

Business establishments that sell and serve alcoholic beverages must be aware of the federal laws that govern the sale of liquor in the U.S., as well as those within their state and local community. The major portion of the federal laws and regulations are concerned with the importation, exportation, distribution, and labeling, while state laws govern the sale, consumption, and distribution of alcoholic beverages within state boundaries.

There have been laws regulating the production, sale, and use of alcoholic beverages as far back as Ancient Babylon, where reportedly the penalty for knowingly selling bad beer was death. As long as there has been alcohol, there have been laws to regulate its production, consumption, and measurement. These laws and regulations reflect the regard in which alcohol has been held in public sentiment through time. When the problems of alcohol consumption become a central issue in a culture, laws are passed to reduce consumption and distribution. As the problems with alcohol ease, the laws are correspondingly relaxed.

The *Volstead*, or *National Prohibition Act,* of 1920 was enacted to curb the problems of over-consumption experienced in the late 1800s and early 1900s. Prohibition ended up *increasing* consumption, rather than the opposite, turning the "Noble Experiment," as Prohibition was called, into a noble failure. The lingering effects of Prohibition can still be felt today.

The threat of liability is inherent in the sale of alcoholic beverages. Nationwide, the sale of alcohol to an intoxicated person or a minor is a criminal offense. The server of the alcohol can be personally fined and arrested for serving such a customer. Both the owner and the manager of an operation that serves alcohol must know the laws and regulations governing the sale of alcohol in their area.

The beverage industry is one of the more regulated industries in the United States. Governments are faced with a dual-edged sword in regard to the sale of alcoholic beverages. On the positive side, governments gain financially from the generation of taxes on the liquor industry; on the other side, they must weigh both the financial and social costs associated with the abuse of alcohol.

Every aspect of alcoholic beverages is regulated, from production, and/or importation, to distribution, serving, and consumption. There are several reasons for the government's high level of involvement in the various aspects of this industry. First, the government at various levels wants to protect its tax base. Alcoholic beverages generate over $6 billion in taxes at all levels annually. More than 50 per cent of the retail cost of distilled spirits is made up of state, federal, and local taxes. Second, some government officials feel it is their role to protect citizens from themselves and others. Unfortunately, some 10–20 per cent of the drinking public cannot control their con-

The U.S. Government gains considerably from the generation of taxes imposed on the liquor industry.

sumption of alcohol, causing problems for those who can. Drinking by minors continues to be a perennial problem. Many feel that strict government control is needed to limit the possible problems arising from "problem" and underage drinkers so they do not harm the public or themselves.

THE DEVELOPMENT OF LIQUOR LAWS IN HISTORY

Almost since the accidental discovery of alcohol, there has been a perceived need to regulate it. Unfortunately, the majority of the population who can handle their consumption of alcohol must be burdened with laws developed in some ways for those who cannot. The strictness and seeming harshness of the laws are not without merit. The misuse of alcohol kills many people worldwide annually. The laws are written to protect the innocent and ensure the quality of products sold to the public.

In Ancient Babylon 4,000 years ago, as we have seen, the penalty for anyone found intentionally selling bad beer was death. Tavern and bar owners were also held liable for the unruly behavior of their guests. Many modern liquor laws can be traced to the sections covering merchants in the English Magna Carta of 1215. Early regulations on standard weights and measures of alcoholic beverages can be traced to this monumental document. There were grave concerns in England about the need for a uniform size of barrels of ale. Care was given to ensure that taverns received the proper amount paid for of this fermented beverage. To this day laws in Britain to protect customers from unscrupulous tavern keepers make it illegal for bartenders to "free pour" or dispense unmeasured, distilled spirits.

The collection of taxes on alcohol has shaped many of the laws in history. The heavy British taxes on imported alcoholic beverages contributed to both the Revolutionary War and to the growth of the production of ale and spirits in early colonial America. The tax on whisky drove illegal stills into the hills of Pennsylvania and was to blame for the *Whisky Rebellion*. The tax on whisky had little to do with the temperance movement, but rather more with the potential for the new government to raise much-needed funds.

PROHIBITION

The consumption of alcohol was widespread in the years of the new republic. Several highly vocal citizens of the new country preached *temperance*, the moderate consumption of alcoholic beverages. The mood of the time, however, was against the consumption of distilled spirits but not of fermented beverages. It was thought that fermented beverages were fine, whereas the problems of heavy drinking could be traced to the more alcoholically potent distilled spirits.

A transportation problem, namely the expense of shipping corn grown in the Midwest areas of the country to the East Coast, is often cited as a reason for increased consumption of whisky. It was cheaper to ship the corn distilled into whisky than it was to ship the corn in its natural state. As consumption grew so did the problems associated with it, ushering in the beginning of the Temperance Movement. The basis of the movement lay with evangelical church leaders. They attacked the problem of alcohol from two angles; they argued first for *abstinence,* which meant no drinking of alcoholic beverages whatsoever, and second for the beginning of control through legal measures, by urging areas to refuse to issue licenses to sell alcohol.

The 1850s ushered in the first powerful efforts to write laws reducing the consumption of alcoholic beverages. Maine was the first state to pass a ban on the consumption of alcohol, with other states soon to follow. These early prohibition laws were squashed by the courts. With the rise of regional controversy concerning slavery, prohibitionists did not excite much attention.

Fresh air and new life were blown into the prohibitionist movement in the 1870s, with the newly formed Anti-Saloon Movement. Religious women crusaded *en masse,* holding prayer vigils in front of saloons extolling the problems of alcohol and its negative effects on society. This movement also waned until it too was revitalized in 1893 with the formation of the Anti-Saloon League.

The Anti-Saloon League grew in popularity from a local movement to the state level. With more states joining the movement, there was momentum for Congress to use federal laws to limit the distribution of alcohol between states. This move towards national Prohibition came in 1913. World War I aided the movement. Food products were conserved to support the war effort and were thus not available for conversion to alcohol; this gave the movement the push it needed.

The *Eighteenth Amendment* was proposed in 1918. Eighteen months later it was ratified by the states of the nation and became part of the Constitution of our land. The National Prohibition Act, or Volstead Act, made it illegal to manufacture, sell, transport, or consume intoxicating liquor in the United States. The penalties for violation of these laws were minor, both first and second offenses being usually treated as misdemeanors.

Prohibition ended in 1933 for several reasons. Public sentiment changed over time after the law was enacted, but first and foremost Prohibition failed because it was not effective in its primary objective of limiting consumption. Alcohol consumption dropped during the first period of Prohibition but grew through the remainder. Lack of enforcement of the ban also contributed to growing public disapproval. Yet another factor that contributed to its demise was the lack of control over the alcohol products being sold for consumption during Prohibition. Since these beverages were being made illegally and sold for huge profits, there was no control over the quality. The injuries to, and potential deaths of, the drinkers of illicit products helped contribute to the end of Prohibition.

The era of Prohibition was a significant chapter in U.S. history and one that has had a dramatic effect on both society and the liquor laws of today. The Eighteenth Amendment, deemed the Noble Experiment and passed in 1920, eventually failed thirteen years later. It is the only constitutional amendment to be repealed in the history of our great nation.

Modern-day retailers of alcoholic beverages have seen the growth of a number of new and stricter laws on alcohol sale and consumption in the U.S. While a return to prohibition has not been advocated, there is a movement toward tightening laws relating to the sale of alcohol. We have seen stronger laws against driving an automobile while intoxicated. States have increased the legal drinking age, with strong federal government intervention. Many states have lowered, or are considering lowering, the measure, the *Blood Alcohol Content* (BAC), that legally defines intoxication.

There are still groups of people today who feel that alcohol is the root of many problems in the nation and that it should again be made illegal. However, Prohibition was a failure. It clearly proved that the law was not enough to stop a country's citizens from doing something they really wanted to do. Prohibition also encouraged and strengthened organized crime organizations who profited hugely from providing illegal alcoholic beverages to a thirsty nation.

LIQUOR LIABILITY AND DRAMSHOP LAWS

The most common liquor liability lawsuits are the so-called *third-party liability* cases where an innocent third party is injured by an intoxicated person. To make the terminology clear, the persons involved are as follows; the *first party* means the person purchasing or consuming the alcohol; the *second party* is the person or establishment selling or serving the alcohol; and *third party* refers to another person who is somehow injured by the first party arising from the alcohol transaction.

IDENTIFICATION OF THE PARTIES
IN A THIRD-PARTY LIABILITY LAWSUIT

1st Party	The drinker or purchaser of the alcohol.
2nd Party	The establishment and seller or server of the alcohol.
3rd Party	Not involved in the above transaction, but somehow injured by the first party.

Liquor liability laws are often based on *dramshop laws*. A dramshop was an operation where alcohol was sold and consumed on the premises. Dramshops are the precursor to today's bars, taverns, and lounges, and the name remains a legal term in England today. The law is based on the belief of negligence regarding the sale of alcohol to a minor or an intoxicated person.

The law was intended to protect the public from the overconsumption of alcohol. Dramshop laws state that the seller of the alcoholic beverage that causes or contributes to the intoxication should be held liable for injury to others by the intoxicated person. The law protects against injury or death caused by an automobile accident, as well as assault, and extends to the family of the injured or deceased third party as well. The first line for recovering the cost of the injuries is the first party (the drinker), but often if he/she does not have enough money to cover the cost of the injuries the injured party goes instead after the owner/operator of the beverage operation.

Establishments serving alcohol are faced with an even greater peril from third-party liability. A suit can also be brought by either the intoxicated patron or the family of the patron. Imagine this situation: a guest visits an operation that serves alcoholic beverages. The guest is overserved alcohol and becomes intoxicated. The intoxicated guest becomes injured after leaving the bar. In some states either the guest or the family of the guest can sue the beverage establishment under dramshop laws for their injuries. In another scenario, two buddies visit their favorite operation that serves alcohol. They both become intoxicated and get into one of their cars to go home. They get into an accident and the passenger is injured. The passenger can sue the beverage operation because its staff should not have let him and his friend become too intoxicated to drive safely.

Dramshop laws are intended to be beneficial to society and may have been more effective in a time when the majority of alcohol was consumed where it was purchased. Nowadays the consumption of alcohol has shifted dramatically from on-premise accounts (bars and lounges) to homes. Consuming alcohol at home (or away from where it is somebody's job to serve them) removes the role of a second party in controlling consumption. Drinkers often underestimate their level of intoxication. Properly trained bartenders act as a type of gatekeeper because they should be able to spot intoxicated guests and cut off service of alcohol to them. Unfortunately, bartenders are often not properly trained, are overworked because of staff shortages, and often do not detect problems. Sometimes owner-operators of bars are more concerned with profits than the well being of guests; this may lead to overserving of drinkers, which makes more money and does not risk offending a valuable customer.

STATE LAWS GOVERNING BEVERAGE OPERATIONS

The sale of alcohol for both *on-premise* and *off-premise* consumption is mostly regulated by state law. Bars and lounges are considered on-premise accounts because they sell alcohol to guests who consume it where it is purchased. Stores that sell alcohol are considered off-premise accounts; customers purchase the alcohol to consume it somewhere other than where they bought it.

The Eighteenth Amendment, which introduced Prohibition, became effective in 1920, and was repealed by the Twenty-first Amendment in 1933, which passed some powers onto states. The Twenty-first Amendment grants states the power to regulate the distribution of alcohol within their borders.

States fall into two distinct groups when it comes to how alcohol is distributed within their borders. States are either *open or license states* or *closed or control states.* In an open state distributors are licensed to disburse their products to both on-premise and off-premise accounts. Distributors are granted exclusive territories within the state for their products so there is no competition. In closed states the state serves as the distributor. Alcohol is sold through state-controlled stores. Delivery to on-premise and off-premise accounts is up to the state. Some states provide delivery while others do not.

Many states allow local communities to make decisions regarding the sale of alcohol in their areas. These laws are called *local option laws.* The state government empowers community or country governments to make a range of decisions regarding the sale of alcohol. The items communities can decide include such things as whether they want to allow the service of alcohol or not (there are still areas in this country that have not legally sold alcohol since Prohibition), the hours of operation, location restrictions, and so forth. The requirement of the state government is that the local laws must at least meet the minimum of state laws or exceed them.

There are a variety of state laws that control those who sell alcohol in the United States. It is often said that the only similarity in liquor laws between states is that they vary considerably from state to state. States take their responsibility to control the distribution and sale of alcohol within their borders seriously. The purpose of the state laws is to promote moderation in the consumption of alcohol and to foster obedience for the law.

State governments treat the possession of a liquor license, granting the legal right to sell alcohol within the state, as a privilege and not a right. State statutes are written to place restrictions on liquor licenses as well as on those who possess them. Above all, states use the issuance of liquor licenses as a way to control the number of outlets selling liquor in their state.

There is a big difference in the eyes of the state laws and regulations between a person who wants to open, for example, a book store and one who wants to open a bar or a store selling alcohol. Many states restrict the location of the bar or liquor store, the age of the employees, the source of the product sold, the days and hours of operation, credit policies, and the number of operations in a certain area. Most states are very careful to whom they issue liquor licenses. In a possible reflection on the influence of organized crime on Prohibition, many states perform rigorous background checks on those applying to operate a bar. Most states will not allow convicted felons to possess a liquor license. Care is also taken to approve the transfer of a license from one person to another. Very few if any of these issues are restricted or controlled in the case of the person wanting to open a bookstore or other type of business that does not involve alcohol.

Liquor laws are generally inconsistent from state to state, with the biggest difference being the level of taxation. The major requirement is that the law must be as strict, or stricter than, the federal law on the issue, if one exists.

SOME ISSUES THAT MAY BE CONTROLLED BY STATE GOVERNMENTS IN OPERATIONS THAT SELL ALCOHOL

Location
Age of servers and staff
Number of businesses in an area
Days and/or hours of operation
Types of identifications acceptable
Warnings to pregnant women
Prohibition of gambling
Prohibition of disorderly conduct
Maintenance of purchasing records
Limitations on promotions
Transfer of liquor license
Who can operate a beverage operation

Since the ability to sell alcohol is a privilege and not a right, granted by states, there are often stiff penalties for those who violate state liquor laws. Violations of state laws often result in arrest, imprisonment, or suspension or loss of the operation's liquor license, which would result in the loss of jobs, and often leads to the failure of the business.

Serving Underage Drinkers/Minors

Unfortunately, an otherwise law-abiding operation can lose its liquor license, and potentially its business, due to an overworked, careless, or untrained server who fails to properly check the identification of an underage guest, resulting in an alcohol-related accident. This is one of the biggest nightmares of both on-premise and off-premise operators. The basis of their business is the license issued by the state granting them the right to sell alcohol. The loss of their liquor license often results in the failure of their business and livelihood.

During the 1970s many states dropped the legal drinking age to 18, partially in response to war protesters of the day complaining they were old enough to die in the defense of their country but not old enough to legally drink alcohol. The trend was later reversed in most states in hopes of reducing the number of alcohol-related traffic accidents and fatalities, which increased dramatically with the lowering of the drinking age. Returning the legal drinking age to 21 came about as a result of strong federal government intervention. In 1984, President Ronald Reagan signed into law a measure that would cut federal highway funds to states who set their legal drinking age below 21. This was an example of the federal government intervening on an issue previously left for states to decide. The federal government did not have the right to set the law but did possess the tools to influence it.

Many state liquor control officers cite their number one problem as the illegal serving or selling of alcohol to minors. To combat the growing problem, some states send in "decoys" or underage police officers to attempt to purchase alcohol. When the decoy is served, the operation is issued a ticket. In most states both the server and the bar can be held liable for serving underage guests.

Identifying Underage Drinkers

Underage drinkers will often go to great lengths to get into a bar to drink illegally. Altered driver licenses, switching identification cards with older friends, and dressing "older" with the addition of makeup are all ploys common to underage drinkers. Bar personnel must scrutinize identification cards carefully to determine if they are legitimate. If they aren't sure, they should ask for another piece of identification to substantiate the first, as well as asking the guest questions to see if the identification is actually theirs.

There are often some clues that bar personnel can look for to help them identify underage drinkers. Staff should weigh all the factors to make a determination. Remember, drinking is a privilege and not a right, and it is better to refuse service than to risk serving an underage customer. First look at their clothing to see if it is indicative of their age. Younger people generally wear more casual clothes. Underage guests often exhibit a behavior that may give their age away. Arriving at the bar at a time before a bouncer is normally working at the door, or sitting in an out of the way location in the bar to escape detection are some things to look for. If a guest is underage they often will carry their driving license without a wallet or any other identification.

CLUES FOR STAFF THAT MIGHT IDENTIFY UNDERAGE GUESTS

Type of clothes
Suspicious behavior
Carrying only one piece of identification

Serving Intoxicated Guests

Serving alcohol to an intoxicated person is illegal; this is the basis for dramshop laws. Servers and bartenders must observe guests to determine if they are intoxicated. Special care must be taken to determine if guests are intoxicated upon entering an establishment. If a guest has consumed alcohol prior to entering the operation, he/she will become intoxicated faster than a guest who has not.

One of the major problems for beverage operations is that servers have to rely on subjective measures, such as observing guests' behaviors to determine if they are indeed intoxicated. Officers of the law have objective measures such as breathalyzer tests to use in their determination. Managers need to encourage their staff to cut off service to guests prior to them becoming drunk to avoid the problems associated with intoxication.

The problems do not end for the beverage establishment when they have either cut off or refused service to an intoxicated guest. They also have the responsibility to ensure the guest does not get into a vehicle and drive, potentially getting in an accident. Bars have been held liable for the resulting damage and injury even though they cut off service to the guest properly, but then allowed the intoxicated guest to leave the location. A country club was still held liable for part of the damages of a guest even though they initially refused to give him his keys because he was intoxicated. They released his keys to his friend, who promised to take him home. The friend tossed him the keys in the parking lot, and for that he shared in the liability for the death of the drunken guest who wrapped his car around a tree on his way home.

Other State Regulations

State regulations severely restrict the relationships between beverage operations and their suppliers. The regulations are intended to level the playing field between suppliers and operators. Imagine if the fictitious National Brewing Company was allowed to own and operate bars in this country. They would generate a market for their products while excluding small companies that are unable to operate their own beverage retail operations. The supplier or producer of beverages cannot own or have any financial interest in an operation that sells alcohol to the public. There are also limits in most states on the value of promotional items that suppliers can give to beverage operations. Depending on the state, some beverage suppliers are not allowed to extend credit to their customers. Without the legal right to extend credit, beverage operations are required to pay for deliveries of alcohol when delivered, rather than in 15–30 days that can generally be negotiated with other non-alcohol suppliers.

Many states require that certain records of the beverage operation be maintained for a set period of time. Of primary concern are purchase invoices. Government officials want to be sure the operator is purchasing from legal sources and has records to prove that. The records are required by federal law to be maintained for three years and they must be surrendered at any time by request of the Bureau of Alcohol, Tobacco and Firearms (BATF) officers.

THE LAW AND THE BAR STAFF

Employees of beverage operations must be aware of the laws that govern the sale of alcohol in their area. "Ignorance of the law is no excuse" is very appropriate here. The bartender or server earning minimum wage, or in some states below minimum wage, can be personally fined for violating a liquor law. Normally when a server is cited for a violation the beverage operation is also cited, so it is to the best interest of the operation to train its employees concerning the law.

Care must be taken to ensure that all employees serving alcohol are aware of the regulations and know how to put them in practice. The transactions of the bar involve both servers and bartenders; some occur at the bar in open view of management or others, while many others occur at the table out of view except for those involved in the transaction. The unsupervised nature of most transactions opens up the potential for problems for the beverage operation's owner or operator. Employees may be tempted to violate some laws for friends or regular customers in exchange for a good tip. Serving underage guests or allowing guests to become intoxicated are two examples. Servers and bartenders may be trying to benefit at the expense of the bar. Managers should spot check the identifications of guests and regularly walk the floor of the operation to spot potential problems before they occur.

THE LAW AND THE CUSTOMER

In many states it is not illegal for a minor to attempt to purchase alcohol. This is unfair to beverage retailers who are fined if they serve underage customers.

FEDERAL LAWS GOVERNING BEVERAGE OPERATIONS

In the beverage trade the following activities are all regulated by federal laws:

> Production
> Importation
> Distribution between states
> Exportation
> Labeling

Control of the products falls under the Bureau of Alcohol, Tobacco, and Firearms (BATF) division of the Department of the Treasury. The three major roles of the bureau are to ensure that proper revenue is collected, to ensure product quality, and to prevent the sale and distribution of illegal products.

THE THREE MAJOR ROLES OF THE BATF

To ensure that proper revenue is collected
To ensure product quality
To prevent the sale and distribution of illegal products

A *tamper-evident closure* is placed on liquor bottles when the taxes are paid and they are ready to be shipped from the warehouse. The closure ensures that the bottle has not been tampered with since it left the warehouse. Care must be taken by receivers of alcohol in beverage operations that the closures are still intact upon delivery. An operator can be fined up to $10,000 if his operation is in possession of a bottle without the closure or remnants of a closure.

Care must be taken with empty alcohol bottles. They may not be reused for any purpose whatsoever. Law forbids their reuse for storing mixers or other items. It is also illegal for beverage operators to *marry* two bottles, or pour from one bottle to another. As innocent as it sounds, combining two like bottles is against federal law, as is adding anything to a bottle of alcohol such as water or another product. The intention is to stop unscrupulous operators from adding no-name alcohol to a call or premium bottle to deceive guests.

SUMMARY

The laws regulating the beverage industry may seem overwhelming to the operator of a beverage operation. The combination of three levels—federal, state, and local—serves several purposes for both the government and the operator. The goal of the government is to protect citizens from themselves and others as well as protect the more than $6 billion in revenue the alcoholic beverage industry generates. The benefit to the operator is that they receive products whose quality and origin they can be assured of.

The heavy regulation of the beverage industry is not a recent occurrence. Some of the first laws in early civilizations related to alcohol. Liquor laws have evolved throughout history. Their primary role was to moderate consumption. The king of all liquor laws was the Eighteenth Amendment, or Prohibition, outlawing the production and consumption of alcohol in this country. It became the first amendment to the Constitution of the United States to be repealed.

State laws regulate the distribution, sales, and consumption within state borders. States can elect to be either open or closed as to the distribution of alcohol within their borders. States also grant local option laws to their communities, empowering them to decide many aspects of the sale of alcohol locally. They control many other matters, including the location of a bar or liquor store, the age of employees, the source of the products sold, the days and hours of operation, credit policies, and the number of operations in a certain area. Most states are very careful to whom they issue liquor licenses.

The federal government has less to do with the actual operation of the bar. Their influence is more on the products that are served. They control the production, importation, advertising, and distribution among states. The federal government is also concerned with collecting the proper taxes due, protecting the integrity of the contents, and preventing illegal beverage sales.

KEY TERMS

Prohibition	Closed or Control	Volstead Act
Temperance	States	Third-Party Liability
Eighteenth	Bureau of Alcohol	Second Party
Amendment	Tobacco and	Dramshop Laws
Blood Alcohol	Firearms (BATF)	Open or License states
Content (BAC)	Marrying	Local Option Laws
First Party	Whisky Rebellion	Tamper-Evident Closure
Third Party	Abstinence	
Twenty-first		
Amendment		

CHAPTER QUESTIONS

1. What was the "Noble Experiment" and how did it come about?
2. What are the two reasons that justify the strict government control over alcoholic beverages?
3. What was the Temperance Movement? What were its goals?
4. What exactly did Prohibition make illegal? What were the penalties for violating it?
5. Name three aspects of serving alcohol that governments are attempting to tighten.
6. Identify the roles of the three parties in a third-party liability law suit.
7. What was a dramshop, and what are dramshop laws?
8. Is a beverage operation just liable for the damage from a car accident caused by an intoxicated guest? Or are they liable for other damages? Explain your answer.
9. Explain the difference between operating a beverage operation in a license and in a control state.
10. What do local option laws grant? Who distributes the power in local option laws?
11. Name four things regulated by state governments regarding the sale of alcohol.
12. Give two clues that may tip off staff to an underage drinker.
13. Can a company that makes or distributes alcohol own a bar? Explain.
14. Name three of the things that federal alcohol laws control.
15. What is the federal agency that is responsible for alcohol? What are their three primary roles?

SUGGESTED READINGS

1. *Coffman v. Kennedy*, 141 Cal Rptr. 267 (Cal. App. 1977).
2. Cournoyer, N. G., et al., *Hotel, Restaurant, and Travel Law; A Preventative Approach*, 4th ed. Albany, NY: Delmar Publishers, Inc., 1993.
3. Goodwin, J. R., and J. R. Gaston. *Hotel & Hospitality Law, Principles and Cases*, 4th ed. Scottsdale, AZ: Publishing Horizons, Inc., 1992.
4. Murchison, K. *Federal Law Doctrines/The Forgotten Influence of National Prohibition*. Durham and London: Duke University Press, 1994.
5. Plotkin, R. *The Intervention Handbook: The Legal Aspects of Serving Alcohol*, 2nd ed., Tucson, AZ: PSD Publishing Company, 1990.

chapter thirteen

COSTING, PRICING, AND CONTROL

chapter outline

chapter objectives

Reading this chapter will enable you to:

- Become familiar with the role of pricing in a beverage operation.
- Calculate drink cost and establish drink selling price.
- Discuss the most common pricing methods.
- Discuss Bar Percentage Costs and profitability.

- Become familiar with the profit margin of various beverage products.

- Use pricing as a marketing tool.

- Know how to set up a pricing strategy.

- Identify today's most frequently adopted product control systems.

- Become familiar with standard customer check handling and cash control procedures.

THE ROLE OF PRICING IN A BEVERAGE OPERATION

The pricing of drinks and beverage menu offerings is one of the most effective marketing and merchandising tools available. In costing and ultimately pricing a drink (the term "drink" refers to cocktails, mixed drinks, wines, beers, cordials, and generally, any beverage item served in a bar and beverage establishment), the business operator often first takes into account the management perspective. It is recommended that the customer's perspective also be considered a priority. As stated in previous chapters, today's American bar and lounge is not only a place to drink an alcoholic beverage but also a place of "social gathering." Today, people visit a bar for a variety of reasons: to discuss terms of business contracts; to renew associations; or to celebrate a festive occasion. Or, perhaps, to temporarily get away from the responsibilities and daily stress that come from our fast paced society. For many, the price of a drink may not be such a concern as it is for others, who are more price/value conscious.

Competently managed, bars, lounges, and other places that sell alcoholic beverages are generally profitable operations. This is largely due to the healthy profit margin of beverages as compared to that of other types of products. An elementary but effective approach to addressing profitability in a beverage operation would be to take note of the "standard sales value" of a well-brand liter bottle of liquor (vodka, gin, rum, etc.). Let's establish that such a bottle will cost the operator approximately $7.50. By serving 33 drinks (one ounce of liquor per drink), and charging $2.00 each, the bottle will give a return of $66.00—about nine times its purchase price—a markup of a factor of nine. Although not all liquor served is of the "well" type, the pouring profit of bar products is generally superior than that of products offered in many other types of business.

When addressing profitability in the hospitality industry, the beverage sector is generally regarded to be second only to the gaming sector. In a restaurant, for example, chefs and food managers are generally satisfied when reviewing a profit and loss statement that reports that the food cost percentage for any given month is within a 28–35 per cent range. By contrast, a bar manager would not be at all satisfied if the same percentage range came out of the income statement of his/her department.

Bar Percentage Cost

More commonly called **"Bar P.C.,"** the Bar Percentage Cost is determined by dividing the purchase cost of beverage goods by their beverage revenue. Although the national average is reported to be in the 28–30 per cent range, the conscientious beverage manager sees the ideal Bar P.C. to be in the 18–25 per cent range. If this percentage is higher there are several areas to consider. One is that drink prices may be too low. If the P.C. is considerably less than 18 per cent, drink prices may be too high. This may please the operator temporarily, but it may also turn out in the long run, not to be a wise business practice. High prices will keep away a certain segment of clientele. This translates into a sales potential that is not maximized or exploited to its fullest degree. Conversely, prices that are too low will certainly attract a large flow of patrons but will not change the high range of the P.C. Another concern of a price structure that is set too low is that it may attract a number of undesirable patrons. In short, a smartly planned and well-calculated pricing strategy will allow the operator to meet the financial objective and please the desired clientele at the same time.

ESTABLISHING BEVERAGE COSTS

Before attaching a definite price to a bar offering, the operator or manager should accurately calculate the **"house cost."** The house cost for any given drink is the purchase cost of all the ingredients necessary to make such a drink. Many operations prefer to separate the various bar beverages into "groups," and decide the drink selling price according to the desired percentage cost for each of the groups. One group can include the most common mixed drinks and standard cocktails. A second group can consist of drinks mixed with more expensive liquor brands. These are usually referred to as **"premium"** brands. A third group could include wines, a fourth could be all beer and a fifth, soft drinks and nonalcoholic beverages such as bottled water, tea, iced tea, coffee, and fruit juices. Today, thanks to the latest touch-screen technology, each of these groups can be easily subdivided into various categories providing management with detailed inventory and sales reports that are more easily subjected to closer scrutiny and accurate controls.

In larger operations, before calculating the house cost, the bar manager establishes a **"precosting"** procedure. Precosting means categorizing all the ingredients necessary to prepare a cocktail and considering the purchase cost for each of the ingredients. Wine and beer do not require precosting but cocktails do. Thus, the preparation of many cocktails will require (taking the example of a Manhattan cocktail):

   a. A main bar product or products—The Bourbon Whiskey
   b. A supplementary bar ingredient—The dash of sweet Vermouth
   c. A garnish—The cherry

The markup rationale is usually decided along the lines of the percentage cost desired. For example, if all the ingredients necessary to make a Margarita cocktail amount to $0.52 (fifty-two cents) and the selling price is $3.00, the percentage cost will be 17 per cent—a markup of nearly six times. (The term "markup" is often referred to by accountants as the "multiplication factor.") In bar operations, a markup of five to six times is generally considered a standard one. There are some beverage offerings that are so popular and in such demand that this allows the operator to feel comfortable in applying a multiplication factor of seven to twelve.

To summarize this example:

Cost of Beverage Product	$0.52
Desired Bar Percentage Cost	17% (100:17 = a markup of 5.8 (rounded up to 6)
Selling Price	$3.00 (0.52 × 5.8)
Gross Profit	$2.48

Consider that the mixing of a standard Margarita requires Tequila, Triple Sec, and Sweet & Sour plus condiments. In breaking down the house cost we proceed as follows assuming 33 portions per bottle of each:

	bottle cost oz./lit.
1 oz. Tequila	$11.25/33 = 0.34
½ oz. Triple Sec	$9.00/33 = 0.13
2 oz. Sweet & Sour	$2.50/33 = 0.15
Total	$0.52

The Margarita also requires approximately a teaspoon of coarse salt for the glass rim, and in some operations, a lime wedge. One teaspoon of salt has a very marginal affect on the house cost, so it is not included here. Some cocktails include a more exotic and costly garnish. If so, its cost should be included.

The bar and beverage operator should consider that not every drink or beverage product offered will give a 17 per cent Bar P.C. Some beverage items are very cost efficient, while others are not as profitable. For example, a glass of an ordinary domestic draft beer would generally give a more favorable percentage cost than a shot of premium bourbon or a fine cognac. Similarly it would be difficult for a bar operator to attach to a glass of house wine the same markup as for a premium single malt scotch.

At this point, it becomes necessary to consider the volume sales for each group of alcoholic beverages and the **Sales Mix** Factor. Alcoholic beverages are generally categorized as discussed in Chapter 6. The sales mix is defined as the sum-total sales of each category of bar offering. The sales mix average will ultimately decide the operator's profit. Although similar in many operational aspects, bar businesses adopt different pricing strategies according to

In costing a drink, the cost of a drop or a dash of these and similar condiments shown here, is generally not included.

the type of clientele and the establishment's specific needs. In some instances, operators feature certain drinks that do not carry a high profit margin. After careful planning, operators may even feature drinks at prices that break even or show a slight loss. In general, this is adopted as a marketing tool to attract more clientele. By means of a positive sales mix, a loss on one or two individual items can be easily absorbed and compensated for by other bar menu offerings, resulting in better sales and overall higher profits.

A typical example of this type of marketing strategy is found in restaurants that offer favorite daily specials such as "steak & lobster." Generally, a steak and lobster dinner is not, in itself, considered a profitable item by chefs and food managers, but it may attract a larger number of patrons who may purchase food offerings other than the steak and lobster. A larger clientele will result in higher beverage sales and, in the long run, a higher check average. Only then, do the high cost-low profit items become justified.

For example:

House Special Cocktail (name)

Total Cost of Mixing Ingredients:	0.90 (main + supplementary)
Garnish	0.05
Selling Price	$2.00
Gross Profit	$1.05
Percentage Cost	45%

House special cocktails, like the example given here, can be quite profitable. They also serve as an effective merchandising tool.

Not a very good one! However, the 45 per cent Percentage Cost is justified if one considers that it takes only a portion of the additional clientele attracted, to compensate for it. Seven customers, who request regular drinks (at 17 per cent P.C. each on average), are sufficient to erase the negative factor (45 per cent P.C.) and bring the average to an acceptable level. In fact it takes six drinks with a 17 per cent P.C. to bring the 45 per cent P.C. house special drink ratio down to 21%. Twenty-one per cent is generally considered a satisfactory Percentage Cost.

PROFIT POURING

As stated earlier, once the cost of the beverage product is accurately determined, a selling price is established according to the desired Percentage Cost. Thus we have:

$$\frac{\text{Operator product cost}}{\text{Desired liquor Percentage Cost}} = \frac{\$.70}{20\%} = \$3.50 \text{ (Customer cost)}$$

This simple equation is the preferred one in most operations. A similar approach is:

$$\text{Operator product cost} \times \text{Markup} = \text{Customer cost}$$

In such a case, the drink house cost multiplied by the desired markup or multiplication factor will result in the final selling price. However, prices can also be established according to the individual disposition of the manager/owner and can be very much personal decisions. This is particularly true in smaller, privately owned operations. Bar owners can establish a drink price intuitively, without the need of calculating drink ingredient costs. Or they may base a price decision on competitors pricing patterns. There are even those who will attach a price to a drink according to the time and effort required for mixing it. Thus, a higher price will be charged for Long Island Iced Teas, B52s, and floated drinks, not because of higher ingredient cost but because such cocktails take considerably longer to prepare.

When pricing a drink a simple and efficient way of breaking down the ounce cost of a specific brand is by using a cost/price chart or any of the "metric quick check" templates. The template shows bottle prices for the most common bottle sizes: Liter, quart, fifth, 750 ml and half a gallon. A quick glance will give the bar manager the cost per ounce for each of the bottles. In the last two decades metric standard measures replaced American standard measures. Thus, the liter bottle size has replaced the quart in popularity, and the 750 ml is often used in place of the "fifth." Liquor dispensing systems often adopt the 1.75 liter size. A quick bottle size/ounce reference is as follows:

Half Gallon	=	64 oz.
1.75 liter (metric)	=	59.2 oz.
Liter (metric)	=	33.8 oz.
Quart	=	32 oz.
Fifth	=	25.6 oz.
750 ml (metric)	=	25.4 oz.
500 ml (metric)	=	16.9 oz.
Pint	=	16 oz.
Half-pint	=	8 oz.
200 ml (metric)	=	6.8 oz.
50 ml (metric)	=	1.7 oz.
Miniature	=	1.6 oz.

Volume operation managers can also benefit from the "volume markup charts" available today. These charts work on the same principle as the metric quick check templates. The only difference is that instead of calculating costs by breaking down the ounces per bottle, they are designed to calculate the cost of ounces per case. This may particularly be helpful when pricing drinks for a large reception or a large banquet such as in a national convention event.

For example, 1 lit. c/s vodka = 405 oz. (1 liter = 33.8 oz. × 12 [twelve bottles in a case] = 405 oz.)

There are countless factors to be considered when calculating drink costs. It is recommended that the following be taken into consideration:

Meeting Projected Sales and Profit
Sales Mix Historical Data
Customer Profile and Drinking Habits
Product Availability
Type of Operation
Price Fluctuation of Goods to Be Purchased

PRICING TO MEET A MARKETING OBJECTIVE OR FOR SPECIFIC PURPOSES

The costing and pricing methods discussed in the previous section are considered standard, and therefore, accepted by most bar and beverage operations. However, situations may arise when the operator finds himself/herself needing to change the standard price structure. This modification might occur during certain times of the day, for a few days, or even longer periods of time. A typical example of price changes for only two or three hours is the "happy hour." During this time prices may be reduced to a half. Maintaining the happy hour on a steady basis has proved to be an effective marketing decision for many operations. Obviously, prices could not be maintained that low for the entire business day. That would result in a consistently high Bar P.C. An example of prices being increased for a few days might be during a special event. In this instance, it would be appropriate and safe from a business aspect to slightly increase prices. This is the true meaning of "supply and demand." Higher prices are often a logical consequence of a large demand for a product.

An additional example of prices being drastically reduced for a period of time (in this case several weeks) might occur when the storage area is becoming overstocked with certain beverage products that according to sales projections should have been sold before a specific time. Bar merchandise that is lying on the storeroom shelves is not producing revenue. These products should be regarded as an *inactive investment*. Merchandise that is not moving occupies space and overloads the inventory, creating a more difficult task for those who maintain it. If a trend of poor sales for a particular product continues, the wise bar manager will look for a way to sell such products as soon as possible. The most effective way of selling the "excess baggage" is to offer attractive drink prices and to set up special drink promotions. To simply feature low prices might not be sufficient. The wise manager needs to brainstorm and display creativity. The following are suggested promotional measures that may serve this specific purpose:

A. Introduce unusual house cocktails and creative specialty drinks using the brands of liquor that are not moving. For example, on holidays or special celebration days, create a new cocktail appropriate for the occasion. Examples might include a Pink Lady or Pink Squirrel type of cocktail for St. Valentine's Day, or creating and naming a cocktail after a habitual and loyal patron.

B. Organize contests that would attract your type of clientele. Darts, billiards, backgammon, chess, and trivia contests could stimulate patrons' interest and at the same time create an interesting atmosphere. The prize for the contest winner could be a bottle of one of the better brands of the products that are not moving.

C. During football season, slightly lower your markup on whiskies and brandies. The same should be done with cooler and refreshing drinks during the summer (Planters Punch, frosted drinks, frozen Daiquiris). Warmer drinks should be launched during the winter months (hot punch, cognacs).

D. Ethnic festivities are always fun for patrons. Serve green beer on St. Patrick's Day, German beer on Oktoberfest, Italian wine on Columbus Day. Create cocktails with Ouzo or Metaxa on Greek festivals and special drinks with Southern Comfort on Martin Luther King Day.

E. Family drinks and children's favorites (Planters Punches and Shirley Temples) served on Mother's Day. Sparkling wines and Spumante served on festive occasions or when celebrating someone's birthday.

F. Invent a new version or make variations of old favorite cocktails such as Margaritas and Pina Coladas incorporating the brands that are not moving. Cocktails such as Screwdrivers and Rusty nails do not offer alternatives and are difficult to modify, but Pina Coladas and Margaritas are versatile, and thus easy to work with.

Pricing Methods

Pricing methods adopted in today's bar and beverage operations vary; the most common are listed here according to the size of the operation:

Pricing by accurate precosting and costing calculations (typical in large properties)

Pricing by intuition (typical in small properties)

Pricing by multiplying the cost of the original product by a factor of five—a markup of five times (typical of small properties)

Pricing by calculating the various costs so that the final Percentage Cost lies in the range of 20–25 per cent (typical of medium size to large size properties)

Pricing without calculating house cost but using the competition prices as a guideline (small and medium size properties)

Pricing by considering external factors such as customer profile, local market demands, specific customer preferences, and consumer trends (small, medium, and large size properties)

Pricing by considering internal factors such as higher wages for beverage staff, building renovation costs, liability insurance costs, and so forth

Pricing by including additional costs such as the cost of entertainment and that of various services

Pricing for specific purposes

SETTING UP CONTROL SYSTEMS

Controlling is a fundamental management function. To exercise control means to make certain that the beverage staff adheres to the policies and procedures established by management. Essentially, the primary objective of controlling is to protect the investment and assets of the owner/operator. Product Control is control of the flow of beverage products, from the time they are received and stored, all the way to pouring and serving them to the patron. Often this "flow" is not quite as smooth as it should be. The operation suffers when the flow experiences problems. Generally, these are caused by failure to follow standard procedures established by management. Standard and actual costs must be similar and should not differ by more than a very few decimal points. Some operations are more lenient and allow the standard and actual cost to vary by a few points of a percentage but by no more than what is considered a "reasonable" amount. If the variance is greater, something is definitely wrong. Management should promptly investigate to determine the culprit area or areas of discrepancy.

Common areas of concern are:

Excessively fast and casual receiving. Lack of comparison of the received product against invoice specifications (typical situation occurring when the receivers of the delivery are in a hurry), inaccurate records of issued products from the storage area to the bar, inaccurate requisitions, improper rotation of bar products such as beer and perishable products (FIFO system = first in first out).

Spoilage. Particularly with dairy products such as milk and cream or perishable beverage products such as fruit juices, which are not handled and refrigerated properly. Although spoilage in a beverage operation is not considered a critical issue as it is with food, careless employees can cause a significant loss of revenue.

Waste. The cost conscious manager never allows the employees to create excess waste. Perhaps not as serious as in food management, this has lately become a growing concern in beverage operations.

Unaccounted beverages. This can occur in various ways:

a. Bartenders who give away sodas, beers, and drinks to employees and do not record the amount or notify management.

b. Drinks that are served to patrons on a complimentary basis for any reason (spillages, complaints, habitual guests, meeting promotional objectives, etc.) and not recorded.

c. Beverages served during employees' meals and staff related events such as employees' special gatherings, training sessions, awards ceremonies, and so forth. Due to the nature of the events, often the amount of the beverages are not properly recorded or allocated.

Pilferage. This area is discussed in detail in Chapter 15. Even the smallest suspicion should prompt the bar manager to apply tighter control methods and to inform both the security department and higher management. In a smaller operation the police should be made aware.

Whether in a large, medium size, or small beverage operation, the basic controlling functions are similar. One of the top priorities is to establish a **par stock** according to operational needs. Once the par stock is determined, an adequate amount of beverages will be available on a daily basis. Replenishing the stock adequately is a very basic task. For example, a small bar operation establishes that par stock for vodka is six bottles. If at the end of the working day four bottles of vodka are left, the next day two bottles must be purchased in order to bring the stock up to par. In smaller operations, the empties system is often adopted. The empty bottles are kept until the end of the shift and broken after each bottle has been recorded for next day requisition. The traditional tag system is still in use today. Small tags containing the bottle brand name that are attached to the bottle's neck are removed, placed in a cup, and recorded at the end of the day for the next day order. In handling wines, the bin-number system has proved to be efficient in most situations. Stored wine bottles are assigned a **bin number** which follows the same placement sequence as listed in the wine list. The bin number of the bottle will be used when ordering the necessary wine bottles to maintain the par stock at a satisfactory level.

A perpetual inventory, if properly handled, will allow the manager to prepare the beverage order for the next day without the need of counting the bottles (See Appendix 2—Perpetual Inventory Form). Thanks to innovative computer software, inventory management systems now have a larger selection of means of effective product control.

The conscientious bar manager or operator always strives to maintain an efficient par stock on a daily basis. As discussed in previous chapters, the ability to accurately forecast product usage and to project business trends can be a deciding factor in profitability. The dangers of overstocking have been pointed out earlier. Understocking will result in disgruntled patrons and fleeing customers. In general, patrons don't like to be told that the establishment has run out of their favorite brand. Smaller bar operations have an easier task in maintaining an adequate par stock. Another advantage of working with a smaller stock size, is the ability to take a daily opening and closing inventory.

Product Control methods are concentrated in four specific areas:

Quantity of products
Quality of products
Cost of products
Employees handling of the products

Control by Standardization

One of the most effective control systems is to standardize every single task that is performed by the staff handling the beverage product. Standardization also means "uniformity." Receiving, storing, handling, and ultimately serv-

These bottles are par stocked. The established amount should be available before opening for business, or for any given period of time as set by management.

ing the bar product should be done with consistency on a daily basis. Two bartenders, for example, who work different shifts, may follow the same basic drink recipe but use different amounts of ingredients and place the garnish on the glass in a different way. The drink that is prepared on the day shift will not look, and certainly not taste, like the same drink that is prepared during the evening shift. The drink's appearance may not represent a problem but the use of different amounts of liquor will.

To standardize the way of placing the olive or lemon twist on a martini or a cherry on a Manhattan may not be considered crucial. However, it may be important for a tropical or an exotic drink where the garnish is considered a major factor in the presentation and the overall appearance. It is recommended that all tasks involved in the handling of beverage products be consistently standardized.

Stacking glass racks, washing, rinsing, and sanitizing glassware, stocking liquor cases in the storeroom, and setting up and breaking down the working stations are vital tasks. Standardizing the handling of the bar products as in free pouring, should be considered a priority task. Free pouring, the direct pouring of a beverage from the bottle into a glass to be served to the patron, can definitely be a problem. Larger beverage operations do not employ free pouring as much as small ones, due mainly to the use of automatic dispensing systems. With the A.L.D.S. (also called L.D.S.), beverages are poured from a gun-type dispenser. Bar products such as premium cognacs or premium single malt scotches are rarely seen in a gun, with the possible exception of some of the 4,000–5,000 room gaming properties in Las Vegas. The bartender must pour directly from the bottle. If five bartenders serving the same brand pour five different drink sizes, management will experience difficulty in implementing the product control system in a satisfactory manner.

For effective Product Control it is recommended that the manager strive to obtain good results from the bar staff by standardizing the following bar procedures:

> Purchasing and receiving the beverage products
> Arranging the products in the storage areas
> Requisitioning and issuing products from the storage area to the bar
> Pouring techniques and consistency in free pouring
> Using the jigger or any other measuring device
> Daily set up and breakdown of the working stations
> Maintaining the same liquor sequencing on the speed rack
> Mixing and garnishing the drink

One can always find bartenders who will claim that it is difficult to adhere to the standards, particularly during "rush hour." They are those who have a tendency to take short cuts and attempt to make their jobs easier. In such cases the manager must intervene and enforce the established standards regardless

Bartender using a jigger for consistency.

of the pace of business. It takes the same time to do things the right way as to do them the wrong way. A standard procedures checklist, to be consulted before and at the end of the shift, is always a valuable tool for this purpose.

Cash Controls

The same standardizing rationale is applied to Cash Control as for Product Control. Customer writing, check processing, cash handling, and completing the daily cash/bank reconciliation are tasks where standardization should be rigidly enforced. If an employee makes a mistake in handling a certain bar product or performing certain tasks, the bar manager can be understanding. If the mistake is made in relation to money, the bar manager should not be understanding or tolerant.

Cash Control and Product Control, although handled separately, should balance together on the register tape at the end of the working day. Thanks to modern technology, processing the customer charge is becoming more practical and expedient. The traditional keyboard point-of-sales system that has been so predominant in larger beverage operations is now upgrading to

Touch-screen systems have proved to provide efficient sales tracking and stock controls.

touch-screen technology. The touch-screen system allows for thorough tracking control of the bar stock and sales breakdowns. It specializes in a periodic track of cash and credit card revenue in relation to goods sold. For example, the manager can access the POS system and check the amount of sales in relation to the number of drinks sold during the working shift. The computerized reports will also allow an easier task should there be the need to follow up an auditing trail.

Although computerized systems become more and more advanced, the basic cash handling procedures have remained unchanged. Bartenders are usually given an opening bank before the shift. The bank includes a sufficient amount of money to handle the volume of business according to the establishment's specific needs. The amount of money is counted, broken down, and recorded by the bill and coin denominations on the cash control sheet. It is recommended that the bartender count the money twice. It is then placed in the register drawer. It is the manager's responsibility to ensure that the cash drawer is never left unattended and that the drawer be left open when the register is not in operation. In a case of emergency or when the bartender leaves temporarily, the drawer should be locked and the key taken or else given to the manager.

Bartenders have the tendency to keep their tip jar close to the cash register. This practice is not recommended (see Chapter 15). Customer checks that have been used should be kept in good order according to serial number and checked periodically by the manager. An experienced bartender, not properly

The practice of keeping tip jars too close to the register is not recommended.

supervised, can be very skillful in illegally misappropriating cash from the employer by reusing checks for a second or third time. To the untrained eye, this type of pilferage may be difficult to catch, particularly during "rush hour." The most common methods of theft and illegal practices are listed in Chapter 15.

CHAPTER SUMMARY

Pricing a beverage product is one of the most effective marketing tools. Generally speaking, the bar and beverage business is a profitable one. To demonstrate this point, the example given is that of the "standard sales value" of a bottle of liquor which costs the operator $7.50 and returns $66.00. Before deciding the price of any bar offering, larger operations adopt a precosting procedure that includes a breakdown of three different categories of ingredients used to prepare a drink. The principal costing procedures are discussed with examples of ingredient costs, selling price, and Bar Percentage Cost. Some operators price their drinks by establishing percentage costs, while others prefer to adopt the markup or multiplication factor method. There are times when drinks are priced for special reasons or for specific purposes. In this case the standard pricing rationale is not applied.

Product control is one of the most fundamental functions of management. It stretches from the time the beverages arrive at the establishment all the way to the pouring into the customer's glass. Par stock and inventory controls are discussed. Standardizing the handling and serving of beverages is an effective way to ensure consistency in product control. The standardization concept is strongly recommended and should be enforced by the conscientious manager, although bartenders at times find it difficult and impractical to adhere to standardization policies and procedures. It is strongly recommended that managers take whatever measures are necessary to ensure that bartenders abide by standardization principles.

Although computerized systems are constantly upgraded, cash handling in a beverage operation, has remained unchanged for the last few decades. Suggestions on cash handling and cash control are provided. Bartenders and bar personnel are, in general, honest, conscientious, and productive employees as are staff in other sectors of the hospitality industry; however, as in other professions, there are exceptions. These may result in loss of revenue for the employer. Occasionally, a manager must face the reality of having a dishonest bartender among the staff. The chapter describes a common method of fraud in a bar and beverage operation.

KEY TERMS

House Cost	Bar P.C.	Multiplication Factor
Drink Groups	Par Stock	Markup
Premium Brands	Overstocking	Standardize
Pre-costing	Understocking	Empties System
Bin Number		

CHAPTER QUESTIONS

1. Define the following:
   - Sales Mix
   - Free Pouring
   - Perpetual Inventory
2. Is the Percentage Cost of beverage about the same to that of food?
3. Why is pricing considered an effective merchandising tool?
4. How are drink groups usually categorized?
5. What is precosting?
6. What is another term for "markup"?
7. What is a par stock?
8. How is a par stock maintained?

9. How can the handling of par stock affect the financial success of the operation?
10. How is the "Sales Mix" concept applied to a bar menu?
11. How does "standardization" relate to Product Control?
12. What is the purpose of the "cash control sheet"?

SUGGESTED READING

1. Coltman, M. *Financial Control for Your Food/Service Operation.* New York, Van Nostrand Reinhold: 1991.

chapter fourteen

PURCHASING, RECEIVING, STORING, AND ISSUING

chapter outline

chapter objectives

Upon completion of this chapter the student will be able to:

- Describe how the greater use of brand recognition affects the purchasing of products in a bar.

- Explain the differences between purchasing and buying.
- Name the two categories of state distribution of alcohol.
- Compare the differences between the two categories of distribution of alcohol within a state.
- Name two advantages of the alcohol purchasing system.
- Name two disadvantages of the alcohol purchasing system.
- State the goals of purchasing.
- Explain the two ways of placing an order.
- Define the function of receiving.
- Define storing.
- State the concerns in storing beer, wine, and distilled spirits.
- Explain the difference between informal and formal issuing.

PURCHASING, RECEIVING, AND STORING THROUGH THE EYES OF THE CUSTOMER

Customers do not see much of the purchasing, receiving, and storing functions of a beverage operation. All three are management functions and do not involve customers. Customers do see the results of the purchasing function. Guests' buy the goods the operation purchases. Some brands of goods are almost standard and are carried in all or most beverage operations, Budweiser beer, Stoli Vodka, Pepsi or Coca Cola, etc. Other items are choices of the management and reflect the goals of management or the operation. There are plenty of products used in an operation whose brand name the guest either does not know or does not care about; things such as glassware, napkins, some well-brand liquors, some mixers, etc. Since guests do not register these brands some operators will tend to purchase the cheapest available. A common phase in purchasing is that "you get what you pay for", and although there is generally no direct relationship between price and quality, i.e., something that costs twice as much is not generally twice the quality, the more you pay for an item the better the quality will be. Guests generally appreciate quality. The more they pay for an item the better the quality they expect.

INTRODUCTION

The purpose of this chapter is to give an overview of the nuts and bolts of the four title topics. The material presented in the chapter is meant to supplement the material on purchasing found in specialist texts. The terms supplier, vendor, and distributor are all used interchangeably.

There is generally greater customer brand recognition of alcoholic beverages than any other category of products served in a hospitality operation. The use of advertising in the beverage industry helps influence customer choice when ordering drinks. Customer awareness of beverage brands helps purchasers decide which to stock to serve in the operation.

Purchasing, Receiving, and Storing are important functions of a beverage operation. Care must be taken in purchasing to pick the brands the "target" market desires. Receiving is the function whereby the ownership of the goods changes hands from the distributor to the retailer. Care must be taken by management to ensure they receive all the goods they are paying for. Storage areas for alcoholic beverages must be secure. Alcoholic beverages are easy to steal and desirable to employees for both personal use and sale.

Beer, wine, and distilled spirits are purchased, and stored differently. Beer and wine products are perishable, have limited and different shelf lives, and often need to be stored in a temperature controlled environment. Distilled beverages are not perishable and have an extended shelf life; although they should not be stored in very warm or cool places, they can be stored at room temperature.

There are some legal restrictions in purchasing that complicate some aspects of the function. As discussed in Chapter 12, states control the distribution of alcohol within their borders. State fall into two major categories in the regulation of distribution; control or license states. Many states regulate by law credit terms, territories for products, delivery, etc. For example, in most areas distributors are granted exclusive territories for products. Whereas purchasers in most areas can purchase lettuce from a number of suppliers, in most areas they can only purchase brands such as Miller Brewery as well as other products from one. There are advantages and disadvantages to this lack of competition in purchasing alcohol.

PURCHASING/BUYING

Purchasing is a formal function and a broad term that can involve many activities. Purchasing involves comparing prices, negotiating terms, etc. *Buying* is generally simply calling up and ordering goods. Buying is informal and involves less activities than purchasing. The decision whether to purchase or buy is made at the operation. Smaller operations will assign the function of procuring goods to one of the managers with other responsibilities. With procuring goods as one of his/her many responsibilities there may be a tendency not to devote much time to it, whereas larger operations may be able to dedicate an employee to the sole, or at least majority, function of purchasing. Purchasing encompasses more than just buying goods. It involves determining with management what items to stock, what quality and quantity to carry, selecting suppliers, negotiating prices and terms, maintaining supplier relations, and paying for goods.

Operations that decide to buy understand they may not be getting the best price on the goods they purchase. They balance that with the reduced labor costs of performing the function. Operations that purchase justify the additional cost of dedicating personnel to the function by the savings they realize.

CONTROL AND LICENSE STATES

States control the distribution of alcohol within their borders. States fall into two categories based on how the liquor, beer, and wine is distributed, control or license states. The process of purchasing alcohol is dramatically different depending on whether you are in a control or license state.

Control States

Alabama	Idaho
Maine	Michigan
Montana	New Hampshire
N. Carolina	Ohio
Oregon	Pennsylvania
Utah	Vermont
Virginia	Washington
W. Virginia	

Control states exhibit the greater restriction on the distribution of alcohol. There are more regulations on ordering procedures and credit policies, and generally a lack of delivery in control states. License states are more open and less restrictive in the ways they operate. The state grants the power to licensed distributors to supply the beverage operations. Establishments doing business in license states operate in an environment of price control at the supplier level. Many states designate minimum and maximum wholesale and retail prices for products.

THE ADVANTAGES/DISADVANTAGES
OF THE ALCOHOL PURCHASING SYSTEM

All alcoholic beverages have a brand name. Some brand names are not recognized by the purchaser, but most are. This differs dramatically from food products purchased, where most are produced by small businesses that do not have a recognized names. The use of brand names reduces the amount of information needed on purchase specifications. For example, a specification for gin would simply state; Beefeaters Gin, 80 proof, 750 ml. bottle, 12 to a case; whereas a specification for oranges would possibly be as follows; California, Valencia, Fancy, 64 count.

A lack of competition among suppliers has advantages and disadvantages for those whose job it is to purchase alcohol. Bar operators generally purchase a wide variety of alcoholic beverages. There are name brand products that are standard in most operations. Absolut Vodka, Jack Daniel's Bourbon, Coca Cola or Pepsi, Rose's Lime Juice, etc. These are products that are well known to customers, generally displayed on the bar, and often the ingredients in the specialty drinks the bar serves. The legally imposed exclusive territory for specific brands of alcohol mean that in each operation certain brands can be purchased at one, and only one, supplier. The purchaser of these products has no choice over who they will purchase them from. They cannot call around to a variety of suppliers to try to obtain the best terms.

There are also products the bar serves of which the guests either do not know the brand or do not care. These include beverages served as "well brands" or served to guests when they order a drink without requesting the brand, and also several mixers. The lack of brand awareness by customers gives the purchaser more flexibility when it comes to purchasing. Although the purchaser cannot call around for the prices of specific brands, they can call around for pricing of generic products; for example, well-brand vodka or gin. They can easily shift between the various well brands of products without the guests knowing or caring.

There are name brand products that are standard stock in most quality beverage operations.

THE GOAL OF PURCHASING

The goal of purchasing is to acquire the proper product and the best price in the needed quantity and the quality desired. The purchasing function does not occur in a vacuum. Purchasing decisions must be made with the assistance of the operational manager. The decisions on which product, quantity, and quality should be made by the managers who deal with customers and not the purchasing agent alone. Often the level of service provided by the supplier is dictated by the price. While it may often appear cheaper for an operation to pick up their purchases at the suppliers warehouse rather than have them delivered, the supplier can probably deliver the products more efficiently and at a lower price than the bar or hotel could.

> The goal of purchasing is to acquire the *proper product* and the *best price* in the *needed quantity* and the *quality desired*.

Proper Product

There are a great variety of products for beverage managers to purchase. In the categories of spirits, beers, and wines there are hundreds if not thousands of brands to choose from. It is both impossible and undesirable to carry all of the available products in any one category. Managers must decide which products their guests prefer. The items carried in an operation should depend on the target market. For example, there will be more differences than similarities between the products carried at a college bar and a country club bar. The college bar will carry a good selection of tequila and imported or microbrewery beers, while a country club bar will possibly carry a good selection of single malt scotches, and vodkas for martinis. The purchaser's role is to provide prices and availability of appropriate products for managers to choose from.

Best Price

The ability to get the best price is more difficult in the purchasing of alcohol than in other products. The lack of the ability to comparison shop for products reduces the possibility of negotiating prices. Prices on many items are flexible, based on the quantity purchased. The more product purchased the greater the discount. Discounts are either given as cash off the invoice or as free product. For example, suppliers may offer a free bottle of wine or $10 off for the purchase of a whole case of wine. Management has to weigh the advantage of a reduced price against the amount of cash they want to tie up in inventory. Since many states do not allow beverage vendors to extend credit to beverage operations, all goods must be paid for when delivered rather than at a later date, which is possible with non-food products. This has serious cash flow implications for operators and care must be taken as to the amount of inventory to carry.

Needed Quantity

The lack of perishability of many beverage products makes it easier to order them than other products. The longer the shelf life the greater flexibility the purchaser has when ordering. If one purchases a couple of extra bottles of bourbon there is little fear that it will spoil before it is used.

Many places use a **Par Stock System** when ordering. A **par,** (see Chapter 13) is the amount of inventory needed to get through a certain period of time. Care must be taken when setting par levels. With the par level operations set a **reorder point.** The reorder point is the inventory level that indicates an order of the item. The amount ordered is enough to bring the inventory level back to par. You do not want to carry too much or too little product, or have the par too high or too low. Most bars have limited storage areas; if you store too much it will get in the way and may increase the temptation for someone to steal; if the par is too low the product may run out causing loss of sales or an employee or manager having to run to restock.

The pars fluctuate by both area and product. The par for the bar area is the amount of product that is needed to get through a shift or a day. The par at the bar will be different for a Monday, which is usually slower than a Saturday, one of the busier days. The par will also fluctuate between products depending on popularity. You may sell five times more vodka than brandy, so you would need fives times more in inventory. There will also be a par for each item in the storeroom. The par for the storeroom will generally be the amount of the product needed to get through until the next delivery day.

Quality Desired

The desired quality is determined by management and should be communicated to the purchaser.

METRIC CONTAINER SIZES

The following tables indicate the equivalent fluid ounces in metric size containers for distilled spirits and wine (see Tables 1 and 2).

ORDERING

Inventory is taken of the storage area on a regular basis, depending on the level of business. Existing inventory levels are compared to par stock levels to see what needs to be ordered. Upcoming or special events planned during the time before the next beverage order are considered to see whether larger

Table 1. Distilled Spirits

Bottle Size	Equivalent Fluid Ounces	Bottles Per Case	Corresponds To
1.75 liters	59.2 fl. oz.	6	½ Gallon
1.00 liter	33.8 fl. oz.	12	Quart
750 milliliters	25.4 fl. oz.	12	⅘ Quart
500 milliliters	16.9 fl. oz.	24	1 Pint

U.S. Government Printing Office: 491–840/4360 ATF F 5100.10 (8–85)

than normal amounts of any products are needed. Orders are then consolidated by distributor. Once the decision has been made on which products are needed and in which quantities, the next step is to place the order with the distributor. The order can be placed in two ways; direct to the salesperson, or called in. How the ordering is done is negotiated as part of the purchasing arrangement. Some salespeople make regular visits to their accounts to take orders, discuss new product offerings, etc. Some managers prefer to meet with vendor's salespeople to discuss business, while other managers prefer to place their orders directly over the telephone. Regardless of how the order is placed the person placing it must follow the procedures of the company they are dealing with.

Most beverage distributors have regular routes; they only come to certain locations on certain set days. Purchasers need to be aware of the delivery schedules of the distributors to ensure they receive the products when they want them. Some suppliers allow ordering by product name, size of container, etc. While others require orders to be placed using the inventory numbers for the products. Many suppliers have minimum order amounts; either numbers of bottles or dollar amounts. The minimum order amount helps them defray the cost of stopping the truck and having the driver make the delivery. The person placing the order must be aware of the minimum order before placing it. It is good practice to make a mark by each item ordered to make sure nothing is left off. Once the order is placed with the supplier the

Table 2. Wine

Bottle Size	Equivalent Fluid Ounces	Bottles Per Case	Corresponds To
3 liters	101 fl. oz.	4	⅘ Gallon
1.5 liters	50.7 fl. oz.	6	⅖ Gallon
1.00 liter	33.8 fl. oz.	12	Quart
750 milliliters	25.4 fl. oz.	12	⅘ Quart
375 milliliters	12.7 fl. oz.	24	1 Pint

U.S. Government Printing Office: 491–840/4360 AFT F 5100.10 (8–85)

order sheet should be put in a convenient place so that the person doing the receiving can find it and compare it with the incoming order.

Goods can generally be ordered as *full cases* or *mixed or broken cases*. Purchasing full cases, a complete case of the same product, is the most economical. Mixed or broken cases, purchasing less than full cases of any one item or the making of cases with several different products, are more expensive, but they relieve smaller operations from having to purchase larger amounts of products then they can use in a reasonable amount of time.

RECEIVING

Receiving is the function where the ownership of the goods shifts from the vendor or supplier to the purchaser [the beverage operation.] It is a key function in the obtaining of goods an operation offers for sale. Once the goods are ordered, they are shipped or delivered by the distributor to the bar. The role of the receiver is not simply to sign the invoice and put the goods in storage, but rather to check to see if it is what was actually ordered, and to ensure the proper amount of goods were delivered. Receiving becomes a key function in the cost control system of the operation. Any product that is included on the invoice or receipt from the vendor, that is not received will increase the costs of the operation.

The high cost, ease of theft, and desirability for personal use or resale of alcoholic beverages forces beverage operation managers to devote time and consideration to the receiving function. Care must be taken to ensure that all the products that were ordered are received and that the products are secured in their proper storage place as soon as possible.

As we have seen, some states do not allow beverage distributors to extend credit to beverage operations. Without the ability to extend credit, orders must be paid for when delivered or COD, cash or check on delivery. Whether the supplier will accept a check or cash depends on the financial arrangements they have made with the purchaser.

Those assigned to the receiving function are generally management personnel. They should be knowledgeable about the products they are receiving. There is the possibility of significant changes in the value of certain products arising from small differences in labeling. The difference in price between one wine and another from the same vineyard but a different year can be very significant.

The delivery should thus be checked for proper quantity *and* quality. Each bottle should be checked in mixed or broken cases to ensure what was delivered was ordered. The condition of the products received should also be inspected (for broken bottles, etc.) Invoices should be checked against the purchase order or list. Operations need to have a specific place to store invoices once they have been checked. Federal and many state laws require beverage operations to store and make available for inspection the invoices of beverage purchases for a certain period of time.

STORING

Storing is the holding of goods from the time they are received until they are issued to the production and or service areas. Storage generally takes place directly after the goods are received. Care must be taken in storage that the goods are protected from theft, maintained at proper temperature, kept in an orderly fashion so they can be retrieved as needed, and rotated to maintain freshness. Different products require different storage conditions or environments to maintain their quality, as well as different levels of security depending on their value.

Most alcoholic beverages are not perishable or have a long shelf life before they spoil. While some require refrigeration, such as keg beer that is not pasteurized, most can be stored at room temperature without seriously reducing the quality. The different types of products; beer, wine, and liquor each require different conditions to maintain their quality, but all require a secure location to discourage theft or pilferage. To best protect the products from theft they should be stored away from non-alcoholic products in separate areas. The key to control is limiting access to the alcoholic beverages.

Concerns when Storing Beer

Beer is probably the most perishable alcoholic beverage served in a bar. It is the only beverage that has a date printed somewhere on the case to let both the supplier and the operator know the date of packaging. It is imperative that beer products get rotated upon delivery of new merchandise. Storage areas should be set up to allow the easy rotation of goods.

The best system to use for rotation is **First In (FI), First Out (FO).** The oldest products get used first. When new products arrive they are placed in the back, while older products are placed in front for quick use. Some beer companies require their salespeople to rotate the stock at each account on their route at least once a month to ensure fresh beer. Some major brewery distributors will terminate salespeople if out of date beer is found at any of their accounts.

Beer has several enemies; heat, freezing, light, and time. Storage in areas of excessive heat will ruin the taste of beer. As care should be taken to make sure beer does not get too hot, care must also be taken to make sure beer does not freeze. When beer freezes and thaws it changes the flavor.

Beer comes in several different types of packaging. These different types require different treatment and storage environments to maintain their freshness. Beer sold in kegs is not pasteurized so it must be kept cold from the brewery to the beverage operation. Bottles and canned beer are generally either pasteurized or filtered to remove any yeast remaining from fermentation. Bottles and cans may be stored chilled or at room temperature.

Concerns when Storing Wine

There are several types of wines carried in most beverage operations and they can come in a variety of packages. Sparkling, still, and fortified wines also require different handling and storage. For example, an operation may serve red or white wine by the bottle in the dining room packaged in 750 ml. bottles with corks. Their house wine may come out of either a 1.5 or 3.0 liter bottle or a "bag in the box". They may serve fortified wines, port or sherry, by the glass in the bar. The different options in packaging require different handling and storage environments.

Wines sold in bottles with corks require the most care. Red wines age longer than white wines. Often wines are purchased at a discounted price, prior to when they are ready to drink, and stored at the operation until they reach maturity. Care must be taken in their storage to insure their quality. Bottles must be stored on their side in a temperature- and humidity-controlled environment. Storing them standing up, rather than on their sides, for long periods of time causes the cork to dry allowing too much air to enter the bottle. The requirement of stable temperature and humidity helps the wine age and mature. An operation that invests in a quality wine inventory and list should also purchase and maintain special storage facilities to protect their investment.

Wines with screw tops, rather than corks, or sold in bag-in-box containers require less careful handling and storage than wine with corks. The wine is more stable and does not improve while in storage. Generally wine should be kept in an area without big swings in temperature and out of direct sunlight.

In order to preserve its quality, wine must be stored in a proper environment.

Concerns when Storing Distilled Spirits

Of all products served in a bar, distilled spirits are the most stable. They are not perishable and require minimum care in storage. Their shelf life, unopened, is almost indefinite. They should be stored in an area with a stable temperature and out of direct sunlight. Distilled spirits do not improve in quality once they are placed in the bottle and sealed with a plastic screw top.

ISSUING

The transfer of products from storage to production and serving areas is called issuing. The goal of issuing is to make sure the right products are delivered to the correct areas. In operations with more than one outlet it is important to track the goods. An accurate record of which goods go to which outlet is imperative to determine costs and profits for each area. With alcoholic beverages issuing is important in tracking and controlling inventory.

Issuing can be informal, with storerooms left open for employees to retrieve products as needed. In formal issuing, requisitions are filled out by the areas needing products, the requisition is presented in the storeroom where the goods are compiled and delivered to the area requesting them. Informal issuing is generally the method used in kitchens where there is only one outlet. Food service operations with more than one outlet fed from one storeroom; for example a hotel with a banquet department and one or two restaurants use the formal system so they can track the flow of goods. More beverage operations use the formal system rather than the informal system regardless of whether there is one or more than one beverage outlet. The use of formal issuing is considered to reduce theft.

CHAPTER SUMMARY

The functions of purchasing, receiving, storing, and issuing are often overlooked in the running of a beverage operation. They are all interrelated and key to the successful running of the business. Purchasing is the function of obtaining goods for the operation to sale. The goals of purchasing is to acquire the *proper product* and the *best price* in the *needed quantity* and the *quality desired*. All four are crucial to the success and profitability of the operation.

State and federal laws make the purchasing of alcoholic beverages different from the purchase of other items used in a food and beverage operation. Most states grant exclusive territories to product suppliers eliminating the ability to compare prices. Credit terms, delivery, prices, and markups are all items that may be regulated by various forms of governments and can make the purchasing of alcohol more difficult.

Once the goods are purchased they are stored until they are needed in the production or service areas. The two keys to storage are maintaining product quality and securing the produce to minimize theft. Different beverage products have different requirements when it comes to storage. Beverage managers need to understand the needs of the various products to effectively manage a bar. Alcoholic beverages are probably the most secured items in a food and beverage operation. Their high cost and desirability forces beverage operations to limit access and store the products under lock and key.

Issuing is the transfer of the products from storage to the areas they are needed. Issuing is normally closely controlled to monitor the flow of alcoholic beverages. Beverage operations use requisitions to "order" goods from the storeroom. The requisitions let the storeroom know what is needed and also generate a paper trail of the flow of goods for easier tracing.

KEY TERMS

Purchasing	License State	Receiving
Supplier	Par Stock System	COD
Vendor	Par	Storing
Distributor	Reorder Point	FIFO
Buying	Ordering	Issuing
Control State	Mixed or Broken Cases	

CHAPTER QUESTIONS

1. How does brand recognition of liquor products affect the job of the beverage purchaser?
2. How does purchasing differ from buying? Why would an operation choose one over the other?
3. What differences are there in purchasing alcohol in a control state compared to a license state?
4. How do legal regulations make purchasing alcohol easier? How do they make it harder?
5. What is the goal of purchasing?
6. What are the two major concerns of storing?
7. What is the difference between formal and informal issuing?

SUGGESTED READINGS

1. Lipinski, R.A, and K.A. Lipinski. *Professional Guide to Alcoholic Beverages.* New York; Van Nostrand Reinhold, 1989.
2. Stefanelli, J. *Purchasing Selection and Procurement for the Hospitality Industry,* 3rd ed. New York; Wiley & Sons, 1992.

chapter fifteen

CONTROLLING INTERNAL THEFT

chapter outline

chapter objectives

Upon completion of this chapter the student will be able to:

- Describe the problem with internal theft in beverage operations.
- Analyze the methods for tighter control possible for bars.
- Critique the lack of controls in bars and how they contribute to theft.

- Judge the 80/20 rule of inventory control and its role in theft control.
- Explain the flow of product through the operation and how to control theft at each point.
- State the three step process to control theft.

INTRODUCTION

Internal theft, of theft by employees, is a widespread but not often discussed problem plaguing food and beverage operations. The National Restaurant Association's Education Foundation estimates about $9 billion a year is stolen by restaurant employees, and as many as one out of every two steal. The U.S. Chamber of Commerce reports that 30 per cent of American business failures are due to employee theft.

Internal theft can take two forms; employees stealing from the operation they work at and employees stealing from guests. Often times customers are the beneficiary of employee theft. Bartenders and servers can use the bar to "go into business" for themselves. For example, a bartender pouring the guest a drink with twice the amount of alcohol, or a double, charging them for a single drink and expecting to be compensated for the "favor" with a larger tip. The general lack of tight controls over inventory allows bartenders to give away alcohol with out much fear of getting caught.

The best opportunity the bartender has of defrauding the guest, greater than in most any other business, is an employee-customer transaction. With each drink the customer consumes his/her observation skills and general awareness is diminished, allowing the bartender greater opportunity to steal from or defraud the guest. A slick bartender can just as easily underpour a guest as overpour them. The bartender will be more likely to purposely underpour the amount of alcohol in the drink, to make up for some of the alcohol they overpoured, on the customers' third or fourth rather than second or third drink.

CUSTOMER PERSPECTIVE ON INTERNAL THEFT

Customers generally go to a bar for a cocktail or beer, to meet some people, and have a good time. Most customers are pleased when a bartender pours them a free drink, or overpours the alcohol in their drink. Some guests may figure the bar "owes" them that for their repeat business. Many guests do not perceive the bartender is actually stealing from the bar. Bartenders often feel they have to give alcohol away to attract and maintain a steady clientele for the bar. Bartenders giving free drinks or pouring generous portions is such common practice in bars that most customers do not think about it as something wrong.

THE PROBLEM WITH INTERNAL THEFT

Much theft goes on because the owners and operators are not aware that it is going on, or do not realize the scope of it. Inventory control in a bar is tougher in most instances than in other types of operation. Loose inventory controls opens the opportunity for theft. For inventory control to be effective the manager must know precisely how much inventory there is on hand at the beginning and the end of the shift, to determine how much is used. An accurate determination of what is sold is then compared with how much has been used.

For Tight Inventory Control the Manager Needs:

1. An accurate measure of how much of each product is available to BEGIN the shift.
2. An accurate measure of how much of each product is available at END of the shift.
3. An accurate count of how much of each product was sold during the shift.

It is often difficult to determine these factors from behind the bar. First, without the use of dispensing technology, it is hard to determine accurately how much liquor is in the bottle at the beginning of the shift; it is equally as difficult to determine how much is left in the bottle at the end of the shift. So management does not have an accurate idea of how much alcohol was used during the shift. Unless the operation is using an advanced **POS,** or point-of-

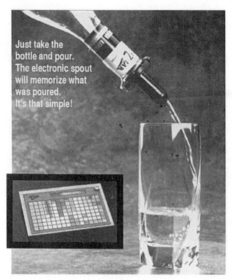

Just take the bottle and pour. The electronic spout will memorize what was poured. It's that simple!

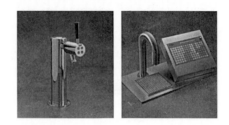

Examples of alcoholic beverage dispensers.

sale terminal, they do not know accurately what they sold. Many operations still use a cash register, on which the bartender simply types in the classification of drink; well, call, premium, domestic beer, etc. Often times, liquors are sold in varying size portions, such as 1.0 oz. or 1.5 oz. Some bars use one size portion for happy hour drinks and another for other drinks. Some drink recipes call for full shots or jiggers of drinks, while others call for fractions of jiggers, making it almost impossible to accurately determine how much of each product was sold.

In Most Bars:

1. It is hard to determine accurately how much of each product is available to BEGIN the shift.
2. It is hard to determine accurately how much of each is available at the END of the shift.
3. It is hard to determine accurately how much of each was sold.

THEFT IN A BAR

Theft can occur in several ways in a beverage operation. Guests can steal both covertly and overtly. Employees can steal cash and inventory from the bar, as well as defrauding the customers and stealing cash from them. This chapter will concentrate on internal theft or theft by employees because it is believed to be the most significant theft in a beverage operation. The chapter will examine two key operations of a bar that can involve theft, the flow of inventory from the supplier to storage in the location, and bar setup and bartender and server transactions with guests. Theft is not limited to these areas, but this is where most theft is thought to occur.

When employees steal they generally do it frequently in small increments. Employees realize that it is unlikely they will be able to "get away" with the theft of a case of liquor or $200–$300 at one time. Instead they take a little at a time and wait to see if it is discovered. If it is not discovered they try to take a little more, again waiting to see if it is noticed. If it is not they will continue to steal until they take the amount they feel they need or deserve. Other employees may catch on that one of their colleagues is stealing. They too will wait to see if management mentions or questions employees about the theft; if not, they will steal too. Theft, gone unchecked, will grow like a cancer in an operation. Once discovered by management the reaction is generally to fire the entire shift rather then try to sort out the guilty from the innocent.

80/20 Rule of Inventory Control

It is unrealistic to try to control all of the inventory in any bar, without exception. Controls must be instituted that limit theft of both cash and inventory without overly interfering with the flow of business. It is impractical to think you can completely eliminate theft at a bar. There are too many things going on that are out of the control of management, too many opportunities for theft to happen. The goal of the control system is to place road blocks in the employees otherwise clear path to theft. So if they are going to steal the operation's money they are going to have to work extra hard at it.

 The general rule is that approximately 20 per cent of the items in inventory make up 80 per cent of the monetary value of total inventory.

The inventory in a bar is made up of both expensive and not so expensive items. The expensive items are mostly the liquor items the bar stocks. The less expensive items are napkins, stir sticks, soft drinks, and mixers for drinks, etc. The general rule is that approximately 20 percent of the items in inventory make up 80 percent of the monetary value of total inventory. So even though you would prefer your employees would not steal from the business you are not going to place the same level of control on a $2.64 box of napkins that you are on a $20 bottle of Jack Daniel's Whisky. For example, liquor products should be locked up in an area for which only managers have the key, while napkins and other items can be left where personnel other than managers can restock them. Your emphasis should be on the items with the highest value.

Flow of Product Through the Operation

It is important to examine the areas of the operation that the products flow through. Remember the strength of the control system is only as strong as the weakest link. By limiting access to stored alcoholic beverages to management there is both a reduced opportunity for theft and less people to question if a loss of inventory is discovered.

Purchasing. There are factors in the purchasing of alcoholic beverages that are both similar to and different from the purchasing of other items in a food operation. The factor that most affects the control system of the bar is the amount purchased. Care must be taken by management not to order too much or too little. What further complicates the matter is the fact that most suppliers offer discounts for volume purchases; the more you order the lower the price per bottle. A storage room that is over stocked is harder to monitor and control. Care must be taken not to purchase too much and open the door for easier opportunities for theft.

Receiving. Receiving is the function whereby the ownership of the products shifts from the vendor or supplier to the purchaser or beverage operation. This is where the control of inventory begins.
Some keys to receiving are:

1. All receiving should be done by a person in management. Because of the possibilities of covering up previous theft, bartenders should not be allowed to check in orders.
2. Care must be taken to make sure all items that are listed on the invoice are received. If not the operation will be charged for goods they will not have available for sale.
3. Goods should not be allowed to remain in the receiving area. They should be put away immediately.

Storage.　Since it is not feasible or practical to purchase and receive items on a daily basis, inventory must be stored between the time it is received and served to the guest. Products are stored in several places as they await service to guests; they are generally placed in the main storeroom, then moved to the bar for service as needed. It is imperative that in each area the products are available for employees to serve to guests as well as secured from theft.

Main Storage.　Products generally are placed in main storage after being received. The main storage for alcoholic beverages should have many of the same characteristics as food storage areas; well lit, well ventilated, sturdy storage racks, clean, shelves labeled, etc. The storage area should be locked, with only management possessing the keys.

Some operations cannot justify the expense of separate refrigeration for bar storage, so they are forced to store beer and some wine in a walk-in refrigerator shared with the kitchen. Although this is not recommended, as some of the aromas from the food could cause "off" flavors in the beverages or vice versa, often it cannot be avoided. If refrigerated space must be shared, it is imperative that the alcoholic beverages are placed in an area that can be locked, limiting access to the proper personnel.

Many operations use a *perpetual inventory* for their supply of alcoholic beverages. Perpetual inventory involves the monitoring of each item in inventory by a written record. A separate sheet for each inventory item is maintained in the storeroom and every time any of the product is received or issued it is recorded. This time-consuming process allows for better tracing of the product and increased control.

Behind-the-Bar Storage.　Storage behind the bar must serve several purposes; to have the products accessible to the employees that need them to serve guests, to limit access to those that do not serve guests, and to secure the items when the bar is closed. Some products can be left out at room temperature, while others are best served chilled or cold. The behind-the-bar area is equipped for both options. The coolers behind the bar make the product accessible for the bartender to serve and can generally be locked at night to secure the goods. The liquor items on the backbar serve both as a display and a place of storage. Some bars have an elaborate backbar display making it hard to secure.

Beer can be served from a keg with either the kegs stored behind the bar or in a remote refrigerated area. There needs to be method to shut off the beer at closing time to eliminate the possibility of employees "tapping" the keg after hours.

Please note: The following section is adapted from *Preventing Internal Theft: A Bar Owner's Guide,* by Robert Plotkin, P.S.D. Publishing Company, Tucson, Az.

CONTROLLING INTERNAL THEFT BEHIND THE BAR

To attempt to control theft behind the bar, management must use a three step process. (Remember, as mentioned earlier we can only try to control, *not eliminate,* theft.) First managers must determine why employees steal, second they must examine how they actually steal, and third and finally they must develop policies and procedures to control the theft. The three steps are like the legs of three-legged stool. For the stool to function properly, or for the control of theft to be effective, it depends on all three legs or steps. Any two steps or legs are more effective than just one, but only if all three steps are followed or three legs used will it be most effective.

Internal theft can affect two things. First, it can affect the liquor cost of the bar. The bartender is giving something away that is not being properly charged for, causing the pour cost of the operation to rise. Depending on how accurately the operation keeps its books, these types of theft may be detected. Second, it can defraud the customer. The money staff are stealing comes from the customer rather than from the bar. Defrauding the customer is generally made easier as the customer drinks more. The affect of alcohol on the guest enables the bartender to take advantage of them. Some bartenders see no problem with this type of theft. Maybe they feel the guest will not leave them a tip, so they take it upon themselves to make sure they get a tip. The problem is that if customers feel they are being defrauded at a bar or taken advantage of, they will probably switch bars possibly costing management a good customer.

Three Steps to Controlling Internal Theft

1. Determine why employees steal/what they do before they steal
2. Examine the methods they use to steal
3. Develop policies and procedures to limit theft

Determining Why Employees Steal/ What They Do Before They Steal

The key to controlling theft is understanding the factors and motivations that lead up to the illegal deed. The assumption managers must make is that most employees are good people and are driven to theft by some factor they may or may not be aware of. Most people must go through a sort of internal rationalization before they steal. Of course, there are those who have no conscience and steal at the drop of a hat, but most people must rationalize the

Liquor bottles are preset as in large banquets, management should carefully monitor tables.

theft as something other than theft. Now people being different, they are also different in the level of rationalization it takes before they steal. The first decision they must make is whether or not the money they are about to take is worth the possibility of losing their job. The chance of getting caught may be sufficient enough to deter them.

Once they have determined the theft is worthwhile, they rationalize the theft as something other than theft.

The Three Most Common Rationalizations

1. Resentment
2. Larceny and greed
3. Financial need

Resentment. Of the three rationalizations, resentment, is the most dangerous and potentially most damaging. It can smolder and fester for a long time with an employee without management even being aware it exists. Employees can resent their employers for several reasons. They may feel they are not being given the best shifts or stations, they may have asked for a day off they were not given, and so on. Whatever the reason they believe that the manager owes them for a perceived slight in the past. They use that to justify stealing.

Larceny and Greed.   Some people steal simply for the thrill of stealing. They enjoy living on the edge outside of the law. While others steal simply for the money, they probably do not need the money. It may be that other employees are stealing, so they feel they need their fair share.

Financial Need.   Many bartenders and servers have trouble budgeting. They leave work with a pocket full of cash tips, go out with friends, and spend most of it. Then as the end of the month comes around and bills are due, they realize their paycheck will not cover their financial obligations and must steal to cover their inability to save their tips. The fear of financial problems overrides their judgment that stealing is illegal.

Examining How They Steal

No program to control theft can be effective without looking at how employees steal both cash and inventory, as well as defraud customers. We will examine how bartenders, servers, and managers can and do steal. The list of methods and techniques given below is by no means exhaustive. It is meant as a sample of some used. Knowledge of the techniques used can benefit management and help them detect theft.

Methods and Techniques

Bartenders.   Bartenders have the greatest opportunity to both steal from the operation and defraud the customer. They handle all phases of the customer-service transaction and have ready access to cash and product.

Misuse of the Cash Register.   Whether stealing from guests or from the bar the bartender needs somewhere to store ill-gotten funds. Most guests would be suspicious, as would other employees and managers if the bartender put money in his/her pocket. So this leaves putting stolen money in the cash register or the tip jar to be retrieved later. If they operate the cash register properly by ringing in the drink they do not get to keep the money. So they devise ways to appear as if they are using the cash register properly when they are not.

Leaving the drawer open between transactions makes it easy to slip in or take money that is not recorded. Taking the money from the guest and hitting the NO SALE key is another way. This is especially easy in operations that have pool tables or other amusements that need change so the bartender hits the NO SALE key many times during the shift. These practices will adversely effect the operation's liquor cost.

Short Changing.   Once the affect of the alcohol has reached the guest they can be an easy target for the unscrupulous bartender. One of the sim-

Practices such as leaving the drawer open between transactions, make it easy for bartenders to deposit money from unrecorded sales.

plest ways for the bartender to increase his/her tip is by short changing. Most guests do not take the time to count their change, and if they do and realize they have been short changed this can be easily shrugged off by the bartender. This does not adversely affect the liquor cost of the bar, although it does defraud the guest and, if they suspect they have been cheated, they may choose another establishment to patronize.

Overcharging. When a guest orders a beverage in a bar they are at the mercy of the bartender in several ways. Most beverage operations do not post the selling price of drinks the way fast food restaurants do behind the cashiers, or a retail operation does with price tags. When a customer or guest orders a drink, in most instances the bartender can charge whatever he or she wants. Then they may enter the correct amount in the cash register and keep the remainder as a tip. For example, a guest sits at the bar and orders a draft beer, the bartender pours the beer and hands it to the guest. The bartender tells the guest the regular price of the drink, rings in the happy hour price, and keeps the difference. The customer is defrauded without any effect on the cost percentage of the bar.

Substituting a Well Brand for a Call Brand. Only a small percentage of the guests of a bar can actually see the bartender pour their drinks. Many guests that order call-brand spirits have difficulties telling the difference between a drink made with a call brand from one made with a well brand. This is made even more difficult with the addition of mixers and ice to the drink. These factors combined open the door of opportunity for a bartender to defraud his/her guests through substitution. For example, the guest orders a Beefeaters Gin and Tonic, the bartender pours him a well brand and tonic, charges for the premium brand of gin, rings the price of the well drink into the cash register and pockets the difference. The customer is defrauded, paying for quality he/she did not get, but the bar's liquor cost is unaffected.

Abuse of Soft Drinks and Fruit Juices. Managers generally have their hands full controlling the alcohol behind the bar. They do not have the opportunity to monitor the amount of soft drinks and juices used. Bartenders, aware of this fact, will use money from the sale of soft drinks and juices to either keep for themselves or to cover for the theft of some other item behind the bar. This method of theft does not defraud the guest.

Abuse of Complimentary Drinks. Some bars allow bartenders to give away free drinks to regular customers as a way to encourage them to return. Some bartenders will provide a drink to a guest, record it as a complimentary drink, and keep the cash for themselves. This method of theft does not defraud the guest or affect the liquor cost of the bar.

Abuse of Draft Beer. It is very difficult to accurately identify the amount of draft beer in a keg. So management does not know how much beer is in the keg before the shift begins or at the end of the shift. It is thus difficult to detect theft. This coupled with the amount of foam coming from the keg, which varies from one keg to another, makes draft beer one of the most difficult things to control. Bartenders can sell a pitcher of beer and keep the proceeds or ring it into the machine as a liquor sale to compensate for previous theft. The bar's liquor cost is affected adversely.

Fraudulent Use of Promotional Materials. If the beverage operation passes out coupons for free or discounted drinks or food, the bartender can use them fraudulently. The bartender can collect coupons on his own to keep with him/her behind the bar then when a guest orders and pays for a drink, the bartender exchanges the coupon he/she has collected for the cash equivalent in the cash drawer.

Cocktail Servers. Cocktail servers have many ways to both steal from the operation and defraud guests. In some ways they have more opportunity because they work throughout the operation rather than in a fixed area like the bartender. The methods of theft for the cocktail server differ depending on whether they are working alone or with the bartender. Although it can be lucrative working alone, cocktail servers have more ways to steal when working in cooperation with the bartender.

Cocktail Server Working Alone (Without the Bartender's Assistance). *Techniques that work similarly to the way the bartender steals:*

Short Changing
Overcharging
Substitution
Fraudulent Use of Promotional Materials

Techniques that are unique *to cocktail servers:*

Spillage. A cocktail server can pick up a drink at the bar and serve it, then when returning to the bar pick up an empty glass claiming they have spilled the drink. The bartender makes the server another drink, which the server sells and collects and keeps the cash.

Destroyed or Missing Drink Tickets. In many operations the bartender simply places a red line or mark on a ticket to indicate it has been used and the transaction is not rung into the machine until later. The server can present the check to the guest and then conveniently lose or destroy the ticket, keeping the proceeds.

Cocktail Server Working With the Assistance of the Bartender. Cocktail servers opportunities to steal increase when they work together with the bartender. The server can use all the methods described above, plus:

Reuse of Drink Tickets. The team of bartender and server can work together to repeatedly resubmit drink tickets without ringing up or recording the sales. The recycled drink tickets can be presented to the unsuspecting guest for payment and then reused, allowing the server to pocket the proceeds.

Overpouring. The server can signal to the bartender when they need a "special drink" for a special guest. The bartenders overpours the drink, the guest leaves a generous tip, and the bartender and server split the bounty.

Unrecorded Sales. The opportunity for unrecorded sales grows dramatically with a team working together. The cocktail server can obtain a round of "unrecorded" drinks from the bartender, serve them to her table of favorite customers and collect the extra tips for the round "on the house."

Managers. Theft in a bar is not limited to bartenders and servers. Although it is less likely, managers can steal both cash and inventory from the operation. A bartender or server caught stealing and dismissed can neglect to include their past employer in their job application, covering up the period between jobs in a number of plausible ways. A manager would generally have more difficulty covering up gaps between jobs.

Bartender and server theft generally goes on in the bar in front of guest or other employees, while managers have access to cash and inventory in storerooms and offices out of sight of watching eyes. Managers also are generally the last people to handle cash, allowing them further opportunities for theft.

Theft of Cash. Managers reconcile employees' cash banks at the end of the night. They can pocket any overages in the banks, or take money from the banks and report it as a shortage by the employee. Managers have the opportunity to void out transactions, and collect and keep the cash.

Abuse or Fraudulent Use of Inventory. Managers have keys to all inventory items in the operation. They have the opportunity to misuse inventory for their personal gain. Often times bars may sell food and bottled beer from a happy hour table for cash. Since the transactions are not ran through the POS until the end of the shift, this opens the door for theft. The manager can purchase beer from the bar for his "personal" use and put it out to sale at the happy hour table and pocket the cash. Liquor wholesalers often give samples of products to the bar to see if they will adopt it as a regular. Since the product is not officially in inventory an unscrupulous manager has the potential to sell the product and keep the cash.

POLICIES AND PROCEDURES TO HELP PREVENT THEFT

We have examined why employees steal, then we looked at how they steal; based on both of these we can now look at preventative measures for controlling theft. Remember, we decided that it is impossible to completely eliminate theft; our goal should be to make it more difficult by placing road blocks between the employee and the theft.

Care must be taken to look at policies and procedures to determine if they are too restrictive. The goal of any beverage operation is to serve guests in a timely manner. No guest will be willing to wait for an unrealistic amount of time while the bartender goes through a series of procedures designed to control theft. An example of a poor procedure would be to have all liquor behind the bar locked up between transactions to eliminate theft. Once an order is placed a manager is called to unlock the supplies and allow the bartender to fill the order. As effective as this procedure may be in reducing theft, it would be too time consuming, causing guests to wait longer then they should to get their beverage. The goal of theft reduction must be balanced with the service and expectations of guests.

Policies and procedures are only good if they are enforced. It is not sufficient to institute them without enforcement. The procedures must be enforced consistently for all employees, management included. The use of such policies and procedures should allow people to watch or "spot" employees to see if they are stealing. With knowledge of the policies and procedures, a person, either management or someone outside the company, can observe to see if theft is occurring. The assumption is that if the policy is not being followed then theft is occurring.

How should management deal with an employee who protests about the new policies and procedures, complaining they are restrictive, interfering with their job serving the customer, or simply feeling bad because they are not trusted? These policies, or ones similar, are designed to limit or reduce theft; if an employee complains it is possibly because it is interfering with his/her theft, and you have just made difficult for them what was once easy. Most likely, once the theft control procedures are instituted, and employees realize they are going to be enforced, employees who are stealing will resign and go work down the street where they can steal without having to get around the policies. The following is a partial list of policies and procedures intended to help control theft.

Examples of Some Policies and Procedures

General Procedures

Bartenders and Servers Not Allowed to Check-Out Their Cash at the End of the Shift. The most common place for bartenders to hide stolen funds is in the cash register. Then when counting the drawer at the end of the shift they just take the money in the drawer in excess of what the register tape says should be there. The inability of the bartender to count his/her drawer at the end of the night, so that they can retrieve their ill-gotten funds, will cause them to find somewhere else to hide them. The time spent by the manager counting the drawers at the end of the night should not be prohibitive. Another option would be to have the bartenders count and record their drawer without the register tape to compare it to. This would also reduce the possibility of them placing stolen money in the drawer.

Location of the Tip Jar. Would you think it peculiar if the bartender placed the money you just gave him/her for a drink in their pocket? If you reduce the attractiveness of placing the stolen money in the cash register using the above policy, the next logical place to place the money without raising too much suspicion would be the tip jar. The key is to place the tip jar far enough from the cash register so that the bartender has to make a conscious effort to place money in it. With the tip jar right next to the cash register the bartender can easily divert money from the register to the tip jar.

Not Allowing Employees to Drink at the Bar When They Are Off Duty. Employees should not drink at the bar of the operation where they work. There is too much temptation for the bartender to give away drinks to their friends. The bartender knows the person, so they can work out an arrangement where the customer gets free drinks in exchange for a large gratuity or some other favor. There also will be a tendency for the bartender to want to socialize with fellow employees at the expense of the other guests. The amount of business the bar will lose will be more than outweighed by the increased control.

Bartenders Not Allowed to Participate in the Physical Inventory Process. The bartender should inventory the products behind the bar but not in the storeroom. Allowing the bartender to have access to alcoholic beverages in the storeroom could provide the opportunity to cover up prior theft. Physical inventory of the storage area should be left to management.

Bartenders Must Obtain Permission to Give a Complimentary Drink Prior to Serving It. By requiring bartenders to get permission *prior* to giving a complimentary drink, *rather than after*, managers invalidate the bartender's excuse, when caught giving a drink away to a friend, that they were going to get permission. It should prevent the bartender from giving away drinks without permission.

Cash Register Control Procedures. The cash register or POS is key to the cost control of the operation. Any time the bartender forgets or intentionally neglects to ring the drink in the register there is no record of the transaction and bartender keeps the money. Procedures must be designed to encourage the recording of the transaction.

Ring in the Drink Prior to Service. If the bartender is required to ring the drink in the register prior to, rather than after, serving the drink, this should result in more drink transactions registered in the machine. The bartender may get busy with another order after serving the drink and either intentionally or unintentionally neglect to ring the drink in the register.

Employees Must Verify the Amount in Bank or Cash Drawer Prior to Shift. This policy will help eliminate the excuse later that the drawer was over or under when they received it. This would prevent the bartender or server from passing the blame to someone else. If employees are going to be held accountable for their cash they should have to count it prior to any transactions.

Cash Drawer Closed Between Transactions. If the drawer is closed between transactions the bartender must ring something into the machine to get it to open. By leaving the drawer open they can deposit money into it without looking suspicious and without any record of the transaction.

Cash/Price Control Procedures

Collect from One Customer at a Time. A common ploy of bartenders is to collect from three separate customers at the bar at once before entering the transactions in the cash register. When he/she goes to the register they then ring in two of the three transactions and keep the money from the third for their own use. By requiring them to collect from only one guest at a time, then ring it in prior to collecting from the next guest, more drinks will be recorded in the register.

Employees Required to State Drink Price to Guests and Amount Tendered with Change Given. Since bars generally do not post drink prices, employees stating prices will let customers know what they are getting charged and ensure that bartenders are charging the same amount to each guest. Talking through the cash transaction will help prevent the bartender from shortchanging the guest.

Theft by employees from the operation and its customers can be lucrative. Unfortunately most of it goes on undetected so it is unchecked. Employees know what is controlled and what is not and what they can get away with. Managers must work to stay one step ahead of them.

Other Factors to Consider in Reducing Theft

Policies and procedures for bartenders and servers can be effective to reduce theft, but there are other factors that beverage operators should consider to fortify the theft control policies listed earlier.

The Hiring Process.   The key to a reduced theft in the work place is the employee. Care must be taken to hire the best employees. Much too often operations hire employees without adequately checking their references. Although the checking of references does not prevent all problems it helps reduce them. If a beverage operation hires an employee without checking with a prior employer they are opening the door to problems. This allows dishonest employees who are caught at one property to easily set up shop at another operation.

Managers should always try to check the claims made on employees' applications. Unfortunately, fear of law suits has reduced the questions managers can ask former managers of an employee. Managers *can* check dates of employment and work positions to see if the employee is telling the truth. The key question they can ask is whether or not the employer would rehire the employee.

Monitoring Employee Productivity.   Managers can place many "roadblocks" in the way of employee theft. Unfortunately it is difficult eliminate all theft. One way to determine if employees are stealing or diverting money from the business for their personal gain is to monitor employee productivity. By tracking the registered sales per hour of employees, management can determine some key information. If an employee is producing less per hour than coworkers on the same shift they are either keeping some of the money or they are slower then they should be. Either way lower than average sales should trigger a flag that this employee needs to be watched more closely. Employees who sell more than others can be rewarded by raises or bonuses.

POSSIBLE OUTSIDE CLASS ASSIGNMENT

Bar Observation Assignment

Assignment: Visit a bar, *for purely educational purposes,* and observe the actions of the bartender[s], server[s] and the operations and set up behind the bar.

Approach your observation of the bar from the standpoint that you are the new manager hired to solve a perceived internal theft problem. Look at both actual problems and potential problems.

1. Briefly describe the bar; the location, the concept, and the target market.
2. Name THREE potential problems that you detect from observing the set up of the bar. Compare what you observe with the material and potential problems that were discussed in class [Be specific]. What are the potential losses

and ways to possibly overcome each of the problems? Suggest at least THREE ways the set up of the bar might be changed to reduce internal theft.

3. Watch the following transactions:

   A Bartender and a few customers

   B Bartender and a couple of servers

   Describe in detail each of the transactions, name two potential problems with each of the observed interactions. For each of the problems that you spotted describe if you think it impacted the bar by either raising the liquor cost or defrauding the customer? Explain. If the bartender acted properly during the transactions explain what he/she did. What can be done to minimize the risk to the bar from each of the problems that you observed?

4. What is your overall reaction to the control systems in the bar? Positive or Negative? Be specific! Explain two of the biggest problems that you spotted. What are two of the strongest parts of the control system that you spotted?

5. Name at least three policies that you would institute in the bar to control some of the problems that you spotted. Explain why you think each policy will work.

SUMMARY

The theft of both goods and money by employees is a problem that plagues both large and small businesses. The money stolen comes directly from the bottom line or profit of the operation. Much of the theft goes on because management does not realize it exists as a result of lack of proper controls. The nature of many aspects of the bar business makes it easier for its employees to steal than employees of other types of businesses. For this reason it is impossible to totally eliminate theft and still operate the business smoothly. Employees must have access to goods to sell to guests. The best a system can hope to do is limit access to valuable inventory items and implement policies and procedures to place roadblocks in the path of the thief. For policies and procedures to be effective they must be enforced.

To attempt to control theft one must first trace the flow of goods through the operation. Care must be taken to look at the areas where goods are stored and to limit access to unauthorized staff. By limiting access there are less people to suspect if a problem arises.

Theft from behind the bar by both servers and bartenders is a particular problem. Employees can steal from both the operation and the guest. The control of all aspects of the transaction by the bartender opens the door of opportunity for them. This coupled with the effect alcohol has on the guest further works in favor of the thief. Bartenders can work alone or with the cocktail server. The combination of the two employees opens the range of theft to all of the customers of the operation.

The three step process discussed in the chapter; Understand Why They Steal, Examine How They Steal, Design Policies and Procedures to Help Control the Theft, will help managers limit theft from their bars by gaining a better understanding behind the process. The three steps are similar to the three legs of a stool, all must be sound for the stool to stand.

KEY TERMS

Internal Theft	Abuse of	Purchasing
80/20 Rule of	Complimentary	Storage
Inventory Control	Drinks	Resentment
Receiving	Fraudulent Use of	Greed
Perpetual Inventory	Promotional Materials	Overcharging
Larceny	Destroyed or Missing	Abuse of Soft Drinks and
Short Changing	Drink Tickets	Fruit Juices
Substitution	Reuse of Drink Tickets	Abuse of Draft Beer
	POS	Spillage
		Unrecorded Sales

CHAPTER QUESTIONS

1. What are the two forms of internal theft? How can guests become a beneficiary of the theft?
2. How is it easier for bar employees to steal from guests than employees of other types of businesses?
3. Why is it unreasonable to expect 100 percent control of theft at a bar?
4. Name two things that must be done for tighter inventory control.
5. Explain the 80/20 rule of inventory control.
6. What are the areas the product goes through in its flow through the beverage operation?
7. What are the two things most employees do before they steal?
8. Why is resentment a dangerous and potentially most damaging form of rationalization?
9. Choose four of the types of thefts listed in the chapter and explain how one or more of the policies and procedures would help control it.
10. What would be the advantage of a bartender and server working together to steal? What is the disadvantage?

SUGGESTED READINGS

1. Plotkin, R. *Preventing Internal Theft: A Bar Owner's Guide.* Tucson, AZ: P.S.D. Publishing Company, 1988.
2. Sympson, R. "To Catch a Thief." *Restaurant Business* 1 Sept. 1995: 72–82.

chapter sixteen

A LOOK AT TOMORROW'S BEVERAGE WORLD
From Industry Leaders' Perspective

chapter outline

chapter objectives

Upon completion of this chapter you will be able to:

- Describe the position of the beverage industry for the new century.
- Discuss industry and education leaders comments on the beverage world immediate future.
- Analyze and better understand the following viewpoints: The wholesaler, ospitality operators, winemaker's and the educational world.

- Discuss industry projection for the next decade.
- Discuss hints and suggestions provided to apprentices, novices and future beverage professionals.

BEVERAGE OPERATIONS FOR THE NEW CENTURY

It is difficult to think of an industry that evolves more than hospitality, and particularly its beverage sector. Forecasting or predicting future trends in the beverage world has always been a tough and challenging task. However, based on the overall picture of the past two decades, predicting beverage trends for the next five to seven years should not require exceptional foresight. Over the past twenty five years the beverage industry has experienced a healthy growth on a consistent basis. There are no immediate signs that this growth is going to decrease or come to a halt. Hotel operators from various parts of the country report that beverage revenue is steadily increasing in such a manner that many claim beverage revenue to be approximately 5 per cent of total hotel revenue.

If one looks at the distinct hotel divisions, the rooms division is generally known to show profits which range from 25 to 40 percent of total room sales. In the same hotel, a competently run food department may show a departmental profit within the range of 15 to 20 percent of total food sales. In comparison, a well run beverage department could easily produce a profit ranging from 50 to 60 percent of total beverage sales!

According to *Restaurant U.S.A.*, the official magazine of the National Restaurant Association, even with the advent of the new century the overall beverage sales volume as compared to that of food is still in the 80/20 bracket (80% for food, 20% for beverage). However, many hotel executives report that their average is gradually approaching the 75/25 level and that beverage sales are steadily gaining ground when compared to food.

In 1999, the National Restaurant Association reported total sales for bars and taverns to be in the range of 12 billion dollars. For the year 2005, sales for bars and taverns are expected to pass the threshold of 15 billion dollars! In states such as New Jersey and Nevada where casino gaming is fully permitted, hotel operators are generally unanimous in reporting that in terms of profitability the beverage sector of the operation is second only to gaming.

PROJECTIONS FOR THE IMMEDIATE FUTURE

For this specific purpose, the authors, rather than pose as prophets or consult the crystal ball, submitted a set of questions to individuals that are recognized as leaders in their field. Who, better than the experts, can competently discuss what appears to be in store for the beverage world over the next five to seven years? Even the experts may not foresee the immediate future with 100 percent degree of accuracy but they certainly are the ones with the potential of coming the closest to reality. Our experts for this sections are going to present a viewpoint according their own area of expertise and they are:

Mr. Larry Ruvo—The Wholesaler Viewpoint

Mr. Bob Smith—The Wholesaler Viewpoint

Mr. Don Carano, and Mr. Brice Cutrer Jones—the Winemaker's Viewpoint

Mr. Tamir Shanel—The Hospitality Viewpoint

Dr. John Stefanelli—The Educational Viewpoint

THE WHOLESALER VIEWPOINT

Name and Title

Larry Ruvo—Senior Managing Director

Company and Affiliate

Southern Wine & Spirits of Nevada, subsidiary of Southern Wine & Spirits of America based in Miami, Florida.

How Would You Describe Your Company?

Southern Wine & Spirits of Nevada is one of the foremost wholesalers in North America. Innovation, creativity and avant-garde describe our aggressive management style and promotions. As an importer of wine, spirits, beer, and non-alcoholic products from throughout the world, we not only import great product, but also provide superb service.

How Will the Beverage Industry Be Affected Over the Next 5–7 Years?

Innovations in Computer Technology.   Computer technology will allow us on the spot detailed information by accounts to provide accounts with a history of their purchases and past promotions. The salespeople are thereby very well armed with information to provide their customers with the best service.

Internet.   This will become very useful for the consumer to track down great vintages and product knowledge.

The Legislative Climate, both State and Federal.   The three tiered-system is ever so important to stay intact. It's not only self-serving, but without it, the large corporations and major accounts would dominate small mom and pop operations. This is what major discount outlets have done to small retail businesses in small towns. Without a three-tiered system and state and federal control, it would be a very, very serious breach of control of the distribution system.

Mergers, Acquisitions, and Globalization.   Continued mergers, acquisitions, and globalization at the import level and wholesale level will allow for reductions in operational costs. Much of these savings will be put into new products. If you look at the typical wholesaler's warehouse today, over half of their sales are to products that were not even in the market 10–15 years ago. Consumer's tastes are changing and as they get more and more sophisticated, these large global companies will be able to meet the changing consumer's tastes.

Do You See Any Industry Changes in the Next 5–7 Years?

Consumer's Expectations.   The consumer is becoming more and more knowledgeable. As they become more informed, they are going to demand the beverage industry supply them with top quality experts. At our company we are presently associated with four master sommeliers and a master of wine. Ongoing training is needed continuously for our staff to relay to our customers the importance of "Knowledge is Power." Through wine periodicals, wine reviews, videotapes, attending trade functions, seminars and tastings, customers receive diligent follow-up on their requests.

Consumption Preferences.   As I said earlier, the marketplace is becoming more and more sophisticated. In certain parts of the country, sweetness is preferred. In colder damp parts of the country, ports are gaining tremendous sales. A big factor in the ethnic preferences is geographical. Consumption preferences will be constantly changing.

What Advice Could You Give a Student Who Is Planning to Pursue a Career in the Beverage Industry?

I will give you the advice that I have just given my daughter, who is considering a career in the beverage industry, "Knowledge is power." Upon graduation from an accredited school, I believe a masters is required, UC Davis is certainly a school to consider. A person should work in all facets of the beverage industry from the distilleries in Scotland, to the breweries and wineries located throughout the world. The knowledge you will receive by working in these would be equivalent to a Ph.D.

To become a well-informed individual, who will have a value to an importer or wholesaler, a person must not only know product, but also must know the importance of matching food and wine. The consumer trends will show in the coming years how important it is to select the right product with the proper foods. The right beverage alcohol with the right food will enhance the dining experience. In years to come, I predict there will be a serious matching of spirits with food, as be well as wine and food. It's an exciting industry, one that I've been blessed to be part of for 30+ years. Now that the next generation, my daughter, is about to start her career, I tell her as I tell novices and students this is a business that will require product information, people skills, innovation and creativity. Good luck!

Brief Profile

Larry Ruvo grew up in Nevada. He is Senior Managing Director of Southern Wine & Spirits of Nevada, North America's largest wholesale liquor, wine and beer importer and distributor. He started this company in 1969 and has glided it to its #1 position.

Larry is a member of the Young Presidents' Organization (Y.P.O.), member of the World Presidents' Organization, Bailli of the Chaine des Rotisseurs, Bluecoats organizer in Nevada (an organization to help families of firemen and police officers killed in the line of duty), Board Member of the Nevada Dance Theater, trustee for the University of Nevada Las Vegas Foundation, member of Legatus and involved with many other civic organizations as both a Board Member and Fund Raising Chairman. He is a supporter of numerous philanthropic endeavors in Nevada as well as nationally and internationally.

Larry has been honored by the United States Congress on two occasions. He was recognized as Man of the Year by MDA and was presented the Altruistic Award by the Meadows School, a school which Larry is very involved with and helped to establish. He has received Man of the Year awards from the University of Nevada Las Vegas, the Food & Beverage Directors Association and numerous other charitable organizations. In November 1998, he was knighted into the Order of Saint John Knights of Malta.

Larry is married to Camille and has three daughters: Nicole, Lauren Marie and Brianna Angelina.

Name and Title

Bob Smith, President and CEO

Company and Affiliate

Allliance Beverage Distributing Company, affiliated with Sunbelt Beverages, Glazier Family Wholesalers, Young Markets Company.

How Would You Describe Your Company?

A wholesale distributor of alcoholic beverages.

How Will the Beverage Industry Be Affected Over the Next 5–7 Years?

Innovations in Computer Technology.   Increased effectiveness in the service and information. Activity based costing will become increasingly more important especially in computing ROI.

Internet.   Orders, EFT (Electronic Fund Transfers), tasting notes, inventory, and vintage availability will be accessible via the Internet.

The Legislative Climate, both State and Federal. Barriers to trade will be broken down as long as the collection of taxes and under-age consumption are not effected.

Mergers, Acquisitions, and Globalization. Will continue at all levels—suppliers, wholesaler, retailer, and restaurateur.

Do You See Any Industry Changes in the Next 5–7 Years?

Consumer's Expectations. More information will be required as consumers continue to gain knowledge. Variety will become a bigger issue requiring new and innovated products.

Consumption Preferences. Consumers will demand higher quality products, with wines, especially reds, leading the charge.

Beverage Product Selection. Will continue to grow in diversity.

What Advice Could You Give a Student Who is Planning to Pursue a Career in the Beverage Industry?

This is still the last and the best of the glamour industries;

- You get to drink and eat well,
- Visit great places,
- It's fun and exciting,

This is the hospitality industry!!

THE WINEMAKERS' VIEWPOINT

Name and Title

Donald L. Carano, Co-owner of Ferrari-Carano Vineyards and Winery

Company and Affiliate

With my wife, Rhonda, I am co-owner of Ferrari-Carano Vineyards and Winery. Our family also owns the El Dorado Hotel/Casino in Reno, Nevada.

How Would You Describe Your Company?

Ferrari-Carano Vineyards and Winery is one of California's most prestigious wineries. It is located in Dry Creek Valley of Sonoma County—a small-to-medium sized winery, we own all our own vineyards, making fine classic varietal wines for restaurants and fine wine shops.

The El Dorado Hotel/Casino is one of Reno's oldest and best-known gaming properties. It has over 800 guest rooms, ten fine restaurants, a theater and conference facilities. We are particularly proud of our fine dining program, which is a consistent award-winner.

How Will the Beverage Industry Be Affected in the Next 5–7 Years?

Innovations in Computer Technology and the Internet. Computers will help us profile and track our customers to a much greater degree than ever before. Internet presence will be absolutely necessary for advertising and promotional purposes. Sales of wine through the Internet will continue to be a controversial issue.

The Legislative Climate, both State and Federal. Alcoholic beverage control is a very complicated legal issue as well as a very emotional one. I think we will continue to see piecemeal attempts at legal change, with far-reaching, uniform legal code reform still far down the road.

Mergers, Acquisitions, and Globalization. The wine industry has become increasingly susceptible to acquisitions and mergers as it has become a more profitable industry, due to the overall economic health of the country. Many small wineries are becoming acquired by larger ones, particularly for their vineyard property. But every day, I still see new, small wineries begin limited production, so there appears to be room for everyone, in all size categories.

Globalization—in marketing and selling of wines—has already become very important for large and publicly-owned wineries. The good part of this is that we are approaching a universal level of wine quality that is substantially higher than it has ever been before. When you have to compete with wines from every major growing region of the world, your product had better be good.

Do You See Any Industry Changes in the Next 5–7 Years?

Consumer's Expectations and Consumption Preferences. Consumers will react to the overall increase in wine quality by refusing to accept anything except very well-made wines. They will expect both value and quality, and wineries will have to work even harder to keep brand loyalty. Consumers will want the wines they drink to make a specific statement—that is, to have a distinctive mark of the place in which they were made. Wine style and quality will be more important than ever.

Beverage Product Selection. More and more Americans will realize that moderate consumption of wine with meals is pleasurable and relaxing. I think the overall percentage of Americans who drink wine will increase because of this.

Beverage Product Availability. Consumers will be so used to ordering merchandise over the Internet that they will demand the availability of alcoholic beverages as well. If this problem has not been resolved, then they will expect their retail shop to make available anything they want.

What Advice Could You Give a Student Who is Planning to Pursue a Career in the Beverage Industry?

I admit an extreme partiality to the wine segment of the beverage industry. It is a privilege to be associated with the dedication and passion of viticulturists and winemakers who work with nature every day to make an outstanding product. This rarefied farming is both a science and an art, and it is constantly fascinating. You can spend a lifetime learning about fine wine and how it is made. Whether you would be on the production or marketing side of the business, it will always completely engage your attention. If you get started in the wine business, you'll probably make it a lifetime career.

Brief Profile

A native of Reno, Nevada, Don completed an undergraduate degree at the University of San Francisco, followed by a two-year stint as an officer in the United States Army. Returning to USF, Don attended law school, graduated with honors and began his law practice in Reno. His legal career made him an expert in both corporate business and gaming law. He then used his knowledge in those arenas to create his own hotel/casino in 1973, called the El Dorado. The El Dorado has expanded from a beginning 282 rooms to its present 817 rooms, now including ten restaurants, a micro-brewery, 70,000 square feet of casino space, a 600-seat showroom, specialty retail shops and a complete convention center. Once was not enough, so Don entered a joint venture with Circus Circus Enterprises to create the Silver Legacy, northern Nevada's first mega-resort with a theme.

In addition to parallel careers as attorney, business owner and restaurateur, Don became a winery owner in 1981 when he and his wife Rhonda founded Ferrari-Carano Vineyards & Winery in Sonoma County's Dry Creek Valley. His commitment to fine wine, long-term vision and search for excellence in wine making has been the driving force behind the success of Ferrari-Carano. Don has consistently been determined to acquire only premium vineyards for estate-grown grapes, the foundation of a fine wine program. He has partnered vineyard acquisition with a tireless exploration of winemaking techniques, equipment and cooperage to elicit the best expression of grapes from the estate vineyards, a combination of missions that will assure the continuing critical acclaim accorded to Ferrari-Carano wines since its first vintage.

Name and Title

Brice Cutrer Jones, President and Founder

Company and Affiliate

Sonoma-Cutrer Vineyards

How Would You Describe Your Company?

A winery that produces estate bottled Chardonnay—exclusively.

How Will the Beverage Industry Be Affected
Over the Next 5–7 Years?

Innovations in Computer Technology. Threats to the traditional three-tier system are for the better.

The Internet. Good for consumers, and for distributors who wish to add value. Very versatile tool for trade. I predict pretty soon it will become universal.

The Legislative Climate, both State and Federal. Will become more difficult and worsening, especially tort system and labor law. I am not pessimistic but it is recommended to those who are in business to be prepared for any eventuality. I sincerely hope that federal and state laws will not become too difficult to abide by.

Consumer's Expectations. Just about everyone will demand higher levels of service. Consumer expectations are on the rise. The product has to be of superior quality and the manner in which it is presented and delivered should not be any less.

Consumption Preferences. There might be a slight change in consumer preferences. People will lean toward products that are trendy and pleasant to the taste. For the most, consumption should remain the same as it has in the past 5 to 7 years.

Beverage Product Selection. We are blessed to see beverage outlets in our country offering so much wider and readily-available selection of beverages than any other nation of the world. Americans like to chose from a variety of products. That's the best way to enrich and refine taste.

Beverage Product Availability. Will become more available through the Internet and by distributors who respond adequately to the net.

What Advice Could You Give a Student Who is Planning to Pursue a Career in the Beverage Industry?

There are countless words of advice I could give. Presently, the best one I can think of for anyone who is starting out, is to save money now, even a small amount at a time, and invest it wisely.

THE HOSPITALITY OPERATORS' VIEWPOINT

Your Name, Title and Company

Tamir Shanel, director of food and beverage, Four Seasons Hotels.

Concerning the Beverage Sector of the Hotel Operation in General, What Do You See Taking Place Over the Next 5 to 7 Years?

Hotel guests will be receptive to try exotic beverage products brought from various parts of the globe. Now is the best time to venture in these beverages as the resources to bring them in are more easily available. Nations who kept their doors closed for many years are now taking a different position. Wine will continue to increase in popularity due to health benefits and smart marketing. Wine's overall quality will benefit due to technological advances and greater winemakers' efforts. Even low-end wines will be improved ultimately.

If included in the beverage menu, hotel guests will ask for lighter, healthier drinks. People in general will be more open minded in trying new bar offerings.

Concerning Your Specific Area of Responsibility, What Do You Anticipate for the Next 5 to 7 Years?

My associates and I will continue to focus on the consistency and quality of the food and beverage products served at the Four Seasons. I will make a special effort to take advantage of technological innovations as a tool to provide even better service standards than we have presently. For example, improving areas such as reservation systems, guest name recognition, guest requests in restaurants, bar and lounges, and keeping track of dates that are significant to our guests.

What Advice Can You Give to Someone Who is Considering a Career in the Food and Beverage Sector of the Hospitality Industry?

Work as server, bartender or bus person while you study. Get familiar with foods and drinks while handling them. Keep asking questions on how they are prepared. It will give you first hand exposure to the very same environment in which you have decided to build your career.

THE EDUCATIONAL VIEWPOINT

Name

Dr. John Stefanelli

What Do You Foresee in Beverage Management Education Over the Next Five to Seven Years?

I believe there will be much more formal instruction at all levels. For example, more beverage suppliers will provide training to their clients and their clients' service staffs. I expect to see more certification programs, such as the ones currently offered by the Culinary Union in Las Vegas to its members for a nominal fee. There will be more emphasis on training that emphasizes responsible alcohol beverage service; I would not be surprised if such training will eventually become mandatory across the country.

There will be more seminars and training sessions included within the many trade shows and conventions that highlight the beverage industry. And I would expect more colleges and universities to expand into beverage education. While many colleges offer a course or two dealing with the beverage industry, currently there are only three college degree programs emphasizing the beverage industry:

> University of California at Davis (school of Enology and Viticulture) offers a degree in wine production,
>
> Sonoma State University offers a degree in wine business (i.e., the distribution and sale of wines), and
>
> UNLV offers a beverage management major (i.e., the sales and service of beverages in the hospitality industry).

What Advice Could You Give to a Student Planning to Pursue a Career in Beverage Management or Food and Beverage Management?

It is critical to determine as soon possible, a particular area of interest. There are so many options. For instance, a person studying beverage management in college could enjoy a career as a:

- bar manager,
- sommelier,
- wholesale distributor,
- liquor store retailer,
- beverage instructor/trainer,
- beverage writer/reporter,
- hotel beverage director,
- cellar master,
- operations/menu consultant,

- alcohol awareness instructor,
- night club/disco manager,
- beverage buyer.

Once a specific career path is identified, the student should seek the school and employer(s) that can assist him or her to accomplish this goal. For example, if the student wants to become a bar manager, he or she should attend a college hospitality management program that emphasizes food and beverage instruction while simultaneously working in bars to gain valuable work experience.

My guess is that the beverage specialist will be much more employable if he or she has a good background in food production and service in addition to a strong beverage background. If, for example, a student wants to become a hotel beverage director, I think it is imperative that he or she understands how the kitchens and dining rooms work and what impact they have on the beverage function. Ideally, a beverage director should understand the big picture.

Brief Profile

Dr. John Stefanelli earned his PhD at the University of Denver, his MBA at Michigan State, his Bachelors at the University of Illinois and an AAS at the College of DuPage.

He is a widely recognized author of two successful books: "Purchasing" and "The Sale and Purchase of Restaurants"; he has co-authored two more hospitality textbooks. He is presently professor and F&B department chair—W.F. Harrah College of Hotel Administration at UNLV. He has been a driving force in obtaining national recognition for the college's food and beverage department. Among the many academic endeavors and innovations, he is responsible for structuring and developing an unprecedented culinary arts management B.S. degree and a beverage management major.

GENERAL INDUSTRY PROJECTIONS

In addition to the gathering of industry leaders and experts opinions as outlined above, various other beverage professional were consulted regarding the beverage world immediate future. Some, did not limit their responses to the beverage area only, but expressed views and opinion on the immediate future of the hospitality industry in general. In summarizing, nearly everyone agreed that the following areas will be affected over the next decade:

- Labor trends are experiencing a setback. The general pool of steady and loyal workers, as we have known it in the past, is decreasing considerably. Employees quit their jobs more easily than ever before. Consequently, adequate staffing has become the most demanding function of management.

- Young people will enter the hospitality workforce at a slower rate compared to the previous decade.
- There will be a considerable increase of women and minorities in the hospitality workforce, particularly in food service and bar & beverage operations. There will be a substantial increase in female bartenders and bar managers. Increase in the number of women-bar owners/operators is also expected.
- Restaurant and bar operators will devote more effort in the creation of safer and cleaner environment for customers. The health district of various cities across the country will make available in local newspapers reports on health inspections of hotels, restaurants and bar/lounges. Fire codes and inspections will more rigidly enforced than in the past century.
- Operators will place a higher emphasis on lounge entertainment
- New business joint ventures between winemakers and distillers are projected, particularly towards the end of the new decade.
- Further expansion of micro-brewing outlets is expected to take place even in medium size rural areas.
- Collaboration with Chinese, Japanese and Korean hospitality executives will intensify.
- Non-alcoholic beverages will experience their largest growth in the areas of: bottled waters, specialty teas and fresh fruit drinks.
- Alcoholic beverages expected to top sales charts will be: Cognacs, aged Bourbons, premium Rums and Grappas, Single malt Scotch, Belgian chocolate cordials, Asian Soju and tropical style cocktails. Vodka will remain the best selling spirit with rum and Bourbon gaining ground over gin and tequila.
- Distillers will seek alternative methods of making liquor and experiment with new grains, seeds, plants and fruit. Traditional ingredients will be partially replaced with substitutes and adjuncts; for example, in the making of rum, southeastern distillers will adopt more citrus molasses as opposed to the conventional sugar cane and sugar cane molasses.
- Beverage products such as aperitifs, medicinals (drinks to aid in the digestion) and specialty-coffee-drinks will appear for the first time in typical small town restaurants and bars. The same will be with espresso-type coffees, cappuccino and latte. (Particularly in Washington State and other Northwestern states.)
- The Agave plant (Blue variety) shortage will cause Tequila price to increase and perhaps double.
- Americans thirst for quality red wines will increase tenfold, partly due to the American Medical Association endorsed reports on the health benefits gained by drinking a glass of wine with a meal daily.

- Improvement of check approval systems will allow a faster processing of checks by means of a rapid scanning a database listing names of "fraud" check writers.
- Improvement of ECA (electronic check acceptance) will enable the funds to be transferred immediately from the buyer's to the merchant's account, resulting in a lower risk for the business.
- Latest POS technology will make it possible for the small restaurant or bar owner to purchase a PC based system for the price of a cash register.
- POS-touch-screen systems will be simplified in such manners that will minimize employees complains about being slowed down during "rush hour."

HINTS FOR BEVERAGE MANAGERS

As pointed out in the previous section, employee turnover is often a major concern for beverage managers. Training and re-training staff can become a costly proposition. What can management do to see that employees, particularly the more loyal and productive ones, stay on the job for longer periods of time? It is recommended to begin with investigating the specific reasons of why they are leaving their job. It is often said that, in general, the principal reason for people to quit their jobs is due to "uncomfortable work environment" rather than wages, or various other kinds of compensation. Therefore it is wise to conclude that, rewards as motivators (Bonuses, paid vacations, employee of the month/year award and so forth), although helpful in many instances, should be regarded of secondary importance. Priority should be given in creating a more comfortable working environment by encouraging teamwork, promoting co-workers rapport and somehow instilling pride and professional satisfaction on the job.

Employees that don't like their colleagues or don't respect their managers will easily self-terminate if other work is available. With the advent of the new century, unemployment rates are lowest than any other time for the past three or four decades. In the U.S. it may be the lowest it has ever been.

Instilling a deeper sense of professional pride can be done in several ways. One suggestion is for management to hold periodical workshops, seminars and get-together sessions so that the staff can interact and form a more cohesive team by collectively discussing job responsibilities. As well as product knowledge and how can better results be achieved in the workplace. This should be valid not only for hotel-beverage departments but for any type of hospitality operation and beverage related business. One good example is the Southern Wine and Spirits of Nevada on-going training program. In addition to holding professional workshops for employees and business associates, the company has recently hired Francesco Lafranconi to lecture in an in-house "Academy of Spirits" class series. Mr. Lafranconi, originally from the Cipriani Hotel in Venice Italy, was the 1998 winner of the international bartenders world championship (Barcardi-Martini Grand prix).

Other events such as the internationally known "John White bartending programs", or the offering of beverage knowledge classes always provide additional stimulus to participants to love and excel in their professions.

Fine examples for this purpose are the wine and wine service classes offered by Sterling Vineyards' Master Sommelier Evan Goldstein and the Organic Wine and Foods appreciation sessions offered by the Fetzer Vinery in Mendocino, California. For the immediate future it is expected that management play a more direct role in "profit pouring" as well as in the delivery of superior quality service. This can only be attained through a high degree of professional competence, dedication and not fearing to "roll up the sleeves" when needed. The more successful managers will be the ones that will commit themselves to go "the extra mile" when necessary.

SUGGESTED READINGS

1. Gerald Lattin, *The Lodging and Food Service Industry,* Educational Institute AHMA, 1998.
2. Tom Powers, *Introduction to the Hospitality Industry,* John Wiley & Sons, 1995.

appendix one

GLOSSARY

Absinthe An alcoholic beverage that contains an extract of the wormwood plant. Absinthe was popular in the 19th century in France among artists and poets but was subsequently banned because of its high alcohol content and the toxic effects of wormwood.

Abstinence Voluntarily refraining, especially from eating certain foods or drinking liquor.

Acetic Acid A sour and pungent substance. Acetic acid is the main acid in vinegar. All wines contain this acid. Small amounts can enhance the taste of a wine, but at high levels it can be perceived as an unpleasant taste.

Acidophilus Mildly soured milk that is easy to digest and considered to promote good health. It is taken sometimes to ameliorate an upset stomach. Some use it to guard against infections.

Adjunct Grains Fermentable material used as a substitute or added to traditional grains such as barley and rye. Used often in bulk brewing.

A la Carte Type of menu where food offerings are individually priced, as opposed to a table d'hôte (fixed price menu) where all courses are included in one price.

Aftertaste The taste that is perceived after drinking the wine. It may be brief or it may linger over the mouth for a period of time.

Aging The span of time that wine, brandy, whisky, beer, or other alcoholic beverages spend in maturing to achieve richer, fuller and more complex characteristics. Wines are aged in a variety of ways from large casks (such as oak or stainless steel) to bottles. Certain red wines greatly benefit from aging whereas most whites should be consumed when they are young. Aging is also applied to distilled spirits; generally before bottling.

Alcohol Ethyl Alcohol or Ethanol. In wine, one of the principal components. During the fermentation, the enzymes created by yeast cells convert the sugar in the grape juice into alcohol and carbon dioxide gas. In fermented grape juice, alcohol combines with acids to produce esters. In general alcohol is defined as "the derivative resulting from the substitution of a hydroxyl radical from an atom of hydrogen in a hydrocarbon". The chemical formula is $C_nH_{2n+1}OH$

Alcoholic Beverages   Beverages created by fermenting or distilling specific grains or fruit to produce the desired chemical reaction. Common alcoholic beverages include: grain alcohol, such as whisky or gin, plant alcohol such as sugar cane alcohol (rum) and agave alcohol (tequila), and fruit alcohol, such as brandy or wine. According to the U.S. Government any beverage containing between 0.5–99.0 per cent of alcohol can be referred to as an alcoholic beverage.

Alcoholism   A chronic illness characterized by the repeated consumption of alcohol to a degree that interferes with physical and mental health.

Ale   Beers distinguished by use of top fermenting yeast strains, Saccharomyces cerevisiae. The top fermenting yeasts perform at warmer temperatures than do yeasts used to brew lager beer, and their byproducts are more evident in taste and aroma.

Amontillado   A dry, golden colored sherry.

Anejo   The Spanish term for aging, referring to distilled spirits such as rum and tequila.

Angostura Bitters   A type of bitters from Trinidad. Bitters are commonly used in mixed drinks to add a very distinct strong flavor.

Anticipation   Anticipate the guests needs which is a fundamental component of service.

Aperitif   A fortified wine, a spirit or sherry consumed before the meal. An aperitif is used to stimulate the appetite.

Appellation   Areas designed by government for the growing of specific grapes. The use of these regions must follow strict rules and guidelines set by both federal and local governments.

Appellation d'Origine Controlée   Literally "controlled place of origin"; on a bottle of French wine the guarantee not only of place of origin but of the quality standards traditionally associated with wines from that place. These control laws represent the most flexible, most enlightened, and most effective body of legislation existing at present for the protection of the wines.

Armagnac   Brandy made in the Armagnac region of France

Asti Spumante   An Italian sparkling wine, made mainly in the region of Piedmont, from muscatel grapes.

B

Bacardi   A brand name for a rum from Puerto Rico. This is the best selling brand of rum, or any other spirit, in the world.

Back Bar   Refers to the area behind the bar where alcoholic and non-alcoholic beverages are displayed as well as other supplies are held.

Bag-in-the-box   This is used for a bulk quantity of beverage dispensing such as soda syrup, wine, and juices. The liquid is contained in a plastic bag within a box.

Bain Marie   A basin that holds water and maintains it at warm to hot temperatures. This device is used to keep hot food, sauces, or liquids hot. It is similar to a steam table. Note: "bain" is a French term for bath.

Baked   Cooked in a certain manner. Also used to describe the smell of warm-earth in a wine.

Balance   When a wine is balanced, nothing can be tasted above another, but all are noticeable—alcohol, acid, tannins, fruit, wood, sugars.

Barrel   Container, usually made of oak, that is used to ferment, store, and age wine.

Bar Mats Used in the bar to avoid any slips and falls while the bar is in use. These mats are laid down to let any liquid soak into the mats instead of a wet floor.

Bar Mixer An electrical piece of bar equipment. The mixer is necessary in a bar for making cocktails such as Margaritas, Pina Colada and Daiquiris. Not to be mistaken with the blender. The mixer kicks the ice around the metal container but it will not crush it as finely as the blender.

Bar P.C. Beverage Percentage Cost. Obtained by dividing the purchase cost of bar goods against sales. Also an electronic piece of equipment used to record customer orders and sales. Necessary equipment in preventing theft.

Bar Towel Towel used to clean up any spills on the bar and to wipe down the bar after use.

Batter A thick beaten mixture of flour and a liquid used in cooking.

Bay Leaf The leaf of the bay laurel tree.

Beer Fermented beverage made with malted barley and flavored with hops. Other grains, such as rice, can be used. Today beer can be made in countless ways including the use of various fruits and vegetables.

Benedictine A very popular liqueur of which the first mixture was made in 1510 at the Benedictine monastery in Fecamp, France, by Dom Bernardino Vincelli, to cheer up and restore the tired monks. The liqueur is greenish-yellow and flavored with a variety of herbs, plants, and peels on a base of brandy and it is claimed that the original formula is still kept secret.

Bercy Sauce (burr-cee) Classic French sauce made with brown stock, wine, shallots, butter, parsley, and lemon juice.

Bernkastler Doctor The most prized Moselle wine. If it is not absolutely first or always first among Moselles, it is nevertheless a great wine. The market pressure of its fame causes it to be somewhat over-priced.

Bitter One of the four basic tastes in Organoleptic Science. In wine bitterness is often due to the tannins in the wine.

Black Rot A fungal disease that affects both the grapes and the vines.

Blended Whisky A combination of straight whisky, grain spirits, light whiskies and neutral spirits. Result is lighter, better balanced, and more consistent than most straight whiskies.

Blending The process of mixing different liquids. In winemaking as many as 15–20 different grapes can be blended together.

Blue Agave The plant that is the source of tequila and mescal; also known as maguey in Mexico.

Blush A pink wine produced from grape juice or must from which the grape skins have been removed before fermentation is completed. Best selling wine in U.S. (White Zinfandel, Sutter Home & Beringer).

Bock Bottom fermented brews. Dark and malty beers that are more ale-like even though they are classified as lagers. Weizen, or wheat beers, are light in color and mildly dry, quite different from the majority of other ales.

Body The feel of a wine in the mouth. Can be light-bodied (watery), full-bodied (sticky and heavy) or medium-bodied (something in between).

Bottom Fermentation One of the two types used in brewing. Bottom fermenting works well at low temperature and ferments more sugars leaving a crisp, clean taste and then settles to the bottom of the tank. Used for making lager-type beers.

Botrytis   A type of disease contracted by grapes. Grapes affected with botrytis make intensely flavored dessert wines because the fruit shrivels, leaving the sugar content extremely concentrated (Botrytis Cirenea).

Bouquet   When referring to wine tasting, the term bouquet is used to describe the scent of a mature wine. The term aroma is used to describe the scent of a young wine.

Bourbon   A type of an American whisky. By American regulation the name applies to any whisky distilled from a fermented mash of grains containing at least 51 per cent corn, distilled at not more than 160 proof, and aged in new charred oak barrels for a minimum of two years. Named after Bourbon County Kentucky.

Brandy   The word alone means distilled wine. It can be made from distillates of other fruits such as apples, pears, plums, and cherries. Cognac and armagnac are the most popular brandies.

Breathing   Term used to describe wine that has been uncorked and has contact with air. There is great debate concerning whether or not this process makes the wine better. Generally vintage red wines benefit from "breathing" for at least half an hour before serving.

Brown Spirits   Scotch whisky, bourbon, Irish whiskey and Canadian whisky, have a more distinctive flavor and are generally consumed straight or with only a splash of water, soda or on the rocks.

Brut   Opposite of sweet, very dry. A term used when referring to sparkling wines such as champagne.

Build   Build layers of spirits and cordials in a cocktail. Examples: Pousse Café, King Alfonse. The building technique is called *Floating*.

Bung   Used to seal a wine barrel. They are usually hammered into the bung hole and can be removed as needed.

Bureau of Alcohol Tobacco and Firearms (BATF)   Records of beverage operations are required by federal law to be maintained for three years and must be surrendered at any time by request of the BATF officers. Control of products fall under them.

C

Cafe au Lait   French term for coffee with milk.

California Menu   A term indicating that breakfast, lunch, and dinner are served 24 hours a day.

Calvados   Apple flavored brandy, from the Calvados region of northern France.

Canadian Whisky   Characterized by its lightness of body and its distinct combination of grains used and their treatment.

Cap   When fermenting grapes, the skins, seeds, stems, etc. float to the top of the juice. These parts of the grape are what give the wine its flavor, color, and tannins.

Carafe   Wide mouthed glass container used to hold and serve wine. ½ liter and liter are the most common sizes. Typically used to serve "House Wines".

Carbohydrates   A group of chemical compounds containing only carbon, hydrogen, and oxygen. These include sugars, starches, and cellulose.

Chafing Dish   A type of equipment used to keep food warm. Used primarily in buffet style service, or sometimes in bars and lounges to offer patrons hot appetizers or hot finger foods.

Champagne Principally white sparkling wines, some still white wine, and a small quantity of red and rosé. District, northeastern France. The classic champagne is made with three principle grapes: Pinot Noir, Pinot Meunier, and Chardonnay.

Champenoise Method The method mostly used in the making of champagne. A second fermentation occurs in the bottle.

Chaptalization Process in which sugar is added to must before or during fermentation. It is important for an adequate amount of sugar to be present because alcohol results from conversions of sugar during fermentation.

Charmat Method Mass/bulk production method for sparkling wine.

Charred The charred oak imparts both a flavor as well as a rich brown color to the final product.

Chef de Rang Equivalent to the dining room captain, sometimes referred to as the front food server.

Cinquieme Cru The fifth growth, or the lowest classification of wines as determined by the Classification of 1855 in France.

Citrus Flavors and aromas in wine that generally resemble citrus fruits.

Classification of 1855 Rating of five classes established in Paris in 1855 for the Paris Exhibition. It was used to determine which Bordeaux wines could be submitted as exhibits. The unofficial ratings stuck and for the most part, have not been changed since.

Cocktail Mixture of one or more spirits and/or cordials with sodas, fruit juice, and other liquids, often referred to as: "Mixed Drink" which is simply a spirit mixed with water or soda. Manhattan, Martini and Margarita are popular cocktails.

COD Cash (or check) on delivery

Coffee A beverage made from the roasted and ground beans of the coffee plant. From "Coffea Arabica" plant–tropical shrub.

Cognac A brandy produced in the Cognac region of France.

Cointreau An orange flavored cordial similar to Grand Marnier, Curacao, and Triple Sec.

Collins A tall drink made of gin and Collins mix. A Tom Collins is a Gin Collins. Vodka and Rum are often prepared Collins style.

Column or Coffey Still Distilling alcohol by using a continuous still.

Commis de Suite Term mostly used in European hotels and restaurants. Person responsible for bringing food items into the dining room, also called the back server.

Competition Analysis A study of competitors methods and style of operating a business.

Condiment Tray A container with several compartments used to keep garnishes for cocktails such as cherries, lemon twists, orange slices, lime wedges, onions, and so forth.

Congeners Non-alcoholic agents that provide specific character and flavor to alcoholic beverages.

Control State (or Closed State) When the state serves as the distributor, they are granted exclusive territories within the state for the products so there is no competition.

Cordials Also called "liqueurs" and "after dinner drinks", cordials can be made in a variety of ways. Most cordials are from mildly sweet to very sweet. Their flavoring agents can be plants & seeds, herbs & spices, fruit, and honey. Grand Marnier, Drambuie, Benedictine, Kalhua, Amaretto, Anisette etc. are classified as cordials.

Cordon Bleu A traditional French cooking school of fine reputation. Also a cognac.

Cork   Used for sealing bottles of wine and other beverages. The bark of the cork tree grown particularly in Spain and Portugal.

Corkage   Term used in restaurants which may charge a fee for opening and serving a bottle of wine that was brought by the guest.

Corn Whisky   Whisky distilled from a mash of fermented grain containing 80 per cent of corn and above. Bourbon whisky must be made with at least 51 per cent corn, aged in new oak barrels for more than two years.

Court Bouillon   A highly seasoned broth made from fish stock.

Creme de Cacao   A chocolate cordial.

Creme de Cassis   A currant cordial.

Creme de Menthe   A liqueur flavored with either white or green mint.

Cuisine   A basic style of cooking, i.e. Mexican, French, Chinese, Italian, Regional American.

Customer   Also: patron, or guest. Someone who exchanges his/her money for goods and services.

Customer-Driven   Customers must be treated as the most important component of a beverage service operation. The whole operation must be designed around the customers and their needs.

Cut Off Service   The decision that management, and sometime bartenders, make to stop serving alcohol to an intoxicated person.

Cuvee (koo-VAY)   French term for "contents of a vat". In France, champagne bearing this on its label indicates a blend of different wines.

D

Daiquiri   A cocktail made from rum, sugar, and lime juice. Daiquiries can be served over ice cubes or mixed into crushed ice. Note: these days, daiquiris are served in a variety of fruit flavors.

Dark Lager   It has a dark brown color, and is full-bodied with a sweet and slight hop taste. It is more aromatic and creamy than light lagers. The color of a true dark lager comes from the addition of roasted barley. Alcohol content in dark lagers approaches 5 per cent by weight.

Decanting   The act of pouring wine from the bottle into another container to separate any sediment or lees from the wine itself. Decanting also allows the wine to breathe. Generally used when transferring red vintage wines from a bottle into a decanter.

Demi-sec   Used to describe mildly sweet to sweet sparkling wines. It is a French term meaning "half dry".

Demi-tasse   A small cup that holds about three ounces of liquid. Used to serve espresso coffee. Note: demi-tasse is French for half cup.

Demographics   Plays an important role in the planning of a business, includes facts and figures of future patrons' age, occupation, marital status, family characteristics, number of children, and personal preferences.

Denominazione di Origine Controllata   (Italian) abrv. D.O.C.—Italian equivalent of *appelation d'origine controlée* of France.

Denominazione di Origine Controllata e Garantita   (Italian) abrv. D.O.C.G.—Similar to D.O.C., but with even more stringent rules. Its primary function is to guarantee the origin of the wine. It is generally regarded as an indicator of fine quality wine.

Dessert Wine Most sweet wines fall into this category. Some of the best known dessert wines come from the Sauternes region in France (e.g., Barsac).

Deuce Term commonly used by dining room personnel when referring to a table that seats two people. Same as a two-top.

Deuxieme Cru Applied to French wines. French for "second growth" as specified in the Classification of 1855.

Distillation A separation process. The alcohol is vaporized by heat leaving the non-alcoholic liquid in the brew.

Distilled Spirits The first distilled spirits were expensive and were reserved for the ruling classes.

Distillery A building in which distilled spirits are made and stored.

Distributor A company that buys goods wholesale from a supplier and resells them to retailers.

Dolce Italian term for sweet.

Dom Perignon Was the name of a monk who is credited with inventing both champagne and the wire cage that goes over the cork to help keep it in the bottle and which is still in use today.

Dosage An addition to sparkling wines that consists of a mixture of sugar and wine.

Double A short, cylindrical glass used for mixed drinks and cocktails on the rocks. It ranges in size from twelve to fifteen fluid ounces. Also called "old Fashioned" glass.

Double Tall A larger than normal sized glass used for cocktails allowing a larger amount of mixer to be added.

Double Tall Highball A tall cylindrical glass used for serving mixed drinks on the rocks, ranging in size from eight to sixteen fluid ounces.

Doux French term for sweet.

Draft Beer The process of dispensing beer from a bright tank, cask or keg, by hand pump, pressure from an air pump or, injected CO_2 inserted into the beer container prior to sealing.

Drambuie A derivative of (Scotch) malt whisky, this liqueur has a light brown color and a honey flavor; originated in Scotland.

Dram-shop Laws Holds the operation that serves alcoholic beverages liable for the damages caused by an intoxicated guest (third party liability).

Dry Term used to describe wine that lacks residual sugar, i.e., the wine is not sweet.

Dry Beer A light beer with less sweetness than most lagers and little or no aftertaste.

Dubonnet A dark red, French aperitif.

E

Earthy A sense of damp soil in wine, usually to the nose and/or the palate. At times, it can be very overpowering.

Eau de Vie (oh-duh-vee) French term referring to any whisky, brandy or spirit. Note: translated means "water of life".

Eighteenth Amendment (also known as Volstead Act), is the only constitutional amendment to be repealed in the history of the United States.

Eiswein German term for "ice wine". It is a prized dessert wine and is very sweet due to the freezing of the grapes while they were on the vine. This freezing caused the sugars in the grapes to become very concentrated. Because the grapes are frozen, not much juice can be extracted from them.

Electra Bar   Electronic pouring which gave the operator opportunity to accurately monitor and record sales by the means of a meter system.

En Carafe   Wine served in a wine pitcher, wine from a cask.

Enology   The science and study of winemaking.

Entree   The main dish. Note: originally it was the food eaten between the heavier courses.

Epicurean   One who has refined taste in food or wine.

Equal Pay Act   Introduced in 1963, the Act establishes that employers provide an equal amount of wage compensation for male and female workers when performing the same type of work.

Estate Bottled   On the label, it is an indication that the wine was made entirely from grapes grown, harvested, fermented, and bottled by the winery and its own vineyards.

Ethanol   (Or ethyl alcohol), the alcohol found in alcoholic beverages. It has a sedative effect on the body. The ethanol consumed as part of a drink gets absorbed into the bloodstream in several places as it travels through the body.

Eucalyptus   Term used to describe the flavors and aromas associated with eucalyptus—spicy and minty.

Evian   The brand name for an uncarbonated mineral water from France.

Extract   Things that add to the color, flavor, and aroma of a wine.

Extra Dry   Term used to describe the residual sugar level in sparkling wines. Although there is sugar in an extra dry sparkling wine, the amount is minimal.

F

Fair Labor Standards Act   One of the oldest federal laws. Introduced in 1938. It protects workers from the age of 40–70 from discharge for reason of age. It also establishes rules for working teenagers and union activities.

Feasibility Study   An extraordinary tool for the operator. Its main purpose is to measure and project what type of operation will have a better chance for success in attracting the desired clientele.

Fermentation   The conversion of sugar into alcohol and carbon dioxide by the action of yeast.

Fermented Beverages   Fermentation occurs when yeast is introduced into a liquid that contains fruits or grain containing sugar. The yeast converts the sugar into carbon dioxide and alcohol. Examples of fermented beverages: beer, wine, and sake.

Field Blend   When a vineyard is planted with different types of grapes and all the grapes are used to create one wine.

FIFO   First In First Out.

First Party   (Legal use); the drinker or purchaser of the alcohol.

Filtering   Winemakers do this to the wine just before it is bottled to remove remaining yeast cells, sediment, and anything else that might affect the quality of the wine while it is in the bottle.

Fining   The process of using an additive to remove small particles from the wine. The additive attracts the particles, and sinks to the bottom as sediment.

Finish   Upon swallowing the wine, it is the flavor and body that lingers in the mouth.

Flinty   Slightly mineral flavor and aroma in a wine.

Floated or Layered Cocktails   Pouring a spirit or other liquid on top of a finished cocktail without mixing it. Specific gravity allows the various liquids to stay separated.

Flor   Yeast that creates a white, frothy layer on the surface of sherries. It acts as a blanket on the wine and prevents contact with air.

Footed Pilsner   A tall, slim, footed glass that is V-shaped, used for serving beer.

Fortified Wine   Wines that have had brandy added to increase its alcohol content. This addition of brandy was originally meant as a technique for preserving the wine. From 17–22 per cent alcohol.

Fraises (frehz)   French word for strawberries.

Framboises (frahm-bwahz)   French word for raspberries.

Free Pouring   Pouring directly from the bottle to the glass.

Frizzante   Italian term for "lightly sparkling". There is less pressure in a frizzante than in a spumante.

Fructose   There are two sugars found in grapes—glucose and fructose. Fructose is supposed to be about twice as sweet as glucose.

Fruity   Term used to describe the flavors and aromas of fresh fruit in a wine. Fruity wines do not have to be sweet wines.

Fumé   Smoked.

G

Garnish   A decorative embellishment to a plate of food or drink. In many cases the garnish may be an important part of the dish.

Gewurztraminer   White wine grapes grown in cooler regions of Europe and California. These grapes are known for their spiciness. Traminer is the grape—gewurtz means spice in German.

Gin   Gin is a juniper-flavored spirit obtained by the distillation and rectification of the grain spirits of malted barley and rye—or sometimes of corn or maize. The two principal gins are British and Dutch.

Ginger   A tropical spice with a strong flavor and sweet aroma. Ginger can be purchased in a variety of forms: pickled, fresh, dried, candied, and crystallized.

Glace   French term meaning iced, glazed, or frozen.

Glassrail   A narrow extension of the counter, usually one inch lower than the regular counter surface. Drinks should be prepared on the glassrail.

Gluco-oenometer   An instrument to test the strength of new musts; used in making port.

Glucose   There are two sugars found in grapes—fructose and glucose. Glucose is supposed to be about half as sweet as fructose.

Glycerine   Colorless, odorless, sweet tasting alcohol formed from glycerol. Used as a solvent to enhance the fattiness of wine.

Goods   The actual food or drink.

Gourmet (or gourmand)   A person with appreciation for, and knowledge of, fine food and beverages.

Grand Cru   French for "great growth". It is the best ranking that can be given to a wine using the rankings of the Classification of 1855.

Grand Cru Classe   French for "great classed growth". According to the Saint-Emilion Classification of 1953, this is the second highest rating for wines.

Grand Marnier   A brand name for an orange flavored liquor.

Grassy   The smell of freshly cut grass in a wine. Often found in Cabernet Sauvignons.

Grenadine   Sweet red syrup, usually non-alcoholic but sometimes with a very slight alcohol content, used as a sweetening agent. Originally made from pomegranates.

H

Halbtrocken   German for medium-dry.

Heady   Used to describe a wine that has a high alcohol content.

Herbaceous   Aromas, and sometimes flavors, of different herbs in wine. Grassy, weedy.

Herbs   Any of a variety of cultivated plants used to improve the flavor of food.

Highball   A long, iced drink, usually whisky and soda. Also the name of a tall glass.

Honeyed   Aroma and flavor of honey. Dessert wines usually have honey characteristics.

Hops   A climbing perennial with rough-lobed leaves like those of the vine. The ripened cones of the female plant are used in brewing, to give flavor to the beer. Cultivated in Europe, Central Asia, and America.

Hors d'oeuvre (awr-der-vruh)   Appetizers, often served with cocktails.

House Cost   The actual cost of goods to an establishment.

House Wine   A table wine, usually served from a large container and presented in a carafe. The house wine is usually less expensive than other wine offerings.

Hydrometer   Device used to measure how much sugar is in the grape musts.

I

Imperiale   A large wine bottle that holds as much as eight regular bottles of wine.

Infusion   Covering food with boiling water and allowing it to stand. This process removes color and flavor. (When you make tea you infuse the water with the flavor and color of the tea.)

Inky   Term used to describe a negative metallic flavor of a wine. This flavor is usually a result of the tannins in the wine contacting metal.

Intermezzo   Usually a fruit flavored sorbet eaten between courses to cleanse and refresh the palate.

Internal Recruiting   Recruiting within your own place of business.

Internal Theft   Stealing within the establishment and pilfering goods that belong to the business.

Intoxicated   The blood alcohol content is above the normal level.

Island Bar   A round-shaped area within an establishment where alcoholic and non-alcoholic beverages are served.

Issuing   Refers to the process of releasing a beverage item from a storage area to the bar.

J

Jahrgang   German for vintage year.

Jammy   Term used to describe a wine that has rich, intense fruit to nose and palate.

Jamaica Rum   Made in the British West Indies, a spirit made from sugar cane molasses, and sugar cane byproducts.

Jeroboam   An oversized wine bottle. In Champagne, France, a jeroboam holds the equivalent of four standard bottles, while in Bordeaux it holds six.

Jigger   Device used to assure the correct measure when pouring.

Jockey Boxes   (or wells), they are located on both sides of the ice bin and are used for keeping all supplementary items needed for proper service.

Juniper Berry   A cedar berry used as a flavoring agent in foods and beverages.

K

Kabinett   The lowest and least expensive classification of German wine, according to the *Qualitatswein mit Pradikat (QmP)*.

Keller   German term for cellar.

Kir   Cocktail made with Crème de Cassis and white wine. Kir Royale is made from Crème de Cassis plus champagne.

Kirschwasser   A brandy distilled from cherries complete with stones. After distillation, it is matured in paraffin-lined casks or earthenware, to prevent it taking on the color that wood would impart; true kirsch is always pure white.

Kosher Wine   Wine that is produced under the strict guidelines of Jewish Rabbinical law.

L

Lage   German for vineyard site.

Lager   Beers produced with bottom fermenting yeast strains; lagering also means maturing.

Late Harvest   Term to describe grapes picked late during the harvest season when they are extremely ripe. Usually, the grapes are picked towards the autumn, at the end of the season.

LBV (Late Bottled Vintage)   Port that is made from a single vintage of grapes.

Leafroll Virus   Disease affecting the grapevines.

Legal Code   Easy to understand written policies that are needed to make management's expectations clear to the staff.

Legs   Swirling a glass of wine up the sides of a glass leaves the inside of the glass coated with rivulets. The streaks of wine down the glass are called the legs or tears.

Liqueur   A strong, sweet alcoholic beverage. Liqueurs are usually served in small glasses as an after dinner drink; often referred to as "cordials".

Local Option Laws   Many states allow local communities to make decisions regarding the sale of alcohol in their areas. These local laws are called local option laws.

London Dry Gin   One of the two basic styles of gin. The other is Dutch. This is the gin of both the United States and England. The base spirit is distilled until neutral and flavoring, from a number of different herbs but chiefly juniper, is added afterwards.

M

Maceration   The period during which the juice of the grape is in contact with the skin and the seeds of the grapes.

MADD   Mothers Against Drunk Driving.

Madeira   A Portuguese white wine. Can be sweet, dry or blended.

Made-to-order   Already made or processed when ordered.

Magnum   Equivalent of two standard bottles, 52 ounces.

Malolactic Fermentation   Also referred to as secondary fermentation. The wine undergoes another fermentation process; however, this time there is no alcohol produced. During this process, the malic acid that is present is chemically converted by bacteria into lactic acid and carbon dioxide.

Malting   The process by which barley is steeped in water, germinated, then kilned to convert insoluble starch to soluble substances and sugar.

Malt Liquor   A legal term used in the U.S. to designate a fermented beverage of relatively high alcohol content.

Maître d'Hotel   French term for the person in charge of the dining room staff.

Manhattan Clam Chowder   A clam stew with a tomato base.

Manhattan   A cocktail made with whisky and sweet vermouth. Garnished with a cherry.

Marc   French for the remains of the grape after it has been pressed, i.e., skin, seeds, stems.

Markup   Multiplication factor.

Market Research   Investigation and research companies do on products and markets.

Market Share   Percentage of the market that the operation has compared with the other operations in an area. It is improved by offering a product different from what a competitor is offering.

Marrying   The process of combining foods and beverages with similar or different textures, flavors, or aromas to produce a more balanced flavor. Also known as the process of complementing foods with particular wines.

Marsala   A semi-dry Italian fortified wine imported from Sicily.

Martini   A cocktail made with vodka or gin and dry vermouth. The less vermouth the drier the martini. Garnished with an onion, an olive, or a lemon peel.

Mashing   Releasing malt sugars by soaking the grains in water.

Mead   An alcoholic beverage made with honey, water, malt, yeast, and spices.

Measured Pouring   Different measurement utensils are used during pouring to deliver an accurate amount.

Medoc   A region of France in which the finest red wines are made.

Metabolize   The chemical or physical process of changing a substance thus releasing energy from living systems.

Microbrewery (Microbeer)   Small brewery generally producing less than 15,000 barrels per year.

Mise en Place   Advance preparation of work stations in the kitchen and in the dining room. The term is French for "to put in place".

Mixer   Used to mix batter or any two or more items to get a smooth look.

Mixing or Broken Cases   A case of liquor that is received from the distributor containing different types or brands of alcoholic beverages.

Mobile Bar   A portable bar unit, of smaller dimensions, which includes some of the same equipment found in a stationary bar such as a speedrack, a gun system, an ice bin, etc.

Mocha   A combination of chocolate and coffee.

Modifying Ingredient   An additive used to stabilize and thicken a food.

Montrachet   A fine quality, well balanced, white Burgundy wine with a tangy dry taste.

Moscatel   A pleasant, sweet after dinner wine. From the Muscat grape.

Mousse   French for froth or foam. Usually used to describe the foam on a glass of champagne or sparkling wine.

Muddler   For crushing fruit, such as an orange slice or a cherry used in preparation of an Old Fashioned cocktail.

Multiplication Factor   The cost of a drink to the customer divided by its cost to the operator. Same as markup.

Muscat   Grape grown all around the world. It is used to make sparkling wines and fortified wines.

Must   Juice pressed from wine grapes before it is fermented.

N

Napa Valley   A famous region of California where wine grapes are grown. The Napa Valley is known for producing some of the finest wines in the world.

Nebbiolo   A classic Italian table wine.

Negroni   An Italian aperitif made with Campari, gin or vodka and sweet vermouth.

Neutral Spirit   Spirits that are distilled from any material to 95 per cent or higher of alcohol, 190 proof.

Noble Rot   A beneficial mold or fungus that attacks grapes under certain climatic conditions and causes them to shrivel, deeply concentrating the flavors, sugar and acid. From the French: *Pourritoure Noble.*

Nose   Term used to describe the olfactory sensations in wine.

Nutty   Term used to describe the flavor of nuts in wines such as sherries or ports.

O

Off Premise   Anything that does not happen on the property, for example, sales that go off property to be consumed.

Open or License States   A state where the government has little over the distribution of alcoholic beverages. Besides licensing distributors and granting them protected territories.

Ordering   Requesting goods from a supplier.

Organization Chart   The diagram which shows the hierarchy in an organization, and also the chain of command.

Organoleptic Evaluation   The tasting and evaluation of a beverage based on smell, taste, sight.

Orgeat   A mixed drink flavoring consisting of barley water flavored with almonds or orange blossoms.

Orvieto   A town in central Italy where the famous Orvieto white wine originated.

Outside Recruiting   Recruiting from outside of your work force, from schools, other places of business, etc.

Overstocking   Having too much stock of the same item.

Oxidation   The chemical reaction that occurs when oxygen is combined with other compounds. It results from overexposure to air.

Palace   An area of France where three famous wines are made: Chateau Lafite, Latour, and Mouton Rothchild.

Palm Hearts   The center portion of the shoots of young palm trees.

Parching   To dry with heat.

Par Stock   The level of inventory that must be kept on hand to maintain a continuing supply of each item.

Pasteurization   Heating of beer to 60–79°C. (140–175°F)

Pasteurized Milk   Milk that has been heat sterilized in order to prohibit bacterial growth.

Pekoe   A commonly used black tea grown in China. Pekoe is commonly used as the main ingredient in a blended tea.

Perception of Value   How customers rate value. Value means different things to different people.

Percolation   The flavoring agent is placed in the upper part of an apparatus, brandy or another spirit is pumped over the leaves or herbs, it is allowed to drain, and is then pumped through again. This process may be repeated for weeks or months.

Perfect Cocktail   A cocktail consisting of gin or whisky (50 per cent), dry vermouth (25 per cent) and sweet vermouth (25 per cent), or any cocktail with an even amount of dry and sweet vermouth.

Pernod   A sweet strong cordial imported from France.

Perpetual Inventory   The process of knowing what is on hand in the store room at all times and its dollar value.

Phylloxera   Tiny aphids or root lice that attack Vitis Vinifera roots.

Pilsner (or Pilsener)   A beer made in the style of Pilsen, Czechoslovakia, light in color, with a prominent hop flavor, with a dry and clean finish. This is the style, minus the prominent hop flavor, most American beers are modeled after.

Pinot Chardonnay   An excellent white table wine originally made from white grapes grown in the Burgundy region of France.

Pinot Noir   A premium grape originally grown in the Burgundy region of France.

Piquant   A French term meaning sharp flavored or highly seasoned.

Piquant Sauce   A classic sauce of white wine, vinegar, pickles, demi-glace, and spices.

Pommard   A red wine from Burgundy.

Pony Glass   A short glass used for cordials.

Port   A sweet, fortified after-dinner wine.

Porter   Beer that is dark and bitter but lighter than a stout.

Port   The classic fortified wine from Portugal.

Positioning   Involves planning to offer future patrons specific items that may make the bar operation unique.

Pot Still   Distilling device. It has two essential parts: the still and the worm condenser. It is designed to process only one batch of fermented liquid at a time, then it must be emptied, cleaned, and refilled between batches.

Pousse Cafe (puskafe)   A layered cocktail.

Pradikat   Refers to wine quality; a German term meaning "attribute".

Premeasure   Measuring beforehand or estimated measurements.

Premium Brands   Alcoholic beverage brands, of high quality and price.

Premiere Cru In reference to wine making, the finest growth.

Privacy Act A 1974 act, it's intended to prevent employers from asking employees questions that may be considered discriminatory and may constitute invasion of personal privacy.

Proactive To make a change in a process without prior incident or condition.

Product Control Refers to the methods used in safeguarding merchandise.

Prohibition (or the Volstead Act) was enacted to curb the problems of overconsumption of alcohol in the late 1800s and early 1900s. To outlaw the production and consumption of beverage alcohol.

Proof One of the terms used to describe the strength of distilled spirits.

Public House A public place (in Britain) where alcohol can be consumed. An abbreviation is "pub".

Purchasing To pay for a product or service based on selection and procurement.

Q

Qualitatswein mit Pradikat (QmP) German wine classification developed in 1971. Loosely translated, it means "quality wine with special attributes".

Quatrieme Cru French for "fourth growth" according to the Classification of 1855.

R

Racking The practice of moving wine by hose from one container to another, leaving sediment behind.

Raisin A dried grape.

Reactive To change responding to a prior condition.

Receiving The act of accepting goods that have been ordered after the amounts have been checked and inspected against an invoice.

Recruitment The function of hiring employees—staffing.

Reorder Point Also referred to as the safety stock, the amount that is always maintained in the inventory to cover for the delivery time.

Residual Sugar Unfermented grape sugar in a finished wine.

Residue The customers' feelings and impressions upon leaving the operation. It will have a lasting effect on whether or not they will return.

Reuse of Drink Tickets Fraudulent use of the tickets more than one time.

Riesling Wine made from a grape that grows along the Rhine and Moselle rivers of Germany. A sweet white wine.

Rum An aged spirit made from the fermented mash of sugar cane or from molasses. Rum comes mainly from tropical islands such as Jamaica or Puerto Rico.

Rush Hour The busiest time in an establishment.

Russian Service Formal service style. Foods are served from a platter onto a plate from the left side of the guest also called "platter service."

Rye Whiskey Whisky distilled from fermented rye.

Saint Emilion   One of the finest grape growing regions of France. It is also the name of a fine red wine.

Sake   A Japanese wine made from rice. Sake is usually served warm in very small cups.

Sales Mix   An average applied to the individual sales of each product or serving, as well as the combination of an establishment's products or services.

Saloon   During the expansion of the Far West, a bar was commonly referred to as a saloon.

Sanka   A brand of instant decaffeinated coffee. The term sanka is often used to refer to any decaffeinated coffee.

Sauternes   Light golden wines varying from sweet to medium sweet. Made in the U.S. or the Bordeaux region of France.

Scotch Whisky   A spirit distilled from malted barley. It is clear, dry, and has an amber head. It must be made in Scotland.

Screening   One of the stages of the staffing process.

Second Party   (Legal use); the establishment, seller, or server of the alcohol.

Sediment   Residual grape solids that collect on the side or bottom of the wine bottle as the wine matures. Also called lees. Note: a fine wine containing lees should be decanted.

Sequencing   In order—the preestablished order in calling cocktails or placing the bar products on the speedrack.

Service   Important role in the hospitality industry. Customers seek good service when they go out for a drink or when they order a drink with their meal.

Service Bar   Bar that is usually out of visibility to patrons whose purpose is to prepare drink for servers only.

Serviette   In the U.S. this term refers to a cloth napkin, in other countries this term is used to refer to any type of napkin.

Shake Mix Method   The method of mixing ingredients by placing them in a covered container and then shaking them.

Sherry   Pale golden or amber hued wine. Dry sherry is often used as an aperitif, and dry and sweet sherry are used extensively in cooking. Can be of "fino" or "oloroso" type from Jerez, Spain.

Short   A wine that has no persistence.

Short Changing   Not giving enough change to the customer.

Single Malt   Whisky that is produced from malt; no grains are added, and it is the product of one distillery.

Slush Machine   Used to dispense premixed and preportioned ingredients particularly for tropical type of cocktails such as Pina Colada.

Soiree (swarey)   An evening party.

Sommelier (soh-mahl-ieyeh)   The person responsible for maintaining the wine cellar and serving the wines.

Sour Mash   A process of making whisky in which yeast from a previous distillation is added to fresh mash.

Sparkling Wines   They are carbonated by the process of a second fermentation where the carbon dioxide remains in the wine. Three main methods are used: (a) Champenios, (b) Charmat, and (c) Transfer.

Speciality Beer   An unusual beer.

Speed Rack Located below the ice bin at waist level. Made of stainless steel, it serves the purpose of lining up the bar products most commonly requested by the customer.

Spillage The amount spilled when pouring beverages.

Spirits Vodkas, whiskies, rums, brandies, gin, and tequilas are referred to as distilled spirits.

Split A six ounce bottle of wine, champagne, or beer.

Spumone A fancy Italian ice cream, it usually has several colored layers and contains nuts and/or candied fruit.

Standardize To maintain things on a regular basis. To do things the same way according to the established standard.

Steam Beer A lager beer made by bottom fermentation but with the higher fermenting temperature of an ale.

Steeping To extract color and/or flavor by soaking in liquid below boiling point.

Stemmed Glass A wine glass with a tall stem.

Stewing Cooked slowly immersed in liquid.

Still A distilling apparatus in which when an alcoholic liquid is heated, alcohol vaporizes and condenses back to form a liquid with a higher alcoholic content.

Still Wines Non-sparkling, table or beverage wines.

Stir Method The method of mixing a cocktail or other types of drinks by stirring.

Storage Used to keep the dry goods in.

Stout A dark colored alcoholic malt beverage with a strong flavor of hops.

Straight Whisky Once it is blended with a neutral spirit, or a light whisky, it is considered a blended whisky.

Strainer Used to drain all the water or liquid out of the product.

Substitution The use of one product for another.

Supplier The person who supplies the consumer with products.

Sweet Mash Whiskey made by the sweet mash method entails using only fresh yeast for the mash mixture, distilled at no higher than 80 per cent whisky and aged in new charred oak barrels for a minimum of two years.

Swizzle Stick A stick used for stirring or holding the garnish in a beverage.

T

Tabasco A spicy hot pepper sauce used as a condiment or a flavoring for sauces, soups, stews, and dressings. Tabasco is the brand name of a pepper sauce made by the McIlhenny Co. of Louisiana, U.S.

Tall Highball Tall highball glass. Can also indicate a tall drink.

Tamper-Evident Closure Placed on liquor bottles when the taxes are paid and they are ready to be shipped from the warehouse.

Tangible Capable of being perceived especially by the sense of touch.

Tannic Acid An acid found in oak. This acid is essential to the aging process of wine and is also present in grape skin.

Tavern Bar or "drinking place". Served multiple purposes. They were often used as courthouses before towns could afford their own courthouse. Besides being where most of the drinking took place in colonial times, they served as lodging places, municipal buildings, and mail distribution centers.

Tea   Dried processed leaves of the tea plant.

Teetotaler   A person that abstains from the consumption of alcoholic beverages.

Temperance   Moderation in, or abstinence from, the use of alcohol.

Tequila   A spirit made from the blue variety of the agave plant.

Texture   A term used for describing the taste or feel of the food or beverage entering the mouth.

Third Party   (Legal use); not involved in the original transaction, but somehow injured by the first party.

Third Party (Civil) Liability   Transfers the responsibility for the damages and injury caused by a drunk driver to the server, manager, and owner of the operation that served the guest.

Tokay   Traditional Hungarian wine. Can be medium dry or sweet.

Tom Collins   A cocktail made of gin, sweet-n-sour and club soda.

Top Fermentation   Method of fermenting brews—the opposite of bottom fermentation. Works better at warmer temperatures; the yeasts are able to tolerate higher concentrations than bottom fermenting yeast. The method is used for making ales.

Triple Sec   Orange flavored liqueur, originally imported from France.

Tulip Glass   A long-stemmed tulip shaped glass used to serve champagne.

Turkish Coffee   A very strong, sweet coffee originating from Turkey.

U

Underbar   Area underneath the bar out of the view of the patron. Serves as a working station where the bar staff keeps the various pieces of equipment and materials for the customer's needs.

Understocking   Insufficient stock.

Unfiltered   Wine that has not gone through the filtration process.

Unfined   Some winemakers prefer to use other methods to remove small particles in the wine. Many believe that fining takes away from the wine's characteristics and they thus choose to use alternate methods.

Unrecorded Sales   An amount that is not recorded in the cash register.

Up (Neat)   A glass in which a cocktail such as a martini is served without ice.

V

Varietal   A wine whose name refers to the major grape variety used in its making, instead of the geographical area where the grapes were grown and vinified. Varietal naming is characteristic of non-European wine making countries. European wines are more commonly named according to the geographical region where they are produced.

Vendor   The person who sells and delivers products.

Vermouth   An aromatic wine, made dry or sweet, served as an aperitif or mixed into other beverages. Classified as fortified wine.

Vin   French term for wine.

Vintage   Refers to a grape or a wine from a particularly successful year or growing season.

Viscosity   Also referred to as the "legs" of the wine. Seen in a glass when swirled and then observed running down the glass.

Vodka   Distilled spirit made from grains. Potatoes are sometimes used.

Voiture   Small mobile carts used in the dining room to serve various foods. Can also be used as a cordial cart.

Volnay   A delicate red Burgundy wine.

Volstead Act   Congress passed the National Prohibition Act in 1920 in order to enforce the Eighteenth Amendment to the Constitution. It prohibited all manufacturing and selling of alcoholic beverages in the U.S.

W

Well   The house brand of a distilled spirit. Usually an inexpensive brand.

Wheat Beer (Weissbier)   Uses up to 60 per cent of wheat in the malt, the remainder being barley. It has a distinctive yeasty or bready aroma and a complex as well as unique spicy flavor.

Whisky Rebellion   Arose from a disagreement over the collection of taxes; unconnected with the temperance movement, which aimed to limit the production and consumption of alcohol.

Whisky Sour   A cocktail with sweet-n-sour and a maraschino cherry.

White Spirits   Vodka, gin, and rum; generally lighter in flavor and made to be mixed.

Wine   Alcoholic beverage made from fermented grape juice.

Worcestershire Sauce   An anchovy based condiment used in drinks.

X

Xarello   White wine grape grown mainly in Spain. Because of its lower quality, it is usually blended with higher quality grapes to add body to the wine.

Y

Yeast   A microorganism of which action permits the process of fermentation to take place.

Z

Zinfandel   Wine made from the Zinfandel grapes grown in California. These produce a pale pink colored, table wine. Not to be mistaken with the pink "White Zinfandel" (blush).

a p p e n d i x   t w o

PRACTICAL AND USEFUL FORMS AND PLANS

1. Standard Bar Set Up Diagram
2. Basic Bar and Lounge Layout
3. Standard Drink Abbreviation List
4. Bar Food Perpetual Inventory Form
5. Liquor Perpetual Inventory Form
6. Beverage Cost Sheet
7. Bar Standard Cashier Report Form
8. Beverage Requisition Form
9. Breakage and Spillage Report Form
10. Typical Bar and Snack Bar Layout and Legend
11. Typical Bar Stock and Inventory Ending Form
12. Beverage Service Employee Performance Evaluation
13. Cocktail Profile Form
14. Bar Staff Schedule Sample
15. Bin In-Out Record
16. Beverage Dept. Schedule
17. Bar Usage Report
18. Bar Product Requisition
19. Inventory Form
20. Inter-departmental Issue Record
21. Monthly Check Average Record

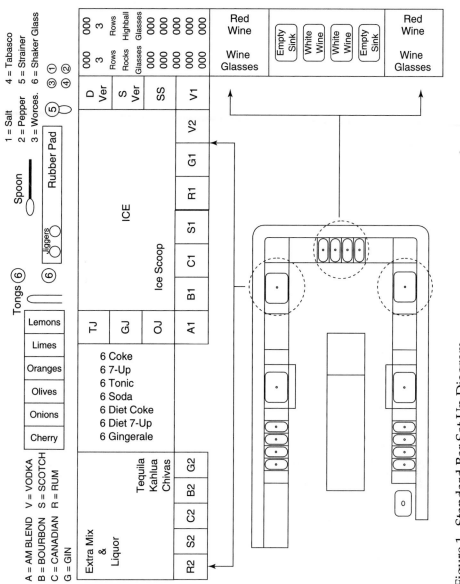

Figure 1. Standard Bar Set Up Diagram

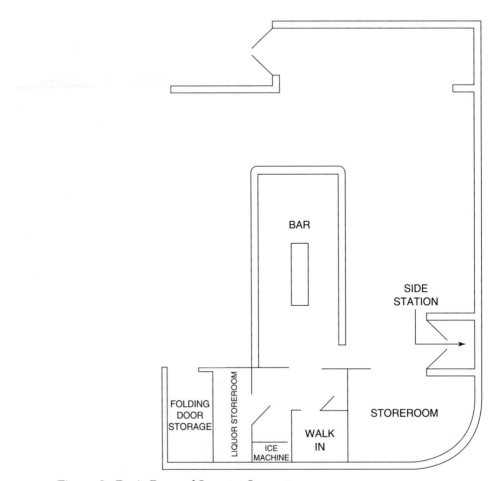

Figure 2. Basic Bar and Lounge Layout

ABBREVIATIONS

COCKTAIL	ABBREVIATION	PRICE
Vodka Tonic	V - T	
Screwdriver	Screw	
Bloody Mary (Salt)	Mary	
Greyhound/Bulldog	Hound	
Vodka Martini (Double)	V - Mart	
Black Russian	Blk Rus	
Salty Dog (Salt)	S. Dog	
Scotch Water	S - W	
Rob Roy (Double)	Rob	
Rusty Nail	R Nail	
Tom Collins	T. Col	
Martini (Double)	Mart	
Gimlet	Gim	
Gibson (Double)	Gib	
Bourbon Coke	B - C	
John Collins	J. Col	
Whiskey Sour	Sour	
Manhattan (Double)	Man	
Old-Fashioned	Old	
Bacardi Coke	R - C	
Bacardi Cocktail	Bac	
Tequila Sunrise	Sunrise	
Margarita	Marg	
Banana Daiquiri	B. Daq	
Strawberry Daiquiri	Straw. Daq	
Daiquiri	Daq.	
White Russian	Wh Rus	
Seven Seven	7 - 7	
Beautiful	Beau	
Brandy Alexander	Br Alex	
Chichi	Chi	
Pinacolada	Pina	
Mimosa	Mimosa	
Kir	Kir	
Kir Royale	Royale	
Stinger	Stinger	

Wine - Glass	GL	
- ½ Liter	½ L	
- Liter	L	

Beer - Domestic
   - Imported

Soda
Juice
Perrier

Figure 3. Standard Drink Abbreviation List

CATEGORY ___BAR FOOD_____

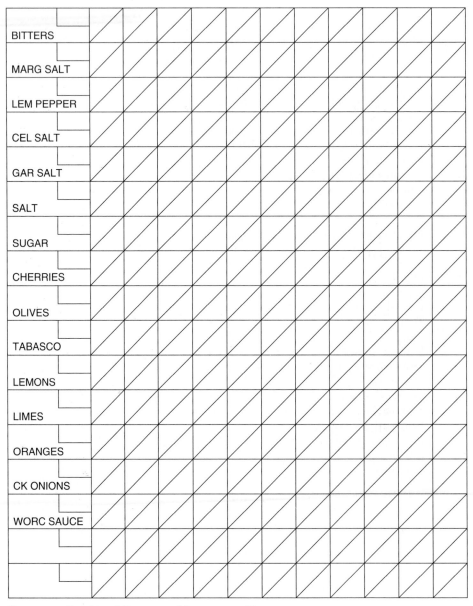

BITTERS

MARG SALT

LEM PEPPER

CEL SALT

GAR SALT

SALT

SUGAR

CHERRIES

OLIVES

TABASCO

LEMONS

LIMES

ORANGES

CK ONIONS

WORC SAUCE

Figure 4. Bar Food Perpetual Inventory Form

PERPETUAL INVENTORY   CATEGORY _____

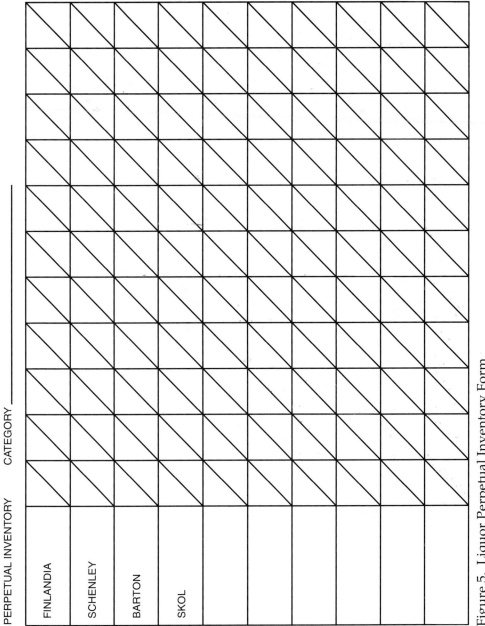

FINLANDIA

SCHENLEY

BARTON

SKOL

Figure 5. Liquor Perpetual Inventory Form

BEVERAGE COST SHEET	EVENT		DATE		NAME			
BRAND	ISSUED	ADD	TOT. AVAIL	END INV.	USED	BOT COS	TOT. COS	COS %
TOTAL								

Figure 6. Beverage Cost Sheet

CASHIERS REPORT				
CLASS: _____		DATE: _____		
	AMOUNT		AMOUNT	
CHECKS:		CASH/CHECKS(closing bank)		
Name CK#		CASH VARIANCE (o) / s		
Name CK#		CASH SALES (register tape)		
Name CK#				
Name CK#		ACCOUNTS RECEIVABLE		
TOTAL CHECKS		COMPS		
CASH:		COUPONS		
100.00		DISCOUNTS		
50.00				
20.00				
10.00		GRAND TOTAL SALES		
5.00				
2.00				
1.00				
0.50				
0.25				
0.10				
0.05				
0.01				
TOTAL CASH				
OPENING BANK	($100.00)			
TOTAL CLOSING BANK				
		MANAGER		
	BAR #	1. _____		
	"	2. _____		
	"	3. _____		
	"	4. _____		
	"	5. _____		

Figure 7. Bar Standard Cashier Report Form

BEVERAGE REQUISITION

CONTROL # 194863

TO: BEVERAGE WAREHOUSE

PLEASE DELIVER TO: ....

CHARGE TO: ....

DATE ORDERED: ....

DATE AND TIME REQUIRED: ....

STOCK NO.	DESCRIPTION BRAND AND KIND OF ITEM *(COMPLETE DESCRIPTION)*	SIZE	PAR STOCK PAR	ON HAND	ORDER	REQUISITION DELIVERED QTY.	✔	SALE VALUE UNIT	TOTAL	COST UNIT	TOTAL

Figure 8. Beverage Requisition Form

PEARSON'S BAR & LOUNGE

BREAKAGE AND SPILLAGE REPORT

Day _____   Date _____

(Mark B for breakage and S for spillage)   **B**   **S**

Bartender's name _____

Item _____

Quantity _____

Reason _____

_____

(BRIEFLY COMMENT WHETHER THIS ACCIDENT COULD HAVE BEEN AVOIDED AND HOW)

_____

_____

Bartender's Signature _____

Supervisor's Signature _____

Figure 9. Breakage and Spillage Report Form

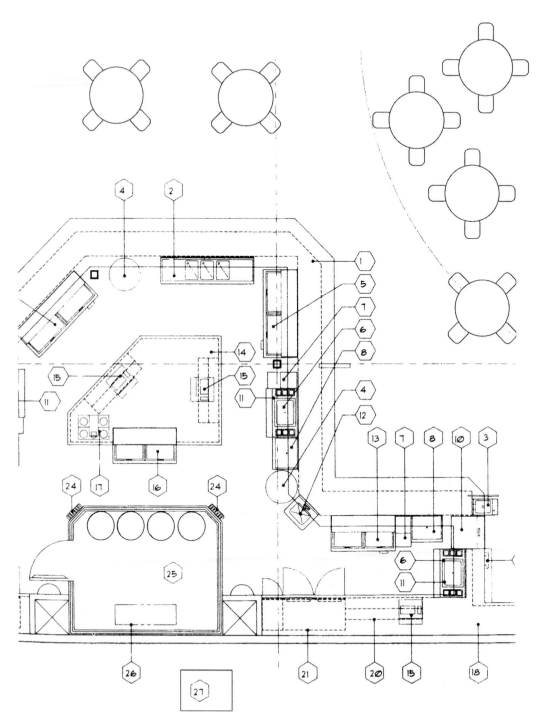

Figure 10.A A Typical Bar Layout

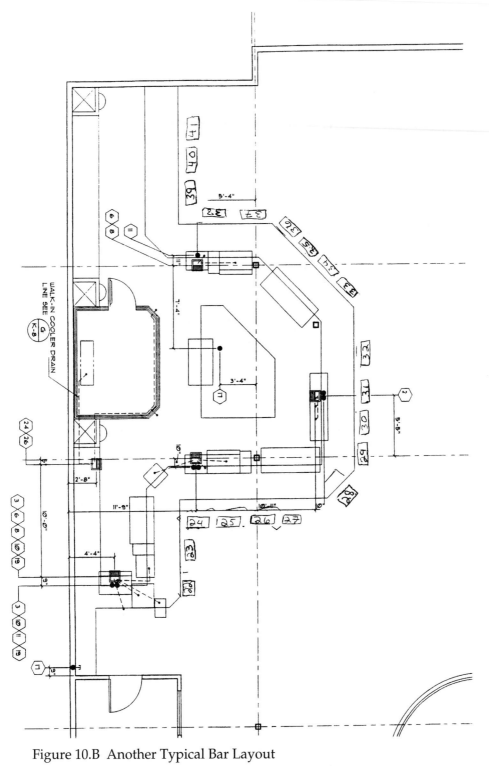

Figure 10.B Another Typical Bar Layout

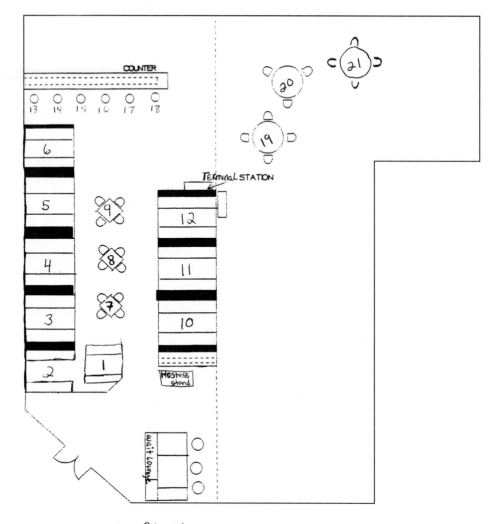

Station Chart

Figure 10.C Station Chart

ITEM NO	QUANTITY	DESCRIPTION
1	1	BAR TOP DIE
2	1	3-COMP. SINK
3	1	DUMP SINK
4	LT	WASTE RECPTICALS
5	2	BOTTLE COOLER
6	3	JOCKEY BOX
7	3	BLENDER STAND
8	3	DRAINBOARD
9		SPARE NUMBER
10	1	GLASSWASHER
11	3	SODA DISP. GUN
12	1	HANDSINK
13	1	BOTTLE COOLER
14	1	ISLAND CABINET
15	3	CASH REGISTER
16	1	MUG CHILLER
17	1	COFFEE MAKER
18	1	BACK BAR CABINET
19	1	UTILITY SINK
20	1	STEPPED LIQUOR DISPLAY
21	2	BACK BAR COOLER
22	1	BACK BAR CABINET
23	1	SODA DISP. SYSTEM
24	2	BEER DISP. UNIT
25	1	WALK-IN COOLER
26	1	COOLER EVAP. COIL
27	1	COOLER CONDENSER
28	1	LUNCH COUNTER
29	2	HANDSINK
30	1	COFFEE MAKER
31	1	HOT CHOCOLATE DISP.
32	1	S/S WORK TABLE
33	1	SALAD TOP COOLER
34	1	HEAT LAMP
35	1	S/S PASS SHELF
36	1	FLOOR MTD ICE & SODA DISP

Figure 10.D Bar Layout Legend

	Product Description	Unit Price Per Case	Cases	Unit Price Bottle	Bottles	Total Amount
	ROAD RUNNER SALOON					
	INVENTORY ENDING:					

Date: _____

By: _____

Time: _____

	Product Description	Unit Price Per Case	Cases	Unit Price Bottle	Bottles	Total Amount
P	Absolut Citron			$ 16.72	LITER	
C	Absolut Vodka			$ 25.44	1.750	
P	Bacardi 151			$ 15.51	LITER	
C	Bacardi Dark			$ 10.11	"	
C	Bacardi Light			$ 10.11	"	
P	Baileys			$ 21.93	"	
C	Beefeater Dry Gin			$ 16.77	"	
C	Black Velvet			$ 9.14	"	
C	Bombay Dry Gin			$ 16.05	"	
C	Bombay Sapphire			$ 17.27	"	
C	Bushmills Irish Wiskey			$ 18.52	"	
C	C.C			$ 13.72	"	
W	Cafe Lolita			$ 9.10	"	
C	Campari Aperitivo			$ 18.52		
C	Captain Morgan			$ 11.43		
P	Chambord			$ 17.30	0.750	
SP	Chartrouse			$ 27.43		
P	Chivas Regal			$ 26.68		
W	Christian Brothers			$ 10.55		
SP	Courvoisier VS			$ 27.89		
SP	Courvoisier VSOP			$ 43.26		
P	Crown Royal			$ 22.27		
W	Crystal Palace Gin			$ 7.45	1.750	
W	Crystal Palace Vodka			$ 11.99	1.750	
P	Cuervo 1800			$ 16.06		
C	Cuervo Gold special			$ 21.54	1.750	
C	Cutty Sark			$ 19.52		
W	De Kuyper Amaretto			$ 10.18		
W	De Kuyper Anisette			$ 8.72		
W	De Kuyper Apricot			$ 9.30		
W	De Kuyper Banana			$ 9.34		
W	De Kuyper Blackberry			$ 9.30		
W	De Kuyper Blue Curacao			$ 9.34		
W	De Kuyper Butterscotch			$ 9.06		
W	De Kuyper Cacao. W			$ 9.55		
W	De Kuyper Cactus Juice			$ 9.06		

Key: W = WELL
　　　 C = CALL
　　　 P = PREMIUM
　　　 SP = SUPERPREMIUM

Figure 11. Bar Stock and Inventory Ending Form

W	De Kuyper Cinnamon			$ 9.06		
W	De Kuyper Coffee			$ 9.30		
W	De Kuyper De Cassis D.			$ 9.34		
W	De Kuyper Hot Damn			$ 9.06		
W	De Kuyper Key Largo			$ 9.06		
W	De Kuyper Menthed D.			$ 9.34		
W	De Kuyper Menthed W.			$ 8.89		
W	De Kuyper Peach			$ 9.30		
W	De Kuyper Peachtree			$ 9.06		
W	De Kuyper Pepschnapps			$ 9.06		
W	De Kuyper Root Beer			$ 9.06		
W	De Kuyper Sloe Gin			$ 9.72		
W	Desert Long Island			$ 7.30		
C	Dewars White Label			$ 19.81		
P	Disaronno Amaretto			$ 21.27		
SP	Drambuie			$ 30.35		
C	Frangelica			$ 15.95		
C	Galliano			$ 11.61		
SP	Glenlivet			$ 31.30		
P	Gold Schlager			$ 16.05		
SP	Grand Marnier			$ 33.18		
SP	Hennessy			$ 27.35		
P	Irish Mist			$ 22.62		
C	J & B			$ 29.49	1.750	
C	Jack Daniels Black Label			$ 25.19	1.750	
P	Jagermister			$ 19.80		
W	Jim Beam			$ 10.07		
C	Johnnie Red Label			$ 19.81		
SP	Johnnie W. Black Label			$ 27.30		
C	Kahlua			$ 18.45		
C	Klar eis Peppermint Schnapps			$ 15.78		
C	Makers Mark			$ 16.59		
C	Malibu Rum			$ 12.77		
SP	Martell			$ 28.60		
C	Metaxa Ouzo			$ 14.93		
C	Midori			$ 17.47		
C	Mount Gay			$ 16.35		
C	Myers Rum			$ 16.10		
W	Old Crow			$ 15.82	1.750	
W	Old Smuggler			$ 11.99	1.750	
W	Old Whiskey Dad			$ 14.47	1.750	
C	Opal Nera Sambuca			$ 17.16		
SP	Patron			$ 32.35		
SP	Remy Martin			$ 46.60		

Figure 11. Bar Stock and Inventory Ending Form (continued)

W	Rio Grande Tequila			$ 11.78	1.750	
W	Ron Rio Rum			$ 10.95	1.750	
C	Rumpleminz			$ 17.02		
W	Saint Brendons			$ 11.59		
C	Sambuca Romana White			$ 17.22		
C	Sambuca Romana Black			$ 17.68		
W	Seagram 7			$ 15.77	1.750	
W	Seagrams VO			$ 13.72		
W	Smirnoff Vodka			$ 14.83		
W	Southern Comfort			$ 10.34		
P	Stolichnaya			$ 15.89		
P	Stolichnayku Orange			$ 13.97	0.750	
C	Tanquery Gin			$ 16.77		
SP	Tuaca			$ 48.05		
C	Wild Turkey			$ 16.27		
C	Yukon Jack			$ 13.28		
	TOTAL A/C 144					

DRAFT BEER					
Bud	$ 48.50		DD	1.00	
Bud Lite	$ 48.50		ID	1.50	
Sierra Nevada	$ 75.00		DP	4.00	
Lite	$ 46.50		IP	5.00	
Samuel Adams	$ 84.00				
TOTAL A/C 140					

DOMESTIC BOTTLE					
Michelob	$ 14.25		0.59		
Michelob Lite	$ 14.25		0.59		
Bud Ice	$ 13.20		0.55		
Bud	$ 13.20		0.55		
Bud Light	$ 13.20		0.55		
Bud Ice Draft	$ 13.20		0.55		
Miller Lite	$ 13.20		0.55		
Miller GD	$ 13.20		0.55		
Miller GD Lite	$ 13.20		0.55		
Miller High Life	$ 10.50		0.43		
Coors Lite	$ 14.25		0.59		
Coors	$ 14.25		0.59		
Red Dog	$ 13.20		0.55		
Red Lite	$ 13.30				

Figure 11. Bar Stock and Inventory Ending Form (continued)

BEVERAGE SERVICE EMPLOYEE PERFORMANCE EVALUATION

Name:
Position:
Date:

PERFORMANCE CATEGORIES	SCORE	COMMENTS
Appearance & Hygiene: Does He/She wear proper uniform and follow proper hygiene procedures?		
Attendance & Dependability: Is He/She on time for class and after breaks? Does not leave station without permission?		
Job Knowledge: Does He/She understand his/her job description, menu items, and service procedures?		
Job Skill: Does He/She perform his/her job properly?		
Timing of Work: Does He/She use time well during set-up, service, and clean-up?		
Work Habit: Does He/She consider safety of work habits, sanitation practices, and good housekeeping in work area?		
Guest Service Attitude: Does He/She take pride in his/her work and genuinely strive for excellent guest service?		
Teamwork: Does He/She work with others as a team and communicate well with fellow students and instructors?		
Adaptability: Is He/She able to perform a wide variety of duties and to adjust to changes?		
Completion of Duties: Does He/She close station properly and finish all storage, inventory, and sanitation assignments?		
Overall Score		

Figure 12. Beverage Service Employee Performance Evaluation

Cocktail Name	Abbreviation	Ingredients (Abbreviation)	Mix. Method	Garnish	Glass	Cost	Sell Price	P.C.

Figure 13. Cocktail Profile Form

BAR STAFF SCHEDULE

Date: _____

RANK	NAME	Mon.	Tue.	Wed.	Thu.	Fri.	Sat.	Sun.
Lead Bartender	Sue	Off	Off	11 am to 9 pm	11 am to 9 pm	1 pm to 10 pm	2 pm to 11 pm	2 pm to 11 pm
Bartender	Mike	11 am 7 pm	11 am 7 pm	11 am 7 pm	Off	Off	11 am 7 pm	11 am 7 pm
"	Bob D.	12 pm 8 pm	12 pm 8 pm	Off	Off	11 am 8 pm	12 pm 8 pm	12 pm 8 pm
"	Jerry	Off	2 pm 10 pm	2 pm 10 pm	11 am 7 pm	12 pm 8 pm	2 pm 10 pm	Off
"	Kate	4 pm 12 am	4 pm 12 am	4 pm 12 am	4 pm 12 am	Off	Off	4 pm 12 am
"	Darrel	Off	Off 12 am	6 pm 12 am	6 pm 12 am	6 pm 12 am	6 pm 12 am	6 pm
"	Lisa	6 pm 12 am	Off	Off	7 pm 12 am	6 pm 12 am	6 pm 12 am	6 pm 12 am
Barback	Bob C.	Off	Off 7 pm	11 am 7 pm	11 am 7 pm	11 am 7 pm	11 am 7 pm	11 am
"	Juan	3 pm 11 pm	3 pm 11 pm	Off	Off	3 pm 11 pm	3 pm 11 pm	3 pm 11 pm
"	Chan	Off	4 pm 12 am	4 pm 12 am	4 pm 12 am	4 pm 12 am	4 pm 12 am	Off
Extra Board Bartender	Bill	11 am 7 pm	Off	Off	5 pm 12 pm	6 pm 12 pm	6 pm 12 pm	6 pm 10 pm
"	Mario	Off	Off	12 am 5 pm	Off	1 pm 9 pm	1 pm 9 pm	Off

Comments _____   Mgr. _____

_____

Figure 14. Bar Staff Schedule Sample

BIN IN-OUT RECORD

Item _____   Item spec. _____

Signature _____   Date: _____

Day-Hr. AM -PM	Purchased	Sold	Plus or Minus from Par

Comments_____

_____

Figure 15. Perpetual Inventory for Products

Beverage Dept. Schedule

Outlet _____

Date: _____

Name	Monday	Tuesday	Wedn.	Thursday	Friday	Saturday	Sunday
Barten.							
1							
2							
3							
4							
5							
6							
Barback							
1							
2							
3							
Cocktail							
1							
2							
3							
ExtraB							

Signature:_____

Comments: _____

Figure 16. Beverage Department Schedule Form

BAR USAGE REPORT

Outlet _____

Date: _____

Item	Open	Issued	Total	End	Total Usage	Unit Cost	Total Cost
Spirits							
1							
2							
3							
4							
5							
6							
Cordials							
1							
2							
3							
Beer							
1							
2							
3							
Wine							
1							
2							
3							
						Total Cost: $	

Signature:_____

Comments: _____

_____

Figure 17. Beverage Usage Tracking Form

BAR PRODUCT REQUISITION

Bar _____ Signature_____

Shift: _____   Date: _____

Product	Prod. Size	Number of Empties	Amount Requisitioned	Par Stock

Figure 18. Product Requisition Form

INVENTORY FORM

Outlet: _____

Date: _____   Signature:_____

Product Bin#	Last Inventory	Unit Cost	Extended Cost
			Total:$

Figure 19. Standard Inventory Form

Inter-departmental Issue Record

Outlet _____ Signature _____

Form #(Last three Digits): _____ Date, Day (AM- PM): _____

Beverage Item	To Kitchen	To Dining Room	To Room Service	Other Department

Figure 20. Inter-Departmental Transfer Form

Monthly Check Average Record

Outlet: _____

Starting Date	Revenue	Number of Customers Served	Check Average	C.A. Previous Month
Week 1				
Week 2				
Week 3				
Week 4				
Person Forecasting	Revenue Forecasted	Number of Customers Forecasted	Check Average Forecasted	% difference (Plus or Minus)

Figure 21. Check Average Tracking Form

appendix three

USEFUL WEBSITES BY CHAPTER

Please use the following websites to complement textbook material. We are not responsible for non-functioning websites.

Chapter One—The History of the Beverage Industry
http://www.health.org/pressrel/jan97/6.htm
Site shows sales of liquor and advertisement in the U.S.

http://www.discus.health.org/weak.htm
DISCUS is the trade association representing producers and marketers of distilled spirits sold.

Commitment to Responsibility
http://www.discus.health.org/commenu.htm

Beer Institute- Responsible Drinking
http://www.beerinst.org/education/respons.html

The Blend website
http:// www.whiskeypages.com/The Blend/story_2/

Prohibition
http://www.cohums.ohiostate.edu/history/projects/prohibition/Contents.htm

Women's Christian Temperance Union
http://www.binghamton.edu/womhist/wctu/intro.htm

Lee McKenzie's Personal Prohibition Web Site
http://hometown.aol.com/utahprohib

The Official web Site of the Prohibition Party
http://www.prohibition.org/

MADD
http://www.madd.org/

SADD
http://www.sadd.org/
www.bohnhoff.com

Chapter Two—Role of the Customer
We were unable to find web reference to this topic

Chapter Three—The Planning Stage
*http://nt01.besco.com/SCRIPTS/hsrun.hse/Aplusweb/aplusweb.htx;start
=HS_index*
Online ordering for bar and beverage equipment
http://www.beverageonline.com/content/products/productcenter.asp
Search Beverage Online's Buyer's Guide by product or by company
http://www.foodanddrink.co.uk/
Target your search by product brand, category, supplier, and item.
http://www.twinlo.com/
More of a small business feel to ordering online
www.beverageworld.com

Chapter Four—Bar Equipment
Mixed Drinks Page
http://www.epact.se/acats/drinks.html
Hospitality Yellow Pages
http://www.inndirect.com/inndirect/yp/barequipment.html
The Recipe Bin: Bartending Guide
http://www.britannia.org/recipes/bartending/
Wunderbar
http://4a2z.4anything.com/4/
Webtender
http://www.webtender.com/handbook/barsetup.html
Stocking a Bar
http://www.epact.se/acats/drinks.html#The
www.mixology.com

Chapter Five—Alcoholic Beverages
Distillation: An Introduction
http://lorien.ncl.ac.uk/ming/distil/distil0.htm
Brewing Beer
http://mollie.berkeley.edu/~jones/calday/barleybiotech.htm
Types of Distillation Columns
http://lorien.ncl.ac.uk/ming/distil/distiltyp.htm
Distillation Process
http://www.canadianmist.com/distillation.htm
How Tequila is Made
http://www.tequila.com/distillery.html

Chapter Six—Spirits and Cordials
The Internet Bartender's Guide
http://tor.klippan.se/~fredrik/guide/
This site provides an introduction to mixology, as well as a comprehensive list of cocktail recipes, organized alphabetically and by spirit.

Webtender
http://www.webtender.com/
Extensive guide offers over 3,700 drink recipes. Search by name or ingredient, or let the Webtender choose a random libation from the database.

Bar-None Drink Recipes
Search for drinks by name or by ingredients, or browse through the drink index. Learn to maintain a home bar, and learn to play drinking games.

Barkeep.net
http://www.barkeep.net/
Complete bartending resource for everyone from the seasoned professional, to the occasional host. Contains tips, tricks, and hints.

Chapter Seven—Wine Fundamentals
M. Trinchero Virtual Winery
http://www.fiorewinery.com/vineyard.htm

Brotherhood Winery
http://wines.com/brotherhood/brother.html

The Sonoma Traveler
http://www.winetravel.com/destinations/virtual2.html

Wines.com
http://wines.com/
Guide to wines, articles and other web sites

WineDay
http://www.foodwine.com/food/wineday/

Online Hospitality Article on Wine
www.smartwine.com

Chapter Eight—Beer
A Brief Overview of the Brewing Process
http://www.crestonbc.com/kokanee/over_ferm.html

Beer History
http://www.compusmart.ab.ca/mcuell/beerhist.htm
North American beer owes its existence to the brewing traditions of the "Old World." As people moved from Europe to America they brought with them recipes and techniques that would produce the style of beer they were used to.

Chapter Nine—Mixology
Bar Drinks
http://www.bardrinks.com/
Look for drinks alphabetically or by category, or search by ingredients
or temperature. Has electronic postcards, drinking games, and jokes.

BarMeister.com
http://www.barmeister.com/drinks.html
View drink recipes and drinking games, or participate in a general discussion forum and exchange cocktail recipes. Visitors may also add
recipes.

Cocktails for Lovers
http://epicurious.com/e_eating/e04_valentine/cocktails.html
Recipes for wonderful cocktails for lovers from Epicurious

Cocktail.com
http://www.cocktail.com/
This attractively presented collection of cocktail recipes comes with a bit
of a twist: it relates each drink to a travel destination, with particular
emphasis on skiiers' and surf. A clever commercial site.

StraightBourbon
http://www.straightbourbon.com/mark.html
This site has lots of info on the history, market, recipes and more on
bourbon.

The Cocktail Collection
http://micro.magnet.fsu.edu/cocktails/
View microscopic photographs of crystallized cocktails, and realize that
a good martini is far more beautiful than you realized. Visually interesting site.
www.allaboutbeer.com/aabmhome.html

Chapter Ten—Staffing Concerns
Keeping Good Employees
http://www.cedmagazine.com/pmr/98sp/98spb.htm

http://www.mybookworm.com/mbw/article/7833048004899616535
Researcher Forecasts Tight Labor Market

http://www.intellectualcapital.com/issues/98/0910/icbusiness2.asp
Tight Labor Markets Remain the Key to U.S. Prosperity

http://www.erc.org/press/fallrecruit.htm
Tight Labor Markets? Recruit With Relocation Programs.

http://www.cnnfn.com/smbusiness/9807/31/hire/
Keeping good employees

http://www.newaus.com.au/econ133us.html
Pollyanna analysts

http://career.olemiss.edu/career/cnpg10.asp
Legal/Illegal Interview Questions

http://chef.fab.albany.edu/deptment/ohrm/operations/recruitment/legal/
Legal/Illegal Interview Questions

*http://www.developer.com/jobs/careerbuilder/interview_handbook_
illegal.html*
ILLEGAL QUESTIONS AND THEIR LEGALCOUNTERPARTS

http://www.nt.net/~hrdc/interview.html
60 INTERVIEW QUESTIONS

http://www.gmu.edu/departments/cdc/job_hunt/illegal.htm
Interviewing Skills: Responding to Challenging Interview Questions

*http://www.cc.colorado.edu/CareerCenter/Publications/
InterviewSkills/Illegal.html*
There are several questions that employers may not legally ask applicants.
www.nightclub-business.com

Chapter Eleven—Promoting Responsible Drinking
Responsible Drinking
http://www.brewers.ca/messages.htm

Liquor Boards and Laws
http://www.azleg.state.az.us/ars/4/111.htm

High Risk Bar that Target College Students
http://www.health.org/pubs/lastcall/index.htm
Article discussing ethical issues of target sales.

Can Drinking Alcohol Affect My Baby
http://www.health.org/pubs/qdocs/alcohol/fas-broc/index.htm

Training Responsible Drinking
http://www.gettips.com/index/html

Reasons for Allowing drinking at Work
*http://www.eyjars.is/~sheepdog/english/part_mars99/reasons_for_
allowing_drinking_at.htm*

Chapter Twelve—Legal Factors
TIPS Web site
www.gettips.com/index.html

Chapter Thirteen—Costing and Pricing
www.beveragesolutions.com

Chapter Fourteen—Purchasing, Receiving, Storing, and Issuing
Smirnoff Online Shopping Site
http://www.shoppinglist.com/sl/p?p=n&by=catg&catg0=Beverages
www.tmsrealtime.com

Chapter Fifteen—Controlling Internal Theft
Theft in the Workplace
http://www.usu.edu/~navigate/Fall98/ringel.htm
www.berg-controls.com/shrink.html

INDEX

Chardonnay, 96, 98
Charmat method, 116
Chenin Blanc, 98
Ciders, 84
Civil Rights Act, 184
Civil Rights Act (2)–Sexual Harassment, 184
Closed or control states, 210
Cocktail server, 177
COD, 243
Coffee Makers, 50
Cognacs, 75
"Collective Bargaining Agreement," 186
Column or Coffey Still, 62
Common Garnishes for Drinks, 153
Comparison Analysis, 39
Components of a Drink, 152
Compounded Spirit, 59
Condiment Trays, 49
Congeners, 59
Control, 238
Controlling, 165
Coordinating, 164
Customer-Driven, 23
Customer-Driven Operation, 22
Customer-Service Transaction, 27
Cutting boards and knives, 49
Cuvinet, 51

D

D.O.C., 105
D.O.C.G., 105
Dark Lagers, 135
Decor, 41
Distillation, 77
Distilled Spirits, 59, 63
Double Bocks 127, 135
Double shot, 48
Draft Beer, 140
Draft Beer Spigots, 51
Dramshop, 16
Dramshop law suit, 194
Dramshop laws, 208
Dry beer, 136

E

80/20 Rule, 251
Electronic/Mechanical Liquor Dispensing, 148
Elijah Craig, 9
Empowerment, 179

English Pub, 34
Enology, 83
Entry Level/Apprentice Positions, 176
Equal Pay Act, 183
Ethanol, 13
Ethyl alcohol, 13, 115
Evaluating, 180

F

Factors Affecting How Customers Judge
    Drinks, 156
Fair Labor Standards Act, 183
Feasibility Study, 38
Federal Laws, 183
Fermentation, 60
Fermented Beverages, 59
Food and beverage director, 176
Fortified wines, 114
France, 103
Free Pouring, 48, 146
Front bar, 36
Front gun system, 47

G

Germany, 103
Gin, 74
Glass washing compartment, 47
Glassrail, 46
Glassware, 52
Goal of Purchasing, 240
Goods and services, 26
Grains, 70, 132

H

Hiring, 180
Hops, 132

I

Ice beers, 136
Ice bins, 46
Ice making machine, 51
Immigration Reform and Control Act, 184
Infusion, 77
Interior Design, 39
Internal staffing, 175
Interviewing, 180
Irish Whiskey, 71
Issuing, 246